RETHINKING MATERIALISM

RETHINKING MATERIALISM

*Perspectives on the
Spiritual Dimension of
Economic Behavior*

edited by

ROBERT WUTHNOW

WILLIAM B. EERDMANS PUBLISHING COMPANY
GRAND RAPIDS, MICHIGAN

© 1995 Wm. B. Eerdmans Publishing Co.
255 Jefferson Ave. S.E., Grand Rapids, Michigan 49503
All rights reserved

Printed in the United States of America

00 99 98 97 96 95   7 6 5 4 3 2 1

Library of Congress Cataloging-in-Publication Data

Rethinking materialism: perspectives on the spiritual dimension
of economic behavior / edited by Robert Wuthnow.
p.   cm.
Includes bibliographical references.
ISBN 0-8028-0789-5 (pbk.: alk. paper)
1. United States — Religion. 2. Economics — Religious aspects.
3. Religion and culture — United States. 4. United States — Economic conditions.
5. Wuthnow, Robert. God and Mammon in America.
I. Wuthnow, Robert.
BL2525.R474   1995
291.1′785′0973 — dc20   95-13191
                                                          CIP

Contents

90839

II. TOWARD A CRITIQUE OF MATERIALISM

Acknowledgments

THIS COLLECTION OF ESSAYS was made possible by grants from the Lilly Endowment and the Pew Charitable Trusts for the support of the Center for the Study of American Religion at Princeton University. These funds made it possible for some of the essays to be presented and discussed at a conference on the theme of the volume organized by the Center for the Study of American Religion and held at Princeton University in June 1993. Several of the essays were also presented at the meetings of the Religion and Culture Workshop, an ongoing weekly seminar sponsored by the Center for the Study of American Religion and the Department of Sociology. Background research for the volume was supported by a grant from the Lilly Endowment for a five-year project on the subject of religion and economic behavior, the results of which are reported in separate books and articles. The editor wishes to thank Fred Hofheinz and Craig Dykstra at the Lilly Endowment and Joel Carpenter at the Pew Charitable Trusts for their support, and to thank John F. Wilson and Albert Raboteau of Princeton University for their involvement as co-coordinators of the Center for the Study of American Religion. Anita Kline merits special appreciation for her role in administering the daily activities of the Center and coordinating the conference, correspondence, and finances associated with the preparation of this volume. Matthew Lawson served as a research assistant, helping to comb through the journalistic literature and providing historical background for the project. Patrick Allitt, Daniel Olson, Jenna Weismann Joselit, Marsha Witten, David Harrington Watt, and Tracy Scott provided helpful comments on the essays that were presented at the conference. Conversations and correspondence with the following people have also been helpful in planning the volume: Paul DiMaggio, Nathan Hatch, John Mulder, Harlan Stelmach, Richard Swedberg, David Trickett, Mary Stewart VanLeeuwen, and Viviana Zelizer.

INTRODUCTION

A Good Life and a Good Society:
The Debate over Materialism

ROBERT WUTHNOW

THE VAST MAJORITY of Americans — about 84 percent — believe that
materialism has become a serious social problem.[1] It is not difficult to
understand why. The American taxpayer is shouldering the bill for more
than $100 billion incurred by the greedy overseers of the savings and
loan industry in the 1980s, an irony made poignant by the fact that
some of the worst offenders were called "thrifts," and an irony made all
the more poignant by the fact that many who *lost* money in the deal
were small investors who were trying to live frugally, building up small
nest eggs for their declining years by opening savings accounts. The
American taxpayer has also been called on to contribute more generously to government programs aimed at reducing the national deficit,
a problem that many believe is attributable to government waste on the
one hand, and on the other hand to a huge delusion created by Rea-
ganomics during the 1980s for the benefit of an otherwise materialistic
class of stockbrokers and lobbyists.

Nor is it difficult to understand why materialism is perceived as a
problem when we consider our personal lives. What Ross Perot described during the 1992 presidential campaign as a giant sucking sound
from the South (referring to the prospect of a free-trade agreement with

---

1. This is a combined percentage from a national survey I conducted in 1989.
Forty-six percent of the respondents said that "too much emphasis on money" is a
serious problem in our society, and 38 percent said that it was an extremely serious
problem; details of the survey are reported in Wuthnow (1991).

Mexico) is more likely to be experienced as a powerful gravitational force from the Far East (especially Japan), targeted directly at the magnetically coded plastic cards in our wallets and purses. It is likely to be heightened by advertisements for the latest wide-screen, flat-screen, image-enhanced, superdigitalized home entertainment center. Or by the newest fuzzy-logic, autofocusing, self-stabilizing, telezoom, palm-sized, wireless-remote video recorder. What was once known as a mere television set, or as a mere camera, is clearly no longer suitable.

The sense that materialism has gotten out of hand is magnified by the pressures facing middle-class American families. Home entertainment centers and camcorders can perhaps be passed by, albeit not without the nagging suspicion that one is needlessly denying oneself (and one's children) the small perks that everyone else in the neighborhood is enjoying already. But other material temptations are much more difficult to withstand. High mortgage payments and property taxes may strap the family budget but seem inescapable, not because the amenities of suburban living are so marvelous, but because the public schools anywhere else are in disarray (if not downright dangerous). A new car that costs fifteen times what a new car cost a generation ago is likely to seem equally essential, not so much for the luxurious pleasure of cruising along exotic coastal highways, but because an older, inexpensive car turns out to be an even worse bargain, given the fact that the local repair-service franchise not only charges ten times the minimum wage for semiskilled labor but also cheats on repair bills and replaces parts unnecessarily. By the same token, frozen dinners, a microwave oven, a dishwasher, and an illegal immigrant hired to clean the house and take one's cat to the vet would have seemed like the epitome of materialism in another time, but now provide the only means available for two-career couples to work hard enough at their jobs to earn the salaries they need to pay for these labor-saving amenities.

Moreover, should the American family happen to be one with children, all these pressures are likely to be multiplied immeasurably. Paying as much as ten times the minimum wage for a ten-minute visit to the pediatrician (required by the school system in order to obtain an excused absence for a routine sore throat) can easily evoke the thought that some class of people somehow is managing to lead an exorbitantly materialistic lifestyle at one's expense. So can the prospect of having to pay four or five times one's entire annual (gross) family income to send one's son or daughter to college. At the same time, children themselves have become a major new voice in the chorus of hurrahs for materialism. Certainly their voices are likely to be heard in the debates concerning home entertainment centers and camcorders. They are also likely to weigh in on such matters as *which* brand of frozen dinner is acceptable, what the advantages are of owning a more luxurious car, and which of the latest movies must be seen and which of the latest compact discs must be purchased in order to be minimally literate in things cultural. They are primed to serve as experts in the war for consumer dollars by the commercials they see on television and by the advertisements they read on every billboard, in every magazine, and on nearly every T-shirt.

All these experiences contribute to the sense that materialism has gotten out of hand. They do so not simply because they place real strains on the family budget, but because they seem essentially to be outside the control of even the most stalwart, hard-working, cost-conscious individuals. They come at the individual, as it were, from the outside, as facts of contemporary life, not as matters of choice or even as subtle promptings of certain internal cravings that, with sufficient effort, can be properly disciplined. They appear as the work of advertisers, of large corporations, of school systems, of the medical establishment, of neighborhoods, of employers, of international trade agreements, of economic cycles, of tax policies, and of governments. Thus it is easy to regard materialism as a *social* problem. It is built into the fabric of society itself, pressuring us to conform to it, shaping our lives by virtue of the sheer fact that we cannot escape living in society any more than we can escape eating and sleeping.

In saying that materialism is a problem, we are of course acknowledging to ourselves that it is something we consider troubling, distressing in our personal lives, and perhaps even unhealthy as far as the good of society itself is concerned. A young woman who works as a personnel manager for a large firm in Los Angeles put it well when she remarked that "more and more people just seem to want more and more things." She finds it troubling that she herself gets caught up so easily in buying clothes. She looks forward to getting something new to make herself feel better. She also thinks that for an increasing number of people, materialism has become essential. "Having things," she says, "makes them feel important, like they've reached a certain level." She worries about where this trend may be heading. When she thinks about the children she knows, for example, she realizes that just getting to go to the movies used to be a treat, but now kids have to go see their favorite movie star in person and have sheets and pillowcases with his or her pictures on them. Asked if things have gotten too commercialized, she responds, "Absolutely. There's too many things out there, too many things to have."[2]

Judging from popular media, materialism is troublesome not only because it threatens our social health, but also because it opposes our deepest values. Clergy argue that we need to turn away from materialism in order to seek true spirituality. Nonprofit organizations extol charitable acts because donors are thereby shown to be nonmaterialistic. Playwrights create characters who give up materialistic lifestyles in order to discover their true identities. Scholars and artists are said to be pure seekers of truth and beauty only when they are not corrupted by materialistic desires. Newscasters paint tragic scenarios around stories of greed, and social commentators charge that whole decades have been colored by a turn for the worse. "What does it mean when life has been devalued to the point where a pair of Reeboks is worth a life?" asks political satirist Diane Ford (Christon 1991). Materialism, she suggests, has taken the place of values, redefining us by what we have rather than by what we are.

Yet, for most of us, materialism is not so much a source of untrammeled regret as of profound ambivalence. We worry about it, bemoaning its hold over us, but we also seem unwilling to do very much to escape its grasp. We decry the fact that so much money is needed to live handsomely in our society, lamenting our lack of free time, and yet we devote ourselves wholeheartedly to earning as much money as we can. And while we are doing this lamenting, we may comfort ourselves by going out to eat at a fancy restaurant or by purchasing a new pair of shoes. Indeed, our behavior seems to reflect the wisdom captured in the bumper sticker that reads, "When the going gets tough, the tough go shopping."

The same public opinion polls that register concern about materialism actually document how deeply committed we are to the pursuit

2. This woman was one of 175 people interviewed in depth about their work, their money, their religious beliefs, their values, and their views of society.

of material interests. For example, a survey I conducted in 1992 among more than 2,000 members of the U.S. labor force revealed both widespread mistrust of materialistic activities and widespread commitment to them.[3] On the one hand, 89 percent agreed that "our society is much too materialistic," and 74 percent said that materialism is a serious or an extremely serious social problem. An equally large proportion (75 percent) agreed that "advertising is corrupting our basic values," and an even larger number (90 percent) expressed misgivings about materialism among youth ("children today want too many material things"). Most (70 percent) also thought American society would be "better off" if there were less emphasis on money. On the other hand, working Americans overwhelmingly register their personal desire for money and their interest in material goods. Three in four (74 percent) say the statement "I wish I had more money than I do" describes them very well or fairly well. An equally high proportion (76 percent) agree that "having money gives me a good feeling about myself." Almost as many (71 percent) associate money with freedom ("having money means having more freedom"). And three-quarters (76 percent) say that "having a beautiful home, a new car, and other nice things" is one of their important values.

Qualitative interviews reveal that the inconsistencies evident in such survey responses are in fact matters of personal struggle. We do not simply deplore materialism at one moment and then go nonchalantly to the shopping mall. Instead, we debate with ourselves. We feel torn. The woman I quoted earlier, for example, admits she has an obsession with buying clothes. But she also wonders if this obsession is really so bad. She figures she deserves some nice things because she works hard, treats other people fairly, and tries not to cause any trouble. She also believes that there are people in her community who are much more materialistic than she is. Other people acknowledge similar feelings. They worry that our society is becoming increasingly driven by materialistic impulses. Yet they are unsure how deeply caught up with these impulses they themselves are, and they wonder what the most effective ways might be of resisting them. Sometimes they engage in token behaviors — for example, fastidiously turning out the lights or

---

3. A copy of the survey instrument and more detail on the findings are presented in Wuthnow (1994b).

buying the deluxe rather than the super-deluxe TV set — and these token activities make them feel better. They are convinced they have at least done something to resist the pressures of materialism. But they are also unsure whether their actions have been enough, or whether they have even been worthwhile.

Part of the reason for this ambivalence is that our concerns about materialism are only part of the cultural mythology with which we live. Messages filter through, to be sure, from churches, artists, intellectuals, and others on the cultural fringe, telling us that materialism is corrupting our values and that we cannot expect to have a good society unless we find a way to curb our material obsessions. But there are more powerful messages telling us that the good life, after all, is one in which material pursuits play an important role. If we only work hard, think wisely, and make use of our talents, the good life will be ours — meaning a comfortable home, opportunities to travel and to enjoy ourselves, good medical care, the means to educate our children, and economic security when we retire. Moreover, the good life, so defined, is not one that government will provide for everyone, but a life that will come to us as a reward for responsible behavior. Indeed, economists tell us that by working hard and by spending our money wisely on the consumer goods of our choice, we are contributing to the betterment of society itself. Accordingly, we do not have to think very deeply about our materialism, other than to deplore it in others. The marketplace more or less regulates itself. Upswings and downswings are largely beyond our control. Living close to our means (if not actually within them) is the better part of virtue.

The debate over materialism is thus a peculiar one. Concerns about how materialistic we have become do not go away. They are fueled by the pressures we face in making ends meet and by the legacy of religious and secular teachings alike which tell us that there are more important things in life than material goods. They are also rooted in long traditions of social thought, defining what America is and arguing that its greatness depends on deep spiritual longings that material abundance alone cannot satisfy. We are, as a writer for the *Wall Street Journal* declared recently, "a nation at the flood tide of history and yet, spiritually, searching for its soul" (Farney 1992). Our concerns reflect our conviction that a good society depends on more than just a good life. "American plenty, to taste right," John Updike (1992) has written, "needs a seasoning of idealism." Yet these concerns are tempered by other messages encouraging us to spend what we have and not to worry so much about whether or not we are doing the right thing. It is thus difficult to think clearly about materialism. It is difficult even to find clear voices speaking about it, arguing strongly against it or in favor of it. Rather, the debate is largely one that remains unjoined. It exists more within our souls, at the level of conscience, than in the public arena. It surfaces as ambivalence, confusion, and in some cases as anxiety and self-blame. These are messages that are easy to submerge, easy to push to the side while the day-to-day demands of the marketplace occupy our attention, issues easy to settle without thinking about them at all by letting economists and policymakers worry about such things while we simply try to purchase quality merchandise and stay within the limit on our credit cards. But, for the good of our society, they are clearly messages and issues that need to be considered.

This volume is an effort to heighten the level of debate about materialism in American society at the end of the twentieth century. It brings together a collection of original essays by leading social scientists and theologians. The authors are a diverse group, spanning the disciplines of sociology, history, philosophy, and theology. They have contributed to a diverse array of specialties within their various disciplines as well, including social theory, the study of education and organizations, gender, religion, and social ethics. What unites them in the present enterprise is a common concern for the growing role that materialism appears to be playing in American society.

Each of the essays seeks to contribute to our understanding of at least one aspect of the problem. They are unified by the assumption that materialism is not fundamentally an economic problem but a cultural one — a spiritual issue. It runs to the depths of our souls and, for this reason, needs to be understood less in terms of budgets or fiscal cycles and more in terms of where we locate the sacred, of where we search for meaning and transcendence, and of how we think about justice, equality, and the future of our world. Collectively, the essays address the ways in which materialism has been understood in recent analyses of American character, how economic theory and the economy itself shape our understandings of ourselves, and the nature of consumerism. They also seek ways in which to move beyond taken-for-granted assumptions about materialism — suggesting, for example, that our understandings of work, goods, economic justice, and moral discourse now need to be rethought.

Throughout these essays, there is an abiding concern for the ways in which religious thought is being reshaped by economic circumstances and, in turn, how it may be able to act against the prevailing materialism of the culture in which we live. These, then, are essays in social criticism, but they are also contributions grounded in hope — in the legacy of religious thought that continues to inspire much of sociology as well as theology, namely, that the hard work of redeeming the social order is not an impossible task, or one that we can afford to neglect.

The Legacy of Ambivalence

Our present ambivalence toward materialism, although acute, is scarcely without precedent.[4] European settlers brought this ambivalence with them and expressed it vividly as they established colonies on American soil. They came in hopes of achieving material prosperity, realizing that a decent living was a vital precondition for pursuing their ideals. Yet they also worried about the excesses such pursuits could lead to and, indeed, had led to in the societies from which they came. They worried, for example, about the willingness of those who were financially well off to care about those less fortunate than themselves. They also worried about the dangers of material pursuits leading men and women away from God and away from their familial and community responsibilities. Puritan clergy espoused an ethic of hard work and spartan living that was often conducive to material success. But they often came into conflict with the merchants and traders in their own congregations who seemed unwilling to remember the needs of the church itself, or of the poor, and who turned readily to government schemes aimed at keeping their taxes low and their profits high (Silverman 1985).

As the small colonial settlements of the seventeenth century gave way to larger industrial communities during the eighteenth century, the nation's ambivalence toward materialism continued to be evident

4. This ambivalence is much in evidence in historical studies of the relationship between Protestantism and economic behavior; for an overview, see Wuthnow and Scott (forthcoming).

(Crowley 1974). Some argued that industrialism itself needed to be curbed, suggesting that it was transforming the world of nature into an artificial realm created and corrupted by human activity. They saw the agrarian life as more in keeping with transcendent ideals and urged citizens to live as simply as they could.[5] Others viewed industrialism with more enthusiasm, regarding it as a way of attaining sufficient material comforts for all so that the higher aims of civilization could then be pursued more effectively. Still, even among the advocates of industrial expansion there was an inherent tension between the pursuit of material well-being as an end in itself and the goals of community betterment, individual happiness, family loyalty, and spiritual perfection that these material pursuits were intended to advance.

The nineteenth century witnessed such inordinate expansion in the material realm that other values were often neglected or at least thought to be facilitated automatically by economic growth alone. Railroads transformed the countryside, turning self-sustained farms into productive units for world markets in wheat, corn, and other commodities. New consumer goods, ranging from prefabricated clothing to mass-produced lighting and toilet fixtures, became more readily available to the rising middle classes. Incomes gradually rose to accommodate the market for such goods. And journalists, scholars, and preachers were often caught up in the enthusiasm of the age for the benefits of economic expansion.[6] Yet, throughout the nineteenth century, social commentators worried about the effects of material "progress," as it was called, on the quality of human life itself. Social reformers led the way in pointing out the ill effects of urban life on the condition of working families, educators struggled with ways in which to balance the rising demand for technical skills against the need to transmit moral values, and clergy were often placed in the position of championing the virtues of the wealthy while trying to elevate their thoughts to a higher spiritual plane as well. Few in any sector of society were able to escape the prevailing ambivalence. They could scarcely curb their enthusiasm for material innovation, but at the same time they also wanted to preserve the health of society (Zuckerman 1991).

In the twentieth century, social science has been among the chief

---

5. Gilmore (1985) is a valuable source on these debates.
6. Examples can be found in Wallace (1978), Rodgers (1978), and Johnson (1978).

beneficiaries of this legacy. Indeed, many of the founders of modern social science were inspired by an attempt to understand human life more fully than it had come to be depicted during the nineteenth century in classical economics (Parsons 1935). Karl Marx and Friedrich Engels (1846), for example, regarded classical economics as a form of false consciousness that helped mainly to legitimate the interests of a dominant capitalist class. In Marx's wider work, he of course contributed significantly to a view of human nature that placed material conditions at the center, and yet his work also contains a powerful critique of these conditions, aiming to show that deeper human qualities, such as cooperation with others and greater fulfillment of individual potential, are corrupted by these conditions. Max Weber (1905) is perhaps best known in wider circles for his attempt to link the rise of modern capitalism with the distinctive ascetic Protestantism of the Reformation. But in his mature work (1921) Weber is concerned even more deeply with understanding the social dimensions of human life that cannot be reduced to economic exchange, and with emphasizing the ways in which a desire for meaning influences the character even of economic transactions. Much of Weber's work is in fact a critique of modern materialism as well, providing tools with which to understand how life has been transformed, demeaned at the same time that it has been enriched by the growth of modern economic institutions. The work of Emile Durkheim (1893, 1937) is less concerned with materialism as such than is the work of Marx and Weber. But Durkheim's work also shows that he was troubled by the ways in which modern economic developments may be altering the character and quality of human life. He follows the classical economists in recognizing that greater specialization is the key to higher productive capacity, and he suggests that this key also creates greater interdependence among the various parties producing specialized goods. Yet Durkheim also wonders if such contractual interdependence can be sufficient to maintain human community. He considers the symbolic and moral dimensions of community and the ways in which these may help to restrain the overzealous pursuit of individual self-interest.

There is thus much to draw on from the sociological tradition in attempting to rethink materialism.[7] This tradition was in turn rooted

7. Further discussion of these points is found in Wuthnow (1994b).

in philosophical conceptions of human nature and of human society that themselves had strong links to Judeo-Christian religious teachings. The classical social scientists were arguing, in effect, that humankind does not live by bread alone. They did not deny the importance of sustaining society in its relationships with the physical environment, but perceived rightly that this quest could become so powerful that everything else would be affected by it. Community might not become impossible to sustain, but it would be subtly transformed once society was composed of apartment buildings, assembly lines, supermarkets, and four-lane highways. Morality was still needed to curb individual behavior, and ways of giving individual behavior meaning were also desperately needed, but morality and meaning rooted in mass advertising was likely to be different from that arising from monasteries, guilds, villages, and parishes.

The legacy of ambivalence toward materialism has also transcended the social sciences, of course, spreading from academic circles into parish halls, labor unions, political interest groups, and critical journalism. Muckraking and settlement houses have given way to lobbying and nonprofit associations, but there is still much in these institutions that carries on the potential for critical discourse about materialism. Many who donate volunteer time to charitable organizations, for example, do so because they fear that society has become too materialistic for its own good (Wuthnow 1991). Many who lobby for political reforms aimed at helping the homeless, providing medical assistance to the poor, or changing tax laws to shift greater responsibility to the rich also do so with an implicit critique of materialism in mind.

Yet there is also something about materialism that makes it difficult to criticize. This difficulty arises any time ambivalence is present. Thus, in the case of materialism, we can seldom criticize its ill effects without admitting that we also want the good life for ourselves and that we regard material advances as a means of attaining other values. But there is perhaps a deeper reason that materialism is difficult to criticize: materialism surrounds us. We might expect to hear a strong critique of it from a religious worker living in Calcutta or from a starving writer in Chile. But it is harder to find the space in which to think about materialism within our own society. Part of the dilemma in trying to think about and criticize materialism, therefore, arises from the conditions that characterize our present situation.

Dimensions of the Present Dilemma

At least three developments in late-twentieth-century America have made it more difficult for us to think clearly about materialism. The first is located primarily in the intellectual sphere itself. The second takes shape within the broader cultural definitions we use to characterize ourselves nationally. The third emerges in the existential conditions under which each of us functions in everyday life. All three are deeply spiritual.

The intellectual development that has done most to erode our capacity to think clearly about materialism is the triumph of economistic perspectives in the social sciences (Wolfe 1989, 27-50). Notwithstanding the legacy of Marx, Weber, Durkheim, and others, social thought in the late twentieth century has been overwhelmingly influenced by instrumental, choice-oriented models of human behavior (Coleman 1990). These models assert the importance of thinking about economic issues in purely economic categories. Understanding materialism is thus a problem that leads us to turn not to philosophy or theology but to economics. This is the discipline that can tell us how to think about goods, markets, consumption, and the forces that drive people to exchange goods or to save or to desire money in the first place. Economics is a highly specialized science that implicitly (or often explicitly) has assumed the irrelevance of many other facets of human behavior or their reducibility to economic factors. In addition, it has also been an imperialistic discipline, seeking to extend its insights into other avenues of social life as well. It is now possible, for example, to find arguments in the social science literature suggesting that caring behavior, such as that exhibited by Mother Teresa, is merely a way of pursuing certain kinds of self-interest, or that the strength of American religion can be understood solely in terms of market-driven competition among various suppliers of spiritual goods. By extension, it thus becomes easier to take for granted that self-interested materialism is simply the only way in which to understand behavior; it becomes harder to find an intellectual perspective from which to examine materialism critically.

The broader national development that circumscribes our ability to understand materialism is the de facto triumph of American capitalism that has come about with the apparent collapse of world communism (Rozman 1993). For all its problems, the existence of communism as a force in world politics throughout much of the twentieth century provided a place from which capitalism could be criticized from without and from which doubts about it could be entertained from within. Those who thought about it carefully could distinguish Soviet-style (or Maoist) communism from Marxism, and thus retain some of Marx's trenchant criticisms of capitalism while recognizing that world communism might be an even worse alternative. In short, capitalism was not all there was. Hopeful analysts on the Left could at least imagine society functioning on socialist principles. Others, less hopeful about socialism itself, could also argue for the possibility of some "third way" (such as democratic socialism or Christian socialism). Indeed, the abuses evident in the Soviet bloc were used to point out the comparable problems of materialism in the West, thereby suggesting the need to think creatively about some other combination of economic and political patterns. The collapse of world communism, however, makes it harder to think that capitalism really is not all there is. We are thus left with having to tinker with minor modifications in capitalism rather than trying to understand materialism as a more pervasive feature of modern life. The success of capitalism appears to provide its own justification (Berger 1986). Indeed, our main concern now is whether we have enough of it, or whether we need to have freer markets, a government that assists businesses more actively, and consumers more oriented toward material goods in order to keep up with our East Asian and Western European competitors. As a result of these developments, any serious criticism of materialism is likely to be branded as utopian or to be regarded as a dangerous departure from the simple facts of life.

In the existential conditions of our everyday lives, the third development that hamstrings us in thinking about materialism is the growing penetration of workplace and marketplace demands into the private sphere.[8] Until even the first half of the twentieth century, two characteristics of everyday life helped to provide a space in which to think objectively about materialism. One was that the workplace and the home were generally separate spheres. While materialism and self-interest

---

8. Habermas's (1987) treatment of the colonization of the life-world provides a general theoretical framework in which to think about these issues; Schor (1992), among others, discusses the increasing demands of work.

might dominate the one, the other could thus be a haven in which cooperation, kindness, decency, and other noneconomic values could prevail. The other (related) characteristic was that these two spheres generally included a gendered division of labor. That is, the workplace was more likely to be the domain of men, while the home was the domain of women. Men could thus be materialistic and self-interested, knowing that women would preserve such virtues as nurturing, hospitality, and the transmission of traditional values. At the end of the twentieth century, however, these divisions have broken down. Work and home are more likely to be joined, and both have begun to be degendered. Consequently, materialism is harder to keep out of the home and more difficult to associate with one gender or the other. In the extreme, workers may now perform their tasks from their bedrooms through modem hookups between their personal computers and the stock market, thereby bringing materialistic concerns into the very sanctuary of their private lives. But in much less extreme cases, advertising penetrates the bedroom via television as well, and both husbands and wives have to figure out how to balance their budgets and maintain the precarious ledgers of their emotions and values as well as their finances.

Each of these developments is profoundly spiritual. Any intellectual development that purports to provide a complete theory of human nature is necessarily spiritual. If modern economics plays that role, it does so not only because it is logically coherent or consistent with empirical data but because it plays on the doubts, the aspirations, and the faith of its practitioners and consumers. In suggesting that people function as rational maximizers of their own interests, for example, it builds on assumptions about the selfishness of human nature that are part of all world religions, but it also denies other religious teachings, such as the corrosiveness of selfishness, the need for forgiveness, and the possibility of redemption. The triumph of world capitalism has a spiritual dimension as well. Communism was of course regarded within the United States as the antagonist of all things sacred, as the epitome of atheistic evil. By implication, capitalism was the defender of goodness. It is now easy for materialism and spirituality to be conflated within American culture. Before religious teachings can become properly critical of capitalism, they will have to attain some distance from it; it is a prophetic voice that is needed, a voice from the outside, calling to the affluent in the wilderness of their excesses. The growing penetration of everyday life by materialism is even more profound in its implications for spirituality. Until quite recently, home and family (with gendered conceptions of both) were considered the haven of contemporary spirituality. If one could not think about God in the workplace, one could at least engage in private prayers, seders, and the religious instruction of one's children in the sacred sphere of the home. And faith provided comfort in the face of illness and death, and a basis for love and marriage, that the marketplace could not offer. But now, materialism pushes even those forms of spirituality aside. Television instructs children in the insatiable desires of consumerism and makes quiet time for prayer less available, pain medicine substitutes for faith, and marriage becomes the domain of for-profit therapists and divorce lawyers.

The danger, then, is that materialism is not only shaping how we live but the way we think as well. It influences our consumer tastes and our preference for high-paying jobs, but it also alters our capacity to pray, the nature of our prayers, and the ways in which religious tutelage instructs our values. It becomes harder for us to hear messages about the suffering of the poor, the need for economic justice, and the desirability of seeing God's handiwork in simple things or in nature. Materialism draws us into its logic not so much by convincing us that material goods are preferable to helping the poor, but by persuading us that we can help them best by buying luxury goods for ourselves (thereby creating jobs). It permits advertisers to sell us more goods, not less, by emphasizing the virtues of high-quality goods that will last, biodegradable goods that will not pollute the environment, and expensive vacations that will give us opportunities to get away and reflect on our values. In fact, materialism becomes so much a way of life that we no longer recognize it as an option, as one value among others that we can decide to choose or to reject. It ceases to raise questions but is taken for granted as an inevitable feature of our society. Without realizing it, Ronald Reagan perhaps said it best when he commented on our obsession with the getting and keeping of wealth: "That is not materialism," he asserted; "that is Americanism" (Raines 1980).

Renewing the Debate

Despite all the reasons for concern about it, therefore, materialism has in recent years occasioned little public debate. To be sure, op-ed essays decry it from time to time. Artists occasionally plead for the virtues of bohemian rather than bourgeois lifestyles. Clergy try to challenge us to think about stewardship and economic justice. And even political candidates have been known to lament the excesses of greed and wealth allegedly encouraged by their opponents. But, compared with the battles launched against other social ills, little in the way of an organized assault on materialism can be identified. For example, pollution is about as widely regarded as a social problem as materialism. Yet there is a sizable environmentalist movement in the private sector, and there are major efforts in the public sector to combat pollution, while nothing comparable is evident for materialism. The same is true of the problems facing the nation's schools. Not only do the vast majority of the public recognize these problems, but there is also a widespread effort to discuss possible solutions; that cannot be said of materialism. Crime, health care, the problems of child abuse, urban decay — they too get far more attention than materialism.

Materialism, by comparison, seems too nebulous to consider as an issue for public debate. How, we might ask, could anyone forge a public policy to deal with it? Materialism is such an integral feature of American life that we cannot imagine living without it. Insofar as we are willing to discuss it at all, we are more inclined to seek solutions that permit us to have our cake and eat it too. As a young woman who had initiated an environmentalist movement in California admitted to a reporter recently, "We haven't given up materialism and we haven't given up having a regular life. It's a different sort of 'having-it-all'" (Koenenn 1990). As long as we avoid overt cheating and stealing, and as long as we pay token obeisance to other values, we feel we are doing our part. Only the more egregious examples of materialism attract public discussion, and then, because they are extreme cases, they seem too exceptional to serve as general lessons. Indeed, most discussions of materialism soon turn to more tractable problems. A discussion of greed, for example, turns into a debate about the savings-and-loan crisis. Or the focus shifts to a now-common lament about materialism — that Americans are paying too much on credit-card debts. But the added problem is that even these discussions devolve quickly into attacks on specific individuals. Thus, a discussion of greed becomes a biographical critique of Michael Milken or Charles Keating. When we engage in these tactics, we give the issue a moral tone, reaffirming our sense that greed is indeed a matter of personal responsibility. But the rest of us are excused from class. We do not see the cultural assumptions that legitimate materialism on a wider scale or the ways in which institutions prevent us from thinking clearly about the meanings of our work, money, and material possessions. Consequently, we have no systematic understanding of materialism.

Research shows, in fact, that few people in the U.S. workforce say they have ever learned not to want a lot of money (even though most say greed is wrong). In my survey of the U.S. workforce, for instance, the statement "Being greedy is a sin against God" evoked agreement from 71 percent of the respondents (83 percent among church or synagogue members). But, when asked if they had ever been taught that it was wrong to want a lot of money, only 12 percent said they had. Research also suggests that money is seldom the focus of any kind of serious discussion. In my study, for instance, only 19 percent said they were clear about how their parents had made decisions about money (nearly half — 48 percent — said they were unclear or unsure). And, as adults, they appear to hide their uncertainties about money as well. Indeed, few ever talk about their money with anyone else, not even with their closest friends. Nor do they seek counsel from financial experts, therapists, or clergy. So they are left with no outside advice other than what they receive from the mass media: buy this, buy that, spend more, focus on brands and prices, not whether to buy something at all.

The spiritual resources that might provide a basis for thinking about materialism also appear to be woefully inadequate. True, much lip service is given in formal religious writings to the problems of materialism and to the need for spirituality as an alternative to materialism. Books and articles abound, for example, in which materialism is condemned as a false sense of security and in which the faithful are called to focus more on their relationship to God. But these teachings run into barriers on the front lines of religious organizations themselves. Clergy admit that it is difficult to talk about work and money to their congregants. They fear the subject may not be appropriate, worry that they do not have an adequate grasp of the issues, and/or are afraid of giving offense. Few clergy in fact have a clear idea about the kinds of work their parishioners do, let alone any idea of how much money they make. The clergy themselves preach sermons that often do more to encourage the pursuit of wealth, or at least to legitimate having it, than to trouble the waters with strong messages about overwork or overconsumption. And yet, parishioners say they would like the churches to be speaking out more on such issues. In my survey, for example, 79 percent of working Americans who were church members said they would like the churches to do more to encourage people to be "less materialistic." In the breach, moreover, a majority of Americans feel anxious or guilty about the ways in which they handle their money, but seem incapable of curbing their material appetites.[9]

What we need, then, are efforts to prod church people, public officials, scholars, and community leaders in the direction of a more serious, sustained debate about materialism in American society.[10] The significance of the topic itself must be recognized. It needs to be placed on the public agenda alongside topics such as individualism, moral decay, and the erosion of spiritual values. We need to understand more clearly how materialism influences our lives, not just in economic terms but in moral and intellectual terms as well. Material things need to be considered more clearly as means to the attainment of better lives and a better society, not as ends worth pursuing in themselves. In spiritual terms, incarnational theology implies that the material realm is important but not final; for Christians, Christ's incarnation provides a means to believers' salvation, a way of gaining a better understanding of and communion with the divine. By the same token, a theology of creation suggests that the material world is created and is in that sense good, but it is not to be worshiped in place of that which created it. Markets may serve morals, but they cannot replace them. Nor should the material means (when they are available) be used to justify the ends to which they are put. These are among the arguments that need to be raised to the level of public debate.

A Look Ahead

The essays that follow take up specific issues which must be addressed in any broader reconsideration of materialism in American society. In

---

9. Further detail on these points is presented in Wuthnow (1993).

10. Several significant contributions to this debate in recent years include McCloskey (1990), Pemberton and Finn (1985), Ellul (1984), Owensby (1988), Block et al. (1982), and Sider (1984).

the first section, the chapters are organized around an effort to understand more clearly what the implications of various cultural developments may be. The chapter by Wilfred M. McClay traces changes in conceptions of American character since the 1950s (with a running start extending a century earlier) in an attempt to see what has been said about materialism. He finds that materialism has often been mentioned in passing, but seldom treated at length or in any systematic fashion. His essay also points to the worrisome conclusion that even our most astute social critics have become increasingly reconciled to the prevailing materialism in American culture.

The chapters by Neil J. Smelser and John Boli turn specifically to the economic realm. Smelser unearths some of the reasons why rational-choice economics has become such a powerful intellectual force in recent decades, showing especially that its practitioners are engaged in a kind of religious enterprise complete with its own priests, rituals, and self-fulfilling prophecies. He also points out that an emerging literature in the social sciences, focusing on the ways in which theoretical perspectives are themselves constructed by stories and rhetorical devices, opens up new opportunities for relativizing and criticizing economistic thinking. Boli focuses on economic conditions themselves, forging an argument parallel to Smelser's. If economic theory has become a kind of religion, as Smelser suggests, Boli argues that economic institutions have also absorbed many of the functions previously fulfilled by religion. Thus, we cannot fully appreciate the depths of materialism unless we understand how economic behavior supplies us with meaning, purpose, and a sense of sacred order. By implication, society may not be as bad off as some naysayers would suggest. For example, markets do reinforce a certain kind of moral commitment, and work, far from being meaningless, is actually a source of great meaning for most people. And yet, religious leaders themselves must ask what their role should be, given these conditions, and social observers more broadly must ask what the source of deeper prophetic wisdom can be. Boli's chapter provides some surprising — and troubling — answers to this question.

Marsha G. Witten rounds out this section by examining religious discourse, focusing especially on evangelical Protestant writings about work, money, and materialism. She shows that there is a legacy of concern about overwork, greed, possessiveness, and other sins of the flesh in these writings, but that there is also a great deal of accommodation in them to the secular spirit of our age. Popular Protestant writing on these topics, she suggests, does much to legitimate the pursuit of worldly success by linking it with personal fulfillment and by offering to alleviate any anxieties that might arise as by-products of the present economic system.

The second half of the book turns to prescriptive essays. Drawing inspiration from Weber, the chapters by Miroslav Volf and Nicholas Wolterstorff take up the question of life in the iron cage, as Weber put it, and how we may be able to move beyond that kind of life. Volf suggests ways in which the insatiability inherent in human nature needs to be identified, and how work may be rethought to focus less on material acquisition and more on contributing to social betterment. Wolterstorff takes up the question of justice, showing that Weber implies its importance but fails to deal with it sufficiently. Wolterstorff suggests that a strong conception of justice as a social ideal may be necessary in order to truly curb individual greed and its negative social consequences.

Albert Bergesen shifts the focus from Weber to Marx, asking what may replace the Marxist vision of social reform now that world communism seems to have collapsed. He shows how environmentalism, animal rights, and related concerns have come to provide a vision of a better tomorrow that has some of the earlier appeal of Marxism. He discusses both the value of these concerns and some of the pitfalls to which they may be subject. The chapter by Alan Wolfe takes its inspiration from the classical tradition of sociological theory more generally. Wolfe argues that sociological theory needs to rediscover its concern with moral discourse. Proposing moral discourse as an antidote to economic theories, he suggests that there are in fact several meanings associated with moral discourse in contemporary discussions, and attempts to show the implications of each of these.

Finally, Martin E. Marty re-examines the historical conversation between American religion and the materialistic environment in which faith has found itself, and calls on religious leaders to think squarely about their message and to address more effectively the challenges associated with the American economic system. He shows that spirituality has often been pitted against materialism, but that the American tradition has always brought the two together in complex ways.

These essays are intended for an interdisciplinary audience including policymakers, religious leaders, laity, and students of the social sciences. Perhaps policymakers cannot be expected to lead the way in rethinking materialism. But it is clear that they have often shaped the public agenda on these matters. Rightly or wrongly, for example, the Reagan administration is popularly blamed for much of the materialism evident during the 1980s, while (at this writing) journalists hope and politicians debate whether compassionate social policies can be reconciled with tough-minded cutbacks in government spending. We hope that these essays can make policymakers and those who study domestic policy aware of the concern that the American public has about materialism, the ambivalence that materialism generates, and the ways in which our thinking about it is often confused.

We hope, too, that religious leaders and laity will be able to glean new ideas from these essays that they can put into practice in the teachings of churches and synagogues. Certainly there is grist here for self-reflection on the part of religious leaders about the ways in which their messages may inadvertently contribute to the prevailing materialism of American society. There are also opportunities for challenging congregations to think more critically about the idolatry of economistic thinking and consumer-driven behavior.

Finally, we hope these essays will help students of the social sciences to initiate new empirical research and new theoretical discussions of the complex relationships between material pursuits and other dimensions of the human experience. Certainly there is a need to carry on the important theoretical and empirical debates initiated by the founders of the social sciences a century ago.

We offer no easy solutions. There are good reasons for our collective ambivalence about materialism. But the time has also come for us to think anew about the meaning and consequences of our love affair with materialism.

I. THE CULTURE
OF MATERIALISM

Where Have We Come Since the 1950s? Thoughts on Materialism and American Social Character

WILFRED M. McCLAY

SURELY NO MODERN NATION has been more prone to chronic bouts of national self-scrutiny and attempts at social self-characterization than the United States. For all that Americans have been collectively satirized as a nation of glib, glad-handing extroverts and shallow materialists, they have also proved a remarkably introspective people. One sees this trait manifested in their persistent search for the nation's special meaning and for the distinctive cultural morphology of "the American." Such a need is itself characteristic; and it reflects persistent cultural and intellectual residues from the American past. The call to rigorous self-examination and redemptive mission implicit in the Puritan errand; the universalistic accents of the Enlightenment, which have resonated especially widely and deeply in the American context; the tendency, whether republican, Enlightened, or romantic, to see American life as a liberation from the corrupt and arbitrary constraints of custom and tradition, and as a recovery of the innocence and authenticity of Nature; the unusual degree of self-conscious deliberation with which "the first new nation" was brought into being and its principal institutions founded; the broadly inclusive "creedal" or ideological (rather than narrowly cultural or racial) basis of American national identity; the identification of America as the prototype and exemplar of modernity — all these conceptions have contributed to, and perpetuated, deep-seated notions of national distinctiveness.[1]

1. I prefer to designate this as a fascination with "distinctiveness" rather than

The cross-cutting diversity, even incompatibility, of these conceptions can seem bewildering at first glance. The New Israel, the City upon a Hill, the Empire of Reason, the New Eden, Nature's Nation, the Nation Dedicated to a Proposition, the Great Refuge, the Melting Pot, the Land of Opportunity, the Transnational "Nation of Nations," the Novus Ordo Seclorum, the Redeemer Nation, the Democratic Experiment, even the Last, Best Hope of Mankind — one can take one's pick of many labels. None of these mythic constructs enjoys anything like unquestioned predominance in American consciousness; but none is entirely dead, either. All cling to, work upon, and endlessly complicate the sense of national identity. And all point to a similar end: a conception of distinctive "Americanness" that is never simply given, in the manner of other national identities, but instead needs to be consciously appropriated, achieved, converted to, or recovered. Americans' firm conviction that they are distinctive supports a perpetual industry; and the very indeterminacy of that distinctiveness ensures that fresh attempts to grasp hold of it will continue to be made.

So the scholarly and popular study of American social character has always been a going proposition in American intellectual life (Wilkinson 1988 and 1992). But business in that sector has not been as brisk of late as it used to be. Indeed, the study of American social character in recent years has followed something of the same pattern of prosperity and decline as the postwar American industrial economy. Beginning, perhaps, with Alfred A. Knopf's republication in 1945 of an inexpensive edition of Tocqueville's *Democracy in America,* his long-neglected classic study of American social character, the study of something called "the American character" began to attract growing interest in the postwar years. Such ruminations not only reflected the process of reassessment that naturally accompanied the nation's rise to geopolitical preeminence. They also reflected a crystallizing sense,

---

"exceptionalism." The latter term suggests the notion that the American nation has been somehow excepted from the forces of history and granted an exemption from the binding force of universal laws. I think it is generally far more accurate to see the United States as universalizing itself rather than exempting itself. It is incorrect, for example, to see Tocqueville as a proponent of American exceptionalism, since he argued that democracy in America was merely the leading edge and exemplar of the future all advanced nations would eventually share.

heightened by the unifying experience of war (and perhaps by intimate involvement with the national cultures of Europe), that American society and the individuals constituting it, for all their seeming diversity, shared a distinctive and relatively homogeneous underlying social character. A steady stream of classic works by talented writers of the 1940s and 1950s, such as David Potter, Ralph Barton Perry, Vance Packard, William H. Whyte, Margaret Mead, Geoffrey Gorer, and David Riesman analyzed this homogeneous American character in ways that, though strikingly different in details, gave evidence of a fascination with the shared psychological and social characteristics of Americans. These writers established an immensely rich literature of social observation and interpretation, a resource upon which subsequent writers have been able to continue drawing to this day.

The tradition those works established, however, has lost some of its authority in recent years, particularly in academic circles, under the force of the progressive deconstruction and fragmentation of American history and society into its component parts that has animated much of the past three decades' scholarship. Not that interesting and influential works in the social-character genre do not continue to be written and read. But anyone who now undertakes such works not only has to do battle with a dauntingly protean subject but must also conquer considerable a priori skepticism in the prospective audience — skepticism as to the very possibility (or desirability) of making broad social and cultural generalizations (Hollinger 1985, 182). That these classic studies of the 1940s and 1950s generally focused upon a small cross-section of the population — educated, white, Northeastern or Midwestern, male, probably Protestant, probably professional (or at least white-collar), and almost certainly middle-class — was usually acknowledged by their authors. But the authors assumed that their studies were no less meaningful or representative for that fact, since such groups were believed to set the tone for the society and hold the key to deciphering the society's future tendencies.

Such an assumption cannot be so confidently put forward today, when more particularist considerations of race, class, gender, ethnicity, and regional identity, among others, loom ever larger in readers' eyes; when the intellectual prestige of nationalism (and therefore the plausibility of notions of homogeneous national identity) is at a low ebb; and when the *nom du jour* for "setting the tone" is the more sinister-sound-ing, power-laden Gramscian "hegemony." This tendency to reject broad social characterizations in favor of deep pluralism is more than just a trend among academic scholars. Indeed, when teaching a book like William Whyte's *The Lonely Crowd* in recent years, I have repeatedly been struck by my students' near-instinctive tendency to ask, a touch impatiently, very early on in the discussions: Yes, but what does this book tell us about working-class men? Or women? Or African-Americans? Or (more rarely) white Southerners — evangelicals, fundamentalists, and "plain folk"? And these are good, penetrating questions, all. But there is a danger that they are increasingly being posed rhetorically and automatically, as if the mere invocation of America's social diversity has become an unanswerable trump card, and the perspectives offered by a book like *The Lonely Crowd* thereby rendered unworthy of careful study — an especially ironic turn of events, since these very students and their families by and large fit *The Lonely Crowd*'s demographic sample perfectly, and could learn a lot about themselves by reading it with care. The invocation of diversity and "difference" ought not serve as an intellectual pretext for an unwillingness to engage in self-criticism.

In short, one can, and should, acknowledge the danger that any broad characterizations of "the American character" or "the American mind" will tend to privilege some voices; and yet one should also acknowledge that recognition of and respect for America's cultural diversity can harden into a dogmatic insistence upon the absolute priority of that fact, with a tyrannical veto power over all generalizations. The force of such an intellectual orthodoxy may well inhibit honest efforts at self-examination by inhibiting the making of meaningful and morally challenging observations about the characteristics that contemporary Americans largely share, and handing out self-granted exemptions virtually for the asking. What historian David Hollinger has written about the external conundrum of America's intellectual relationship with Europe, albeit with intellectuals specifically in mind, applies equally to the internal conundrum of the American nation's relationship with its consitutent elements: "If it will not do to assume that everything written in America expresses some mystical American spirit, neither will it do to assume that Americans . . . can be fully understood without assessing their simultaneous involvement in their national community" (Hollinger 1985, 182-83). What it means to be an American may be more complex than ever — and it never has been simple — a meaning that, moreover, surely does not begin to exhaust all one's sources of identity. But it is not without its own irreducible importance, either.

The *pluribus* remains in symbiosis with the *unum*, in short. If the concept of "social character" is to be a valid analytical tool, then it must represent something one participates in, whether or not one does so consciously or willingly; and there is a powerful (and I daresay typically American) impulse to wriggle away from any such characterization, rather than allow oneself, like J. Alfred Prufrock, to be pinned to it. Just as Americans seem prone to engage in acts of grand national characterization, they also seem prone to leave themselves personally out of the pictures they draw, as a way of preserving their sense of autonomy and free agency. The impulse to do anthropology is generally directed at others, not at ourselves; and the image of the Tocquevillean foreign traveler, the not-unsympathetic ethnographer who nevertheless stands cleanly apart from his or her subject, is the archetypal stance for American social-character speculation, especially that undertaken since the Second World War. Perhaps the best way, then, to ensure balance and *mesure* in the use of such generalizations is by paying close and critical attention to the way they have been propounded and to those doing the propounding. By that standard, my students' vivid and heartfelt reactions are themselves important signs of the Zeitgeist, undeniably indicative in their own way of where we have come since the 1950s.

1

Perhaps, then, the examination of evolving American social character is a question of intellectual history as much as it is one of social physiognomy. In that case, the "we" in my title can be taken, at least initially, to refer less to American society as a whole than to those writers and thinkers who have attempted to interpret it; and the guiding perspective in what follows will be the evolving conceptualizations of American social character.[2] I am under no illusion that "theory" and "empirical

2. Although the concept of social character is not hard to grasp in an approximate sense, it is not easily defined with precision; and many of the writers who have employed the term have declined to offer definitions. It would be difficult, therefore, for me to undertake to do so in a sustained analysis of these writers. I can, however, relate the

reality" (or for that matter, fact and value) are so easily separable, and I recognize that this heuristic distinction will prove difficult to maintain in the end. Nevertheless, I propose in what follows to concentrate upon the ways in which a number of influential scholars and writers have described the social psychology and characteristic value orientations of contemporary Americans. In keeping with the overarching theme of "rethinking materialism," I shall be especially interested in examining the role that materialism, in both the philosophical and the moral acceptations of that term, plays in these constellations of the American self, past and present. And, as a historian by training, my disciplinary bias draws me to look for long-term continuities, continuities that can be found in abundance.

It is perhaps fitting, therefore, to begin the analysis with Tocqueville, who is not only the premier nineteenth-century analyst of American social character, but also a writer who gave a great deal of prominence to the social consequences of materialism. In addition, Tocqueville distinguished, as I too wish to do herein, between the two principal senses of the word: *materialism* as a philosophical doctrine that there is no reality but matter, whose motions are governed by immutable physical laws; and *materialism* as an excessive regard for the acquisition and consumption of material things and, more generally, for the means and ends of what Christians call "the world." Even though we tend to use the word rather freely and loosely, these two meanings are distinct; and even though the two meanings are related to one another, the relationship is not an obvious or uncomplicated one. One can be, as George Santayana was, a philosophical materialist who lives like an ascetic. One can be a Pentecostal Christian who lives like a sybarite. In either case, there is an intelligible connection between abstract thought and concrete behavior; but one must first be careful to distinguish them in order to understand that connection.

---

useful characterization made by Erich Fromm, repeated by David Riesman et al. in *The Lonely Crowd* (1969), p. 5: "In order that any society may function well, its members must acquire the kind of character which makes them *want* to act in the way they *have* to act as members of the society or of a special class within it. They have to *desire* what objectively is *necessary* for them to do. *Outer force* is replaced by *inner compulsion,* and by the particular kind of human energy which is channeled into character traits." Both here and throughout the text, I have used for quotation the abridged 1969 edition of *The Lonely Crowd,* which is more readily available than the 1950 edition.

I trust that Tocqueville's general rendering of the American social character is familiar enough that it need rot be rehearsed in detail here. Indeed, his memorable portrait of a feverishly commercial, acquisitive, middle-class, egalitarian, practical-minded, privatistic, restlessly mobile, incurably (and sometimes fanatically) religious, and present-minded American character has so thoroughly permeated all our subsequent notions that many, if not most, seem unavoidably derivative. It is especially fitting to begin our discussion with him because *Democracy in America,* for all its unquestionable prestige, epitomizes the difficulties encountered by all practitioners of American social-character analysis. Indeed, it is for that very reason that the volume has attracted growing fire over the years from revisionist scholars who reject its portrayal of Jacksonian America (and, by extension, of the America of our own day) as an overwhelmingly homogeneous and egalitarian "middle-class democracy" (Wilentz 1988; also see Blumin 1985). But, *pace* such critics, I would argue that the most trenchant recent examinations of American social character have increasingly tended to cast the problem in the same terms that Tocqueville did; and that Tocqueville's answers to the problems of materialism in American life have never been more pertinent than they are today.

It is important, then, to re-emphasize some features of Tocqueville's understanding of political society that have been comparatively neglected, both by his supporters and his detractors. André Jardin has made it clear in his recent biography that Tocqueville, for all his concessions to the classical-liberal worldview and to the driving force of self-interest in modern politics, never abandoned an intensely classical, civic-humanist, even republican view of the proper ends of political society, and an exalted conception of citizenship that stressed the need to participate fully in public life in order to fully realize one's nature (Shalhope 1972 and 1982; Pocock 1975, especially pp. 506-52). Tocqueville took great pains to distinguish selfishness, which was a perpetual but universal vice, from individualism, which he regarded as a particularly novel and worrisome by-product of democratic social relations. Unlike selfishness, individualism was an embryonic philosophy of life, tailored to democratic sensibilities — a "mature and calm feeling" that disposed each person to "sever himself from the mass of his fellows and to draw apart with his family and friends" (Tocqueville 1945, 2:104; subsequent page references come from this edition). Nothing about the coming of democracy worried Tocqueville more than the eventual possibility of an evacuation and collapse of the public sphere: the possibility that individuals, directing their lives by the motive force of their acquisitive desires, would withdraw from public life and thereby abandon the pursuit of anything higher and more ennobling than the comfort and enrichment of themselves and their coteries.

So concerns about materialism, and the tendency toward materialism he found at the heart of the American ethos, were at the very heart of Tocqueville's understanding of American social character and of American religion. Democratic societies, he believed, were especially prone to fall under materialism's spell. He argued that it was in the nature of such societies, given their formal commitment to the egalitarian social ideal, that their inhabitants would become increasingly focused upon the pursuit of their own physical well-being. "The passion for physical comforts," he declared, "is essentially a passion of the middle classes"; hence, in the overwhelmingly middle-class, democratic United States, "the love of well-being has now become the predominant taste of the nation" (2:137-38). In the particular American context, where the principle of self-interest rightly understood *(intérêt bien entendu)* had served to combat the pathologies of individualism by providing a low but serviceable criterion of moral deliberation, such a passion had so far proved largely compatible with the requirements of public order. Yet Tocqueville worried about the longer run and its less visible problems. He wondered at the "strange melancholy," "secret disquietude," and "inconstancy" that afflicted the hearts of so many Americans, who remained restless in their prosperity because no degree of equality was sufficient to still the ever-churning desires of their covetous hearts (2:144-47). He also worried that the exclusive pursuit of worldly affairs would eventually blind Americans to the pursuit of loftier goals, degrade their highest faculties, and — worst of all — sap their sense of free will. "[A] kind of virtuous materialism may ultimately be established in the world," he brooded, "which would not corrupt, but enervate, the soul and noiselessly unbend its springs of action" (2:141). With that gloomy prospect in mind, he urged democratic legislators to support, by their words and their example, religious beliefs and practices, which he believed would counteract such untoward tendencies (2:152-56).

In the above context, then, Tocqueville's use of the term "materialism" refers not merely to a passion for physical gratifications but to doctrines of philosophical materialism: "those pernicious theories . . . which tend to inculcate that all perishes with the body." To his mind, the distinction was all-important. Although he was quite willing to accept the pervasive taste for physical gratifications that democracy seemed to breed, he reserved some of the harshest language in the entire *Democracy* to attack materialist theories and those "by whom such theories are professed." He labeled these "offensive" materialists "brutes" and "natural foes of the whole people"; they left him "disgusted at their arrogance." Materialism as doctrine was nothing less than "a dangerous disease of the human mind," whose effects were especially to be dreaded in a democracy, which already had profound tendencies in that direction. So far, Tocqueville conjectured, the pervasive religiosity of Americans had protected them against this disease, so that "among them materialism may be said hardly to exist," despite their enormous appetite for physical gratifications. But without the bulwark of religion, and particularly without an elevating belief in the immortality of the soul, Americans' taste for physical gratification would easily become all-consuming, fed by the "pernicious" belief that perishable matter is all there is. The mutually reinforcing nature of such harmful beliefs and passions would lock the nation to a "fatal circle," which would spiral downward into paralysis and ignominy (2:154).

Despite the vituperative language, it is not entirely clear whether Tocqueville ultimately esteemed religion for its truth or its utility. Perhaps if materialism could have served the civic purposes for which he looked to religion, he would not even have excoriated it. In any event, Tocqueville's basic requirements for an acceptable religious faith were fairly simple and not terribly demanding: above all, it had to support belief in the soul's independence of, and persistence beyond, the body.[3] Such an emphasis reflects one of the central themes of the *Democracy*: Tocqueville's fear that philosophies of materialistic determinism were not only false but disastrous in their moral effects. Although he spent much of the book examining the ways in which the structural shift toward equality led to profound changes in individual and social character, his trenchant final words left no doubt that the study of such material factors and their effects did not negate the imperative reality of free will:

3. He was even willing to prefer belief in metempsychosis to materialist unbelief; it is better to believe "that the soul of man will pass into the carcass of a hog" than to believe "that the soul of man is nothing at all" (2:155).

It is true that around every man a fatal circle is traced beyond which he cannot pass; but within the wide verge of that circle he is powerful and free; as it is with man, so with communities. The nations of our time cannot prevent the conditions of men from becoming equal, but it depends upon themselves whether the principle of equality is to lead them to servitude or freedom, to knowledge or barbarism, to prosperity or wretchedness. (2:352)

At the heart of Tocqueville's work, then, was a sense of the contingency of human affairs, and of the moral responsibility such contingency necessarily enjoins upon us. Americans needed a non-materialistic philosophy to counter their tendency toward materialistic behavior. The pursuit of physical well-being was not in itself fatal, but it could readily *become* so if supported by a materialistic philosophy. Tocqueville had identified a potentially disabling cultural contradiction inherent in materialism. Even if one were to live one's life purely in "the service of the body," he argued, such an undertaking required a "great and strong soul" to be successful; and a materialist philosophy would, in due course, erode that strength and render it ineffectual. If Americans "were ever to content themselves [solely] with material objects, it is probable that they would lose by degrees the art of producing them" (2:157). Even the preservation of the American style of material acquisitiveness eventually required a compensatory dose of religion, not merely as an antidote but also as an indispensable source for the renewal and empowerment of the free will.

2

It was no coincidence that the revival of interest in Tocqueville's reflections upon Jacksonian America reached its peak in the years after the Second World War — another era of unprecedented affluence and immense physical and social mobility, in which Tocquevillean characterizations of America as a restless middle-class democracy seemed especially apropos. Tocqueville's somewhat bland and functionalist advocacy of an American religion-in-general (and disdain for sectarian fanaticism) also seemed in keeping with the religious temper of those years, and is somewhat crudely approximated in President Eisenhower's famous remark that "Our form of government has no sense unless it is founded in a deeply felt religious faith, and I don't care what it is" (Henry 1981, 41; Herberg 1955, 84). Indeed, as Will Herberg pointed out in *Protestant—Catholic—Jew* (1955), wherein Eisenhower's statement was immortalized, the postwar era saw the boundaries separating conflicting faith communities being progressively blurred or breached. The inexorable process of Americanization was transforming these formerly separate or antagonistic communities into hearty fellow exponents of the "American Way of Life," a generalized civil-religious faith in democracy, individualism, tolerance, idealism, and so on, whose genial inclusiveness increasingly took precedence over the more strenuous and particularistic truth claims of the traditional faith communities (Herberg 1955, 75-90).

The concept of "civil religion" itself, though it was not widely used by American scholars before the appearance of an influential essay in 1967 by the sociologist Robert Bellah (Herberg himself had used the term "civic religion"), had been adapted for a use that was thoroughly Tocquevillean in its thrust (Bellah 1967; Herberg 1955, 263). "Civil religion" aimed to secure legitimacy and moral credibility for the secular political and social order by linking it to a transcendent order, which would serve both as a transcendent source of validation and a transcendent standard by which the nation's actions in the world would be judged. While the American version of civil religion, unlike Rousseau's, did not require the suppression or subordination of anterior faiths, it presumed a high degree of willing adaptation and cultural accommodation. More specifically, it presumed that energies formerly enclosed within denominational and confessional barriers would now be made politically available, canalized into a sacralization of the state and the extant social order.

One can identify, then, a distinctively Tocquevillean approach to the phenomenon of American materialism, to its place in the American social character, and to the role of religion (and civil religion) in countering it. None of this, however, was much cause for celebration in the eyes of Will Herberg. His scathing critique-cum-lamentation over the deplorable state of American religion concluded with a reminder that, though Americans seemed to be incurably religious, as evidenced by their swelling congregations and growing denominations, the quality of their faith (which was at bottom, he contended, little more than a "faith in religion itself") had descended into something highly questionable. The American Way of Life, however worthy it might be in many respects, was not an appropriate object of religious piety; indeed, Herberg claimed, the Jewish and Christian traditions had always regarded "civic religion" as nothing less than idolatry. He contended that American religion had been adulterated into a "man-centered" spiritual system, a "cult of culture and society, in which the 'right' social order and the received cultural values are divinized by being identified with the divine purpose." Herberg lamented the disappearance of a more authentically biblical sense of a God whose awesome, transcendent, and inscrutable Being stood over, and in judgment of, all worldly and human institutions. The absence of such a sense, he averred, was secularism in all but name (Herberg 1955, 262-70).

One could, of course, argue that a truly biblical Judaism was nothing if not civil-religious; but Herberg's cultural point was clear enough. Even so, for all the dissimilarity in tone and emphasis of Herberg's critique, the terms of his analysis of American religion and its relationship to society were not yet dramatically dissimilar from Tocqueville's. Nevertheless, the two had markedly different viewpoints. The latter was well aware, for example, of the this-worldly, results-oriented tendencies of American religious practices and beliefs; but he interpreted these as inevitable by-products of the principle of self-interest rightly understood and not, therefore, to be discouraged or disparaged (2:129-35). Not so Herberg, who felt that the avid American pursuit of "sociability," "belongingness," and "peace of mind" were betrayals of the stern otherliness of the biblical prophets, and that the civil-religious covenant between the Kingdom of Heaven and the United States of America shamelessly ignored the proper boundary between the sacred and the secular, debasing both in the process. What Tocqueville found to be pallid virtue, Herberg saw as flagrant vice. The former saw civil religion's benefits, the latter only its liabilities.

Whence the great differences between two writers whose fundamental terms of analysis were so similar? Especially in light of the intense and widespread interest in Tocqueville's work at the very time that Herberg was writing?[4] Although these questions admit of a multitude

---

4. It should be noted, however, that *Protestant—Catholic—Jew* showed virtually no influence explicitly deriving from the *Democracy*.

of possible answers, especially when the writers in question are separated by nationality, religious tradition, and more than a century's time, one point stands out; and this point directly bears on the question of materialism and its proper place in American life. Tocqueville extolled the principle of "self-interest rightly understood" because he saw in it an answer — in fact, the only plausible answer — to the problem of achieving and preserving a modicum of social cohesion in an increasingly fluid, egalitarian, individualistic, and potentially disorderly society. "No power on earth," he asserted, "can prevent the increasing equality of conditions from inclining the human mind to seek out what is useful or from leading every member of the community to be wrapped up in himself." It was inevitable, he felt, that Americans would be drawn to *acquisitive* materialism. The only real option left, then, was to teach citizens the proper *understanding* of their self-interest. In the past, they might have been taught that behavior can be virtuous only if it is sacrificial or disinterested; but that appeal was no longer effective. Now they must be persuaded that it is in their own interest to be virtuous. Without such education, "the time is fast approaching when freedom, public peace, and social order itself will not be able to exist" (2:132). Tocqueville was, in a word, more concerned with promoting social order than promoting a profounder faith and a deeper spirituality.

But such were not the priorities of Herberg; nor were they the priorities of most of the distinguished social critics of the postwar era, such as Reinhold Niebuhr and David Riesman, who were among the most visible intellectual influences in the background of *Protestant—Catholic—Jew.* Such writers did not worry about the possibility of an American society that lacked fundamental cohesion. Far from thinking that America faced the prospect of individualistic disorder, nearly all of them worried about a diametrically opposite prospect: that modern Americans were being socialized within an inch of their lives, at great peril to their dignity as free and autonomous human beings. These writers perceived the great task of the postwar era as the preservation of the possibility of genuine individuality in the face of a world increasingly smothered or hemmed in by vast corporate business organizations, impersonal public bureaucracies, and the relentless intrusions, manipulations, and impertinent psychic demands of modern social existence. Although Tocqueville did not neglect these potential pitfalls, and indeed warned darkly of the tyranny of the majority and of the possibility of a "democratic despotism," he thought those tendencies were for the moment largely checked by mitigating counterforces, so that the problems they might create lay, for the most part, well in the future (1:264-95; 2:334-48). For the critics of postwar American life, those problems had now come to the fore.

A number of factors contributed to the postwar critics' state of mind. Clearly, as Rupert Wilkinson has pointed out, they were tapping into longstanding habits of antinomian, anti-institutional, anti-group suspicion among American thinkers — what Wilkinson has called the great American "fear of being owned" (Wilkinson 1988, 48-50; also see Elkins 1959 and Fredrickson 1965). A tradition of nervous but resolute independence and fear of authority had been evident in American society since the founding of the Republic — and indeed, even earlier, in the radical Whig and libertarian rhetoric that was so important in catalyzing the Revolution (Bailyn 1967). Tocqueville himself derived some of his notions about the tyranny of the majority and other features of American political institutions less from observation than from a careful reading of indigenous American sources, including James Madison's *Federalist* 51 (Jardin 1988, 201-2, 216; the quotation from the *Federalist* appears on 1:279 of the *Democracy*). The radical individualism of a figure like Ralph Waldo Emerson, who boldly disdained institutions and organizational constraints as impertinences to the spirit, has always loomed large and influential in the past century and a half of American experience. Without doubt, too, the spectacle, in the twentieth century, of the rise of European totalitarianism and its doleful effects played a decisive role in rekindling Americans' primal fears of a collectivist imprisonment, causing them to identify the preservation of the very possibility of individual integrity with the cause of American civilization. It is especially striking to note that this individualist tradition seems only to have gained strength as modern America has become more visibly organized and corporate; and that the centripetal and corporatist offerings of American social thinkers in the decades after the Civil War, ranging from Edward Bellamy and Lester Frank Ward to Herbert Croly and John Dewey, have proved so fragile and ineffectual. That a conscious ethos of individualism has only gained ground as American life has become more palpably corporate suggests a relationship between social thought and social reality that is, to say the least, complex and problematic, an issue to which we shall return later (McGerr 1993).

Such a seeming paradox again should remind us that our images of social reality are mediated by those who map and interpret it. Such a consideration is particularly relevant in the postwar instance. The most perdurable images we have of the postwar era were themselves the productions of an increasingly prominent, self-conscious, and self-confident American intellectual class; hence, those images were likely to be especially reflective of those intellectuals' most characteristic concerns. G. M. Young once observed that Victorian Britain was condemned to be known primarily through the images put forward by its satirists, notably the acid portraiture in Lytton Strachey's *Eminent Victorians* and *Queen Victoria*. Is it possible that our images of the postwar years, especially the fifties, are similarly filtered by influential books like David Riesman's *The Lonely Crowd*, William Whyte's *The Organization Man*, Sloan Wilson's *The Man in the Gray Flannel Suit*, Vance Packard's *The Status Seekers*, C. Wright Mills's *White Collar*, and John Keats's *The Crack in the Picture Window?* It is never easy to distinguish between structures of meaning and the meanings they have structured, to know where intellectual history leaves off and social history begins, to separate reportage from the event reported. It is even more difficult to do so in an era in which skillful use of the organs of mass communications can impart a palpable, even heightened sense of reality to nearly any interpretation of social conditions.

3

For our present purposes, though, it is sufficient to observe that many of the most influential analysts of social character in the postwar years seemed obsessed with the specter of a soft-totalitarian social tyranny in America. This tendency was especially evident in *The Organization Man*, perhaps because of the lucid, hard-hitting journalistic style of its author, William Whyte. If Americans had an ingrained fear of being owned, the advent of the modern organizational society had now really given them something to be afraid of. The new men who worked in The Organization, Whyte asserted, "*belong* to it as well." They had "left home, spiritually as well as physically, to take the vows of organization life." Such men were now "the mind and soul of our great self-perpetuating institutions" and "the dominant members of our society." They were the most prominent example of a process of "collectivization . . . af-fect[ing] almost every field of work" in modern America. They had abandoned the Protestant ethic of their elders, which had prescribed hard work and competition as the route to individual salvation, for the security of a social ethic, which "rationalizes the organization's demands for fealty." The social ethic more generally "makes morally legitimate the pressures of society against the individual." Man, in its view, is essentially a social creature who becomes worthwhile only "by sublimat-ing himself in the group." Therefore, what we think of as legitimate conflicts are in fact merely "misunderstandings" and "breakdowns in communication," which can be resolved by the techniques of those skilled in the science of "human relations" (Whyte 1956, 3-15).

Such quotes should not lead one to think that Whyte was nostal-gically advocating a reversion to the Protestant ethic and a wholesale return to the pre-organizational ways of the eighteenth or nineteenth centuries. Such was clearly not the case. As an editor and writer for *Fortune* magazine, he knew too much about the organizational require-ments of modern business for that. Nor should the book be regarded simply as a tendentious and hostile caricature of organizational life, for it is more than that. Taken as a whole, it offers a rich, detailed, complex, and largely sympathetic portrait of the life of The Organization Man as he moves through all his stages and habitats of life, ranging from his formative experiences of socialization in college, to the stresses and behavioral requirements of his workplace, to the unique texture of his home and family life, with special extended attention given in the last case to the "package suburb" of Park Forest, Illinois. But when all was said and done, Whyte's judgment upon that organizational way of life was harsh. He concluded the book by warning his readers that they must actively resist the possibility of "the dehumanized collective that so haunts our thoughts."

[The Organization Man]. . . must *fight* The Organization. . . . For the demands for his surrender are constant and powerful, and the more he has come to like the life of organization the more difficult does he find it to resist these demands, or even to recognize them. It is wretched, dispiriting advice to hold before him the dream that ideally there need be no conflict between him and society. There always is; there always must be. Ideology cannot wish it away; the peace of mind

offered by organization remains a surrender, and no less so for being
offered in benevolence. That is the problem. (448)

The Lonely Crowd, though it was published six years before *The
Organization Man* and was a notable influence upon Whyte's thinking,
was in many respects a more intellectually ambitious and sophisticated
work, with more interesting implications and more lasting intrinsic
value. Yet it was, in the end, aimed at similar phenomena and evinced
similar sets of concerns. Riesman and his collaborators, Nathan Glazer
and Reuel Denney, used the concept of social character as an analytical
tool for the description of "the changing American character," attempting to correlate three different typologies of social character (or "modes
of conformity") with three successive stages in the social, economic,
and, most importantly, demographic development of the West.[5] The
stages were identified by the source of the sanctioning power that
directed the individual: for the static, premodern, feudal, ascriptive
social order, *tradition-direction;* for the mobile, modern, capitalistic,
fluid, expansive, achievement-oriented and production-driven social order, *inner-direction;* and for the emerging new world of large
corporations, mass communications, advertising and salesmanship,
information and symbol manipulation, "human relations," profession-
alized management techniques, personality-oriented workplace, and
consumption-driven economy, *other-direction* (Riesman et al. 1969,
5-36). The endlessly suggestive dichotomy of inner-direction and
other-direction was the core of Riesman's achievement, and that dichotomy was beautifully captured in a pair of memorable images: the
inner-directed man was guided through life's storm and stress by the
unfailing inward gyroscope of his internalized values, while the other-
directed man employed a radar device to orient himself by reference
to the shifting needs and expectations of his peers.

One of the many things that made *The Lonely Crowd* so complex
a work was its ambivalence toward other-direction, which was in part
a consequence of its focus upon social character. Although Riesman's

5. This statement needs to be qualified, since Riesman also clearly suggested that
the pattern of successive forms of "directedness" might be enacted within a single culture
or civilization; see, for example, his discussion of ancient Athens on pp. 25-27. While it
is tempting to see in *The Lonely Crowd* a repackaged version of Marxian metahistory,
Riesman's use of his categories does not lend itself to that reading.

conception of the "other-directed" type is borrowed from Erich Fromm's notion of the "marketing orientation," as well as from John Stuart Mill's notion of "other-regarding" conduct (and possibly even the Kantian notion of "heteronomy"), its use was reinforced by Riesman's considerable familiarity with cultural anthropology, which offered a non-evaluative style of social inquiry that greatly appealed to him. The chief use of the concept of social character, if rigorously employed, was in providing a non-evaluative way to conceptualize large-scale social-psychological change, without reference to the tendentious and value-laden categories of "progress" or "decadence." In this view, an alteration in social character merely represented a change from one state to another, like an organic evolutionary adaptation, without any ultimate judgment being attached, one way or another, to the significance of that change. The concept of social character certainly enables, and to some extent entails, such strict Weberian social-scientific neutrality.

But if Weber himself was never as neutral as he aspired to be, neither did *The Lonely Crowd* consistently sustain a neutral tone toward the change from inner-direction to other-direction. In some places, Riesman seemed to suggest that the flexibility and sociability of other-direction represented a considerable improvement over the rigid and asocial compulsiveness of inner-direction. In many other places, however, he found it difficult to refrain from criticizing the other-directed personality type — sometimes directly, more often implicitly in the diction and imagery used, and nearly always in ways that would later be amplified in a text like *The Organization Man*. Adding to the undercurrent of critique were *The Lonely Crowd*'s concluding pages, which put forward an alternative characterological ideal — called "autonomy" — to that offered by other-direction (*and,* though many of Riesman's readers miss this point, also to the compulsiveness of inner-direction). The introduction of "autonomy" as a prospective individual and social ideal suggests that *The Lonely Crowd* was in fact a hybrid work, part descriptive social science, part prescriptive moral critique. Such multiplicity probably contributed to the book's popular success, for it ensured that the book would be read in different ways by different readers. But a surprising number of them, including some highly intelligent readers, read *The Lonely Crowd* as a lament for the passing of the solid, individualistic, inner-directed Victorian character, and its replacement by the shallow, glad-handing, other-directed hollow man of today. Such readers may have misread the book in important ways, failing to note the important distinction between inner-direction and autonomy, or failing to give the latter concept sufficient independent weight; but they did not misconstrue the book's gravamen (McClay 1993). Just as *The Organization Man* urged individuals to "fight the organization," *The Lonely Crowd* promoted the ideal of autonomy as a personalized psychological answer to an oversocialized world.

4

Such similarity also is evident in the two books' treatment of the American tendency toward materialism, a treatment that, not surprisingly, takes us some distance beyond the Tocquevillean emphasis upon the need for a religious "check" upon acquisitive impulses. It is a historiographical truism that, by the middle of the 1920s, the behavioral center of gravity in the American economy had shifted from production to consumption; and *The Lonely Crowd* appropriately devoted much attention to the social psychology of consumption, anticipating in many particulars the abundant scholarship on consumer culture in our own time. Riesman even endorsed Leo Lowenthal's claim that postwar American popular culture was dominated by images of "heroes of consumption" rather than the "heroes of production" of former, inner-directed times (209). Riesman was therefore keenly interested in the process of consumer training, one of the critical tasks of the other-directed orientation in an economy of abundance. But he concluded, perhaps surprisingly, that in the contemporary setting, the extreme importance placed upon "the socialization of consumer preferences" clearly showed that neither possession and consumption of the objects themselves nor the egoistic opportunity to publicly display one's discriminating tastes constituted the deepest motive for this brand of consumerism.

On the contrary, Riesman argued, other-directed preferences in consumption reflected fundamentally *social* values, not individual or personal ones:

> For the objects [of consumption] are hardly given meaning in private and personal values when they are so heavily used as counters in a preferential method of relating oneself to others. The cultural objects,

whatever their nature, are mementos that somehow remain un-humanized by the force of a genuinely personal, idiosyncratic attach-ment. (77-78)

This kind of consumer, he believed, was far removed from the spirit of pure acquisitiveness that one encounters in the Tocquevillean portrait — though not at all removed from the tensions of status that Tocqueville saw as an inevitable result of social equality:

> The consumer today has most of his potential individuality trained out of him by his membership in the consumer's union. He is kept within limits on his consumption not by goal-directed but by other-directed guidance, kept from splurging too much by fear of others' envy, and from consuming too little by his own envy of the others. (79)

In other words, in modern American society, the act of consumption itself had been transformed into a means of constituting and maintain-ing community and relatedness; and consumer preferences had there-fore become agents and products of socialization (73).

It is perhaps evident from these remarks that Riesman felt little of the standard-issue Puritan-republican moralistic hostility to consump-tion per se. Indeed, *The Lonely Crowd* took a very sunny view of con-sumption and, more generally, of leisure and play, as potentially superior avenues toward free personal development. His chief regret about Amer-ican materialism was the narrow, passionless, ovine, and status-obsessed way that Americans made their consumption choices.[6] As he put it in a discussion of the role of education in shaping the outer-directed round of life, "the peer-group becomes the measure of all things; the individual has few defenses the group cannot batter down" (82). Nor did Riesman feel any need to offer religion — about which *The Lonely Crowd* said next to nothing and seemed to regard as irrelevant — or any other notions of moral accountability as counterweights to the American tendency toward material acquisitiveness. On the contrary, his discus-

6. Riesman's correspondence with Hannah Arendt during the composition of *The Lonely Crowd* reveals that "Passionless Existence in America" was the original work-ing title of what became *The Lonely Crowd*. See Young-Bruehl 1982, 252.

sion of the moralistic style in politics reflected a rather unfavorable view of the public uses of such moralizing (172-80). One certainly should not conclude from this that Riesman was writing as a kind of genial American Nietzschean; in fact, much of his work, not excepting *The Lonely Crowd*, was deeply concerned with moral and political issues, although the issues were addressed in a highly individualistic, critical fashion that rigorously eschewed expressions of moralism.[7] Rather, it is an indication of how profoundly Riesman felt that the most serious threat to the social character of Americans, circa 1950, was the prospect of excessive socialization that other-direction seemed to portend; and that the way to address this threat was by appealing to a new counterideal of autonomy that would open up a *more* uninhibited, and individualized, exploration of the possibilities for personal expression through consumption and leisure activities (see especially 239-307). The Tocquevillean anxiety that materialism and individualism in American life might need to be forcefully countered is simply absent, not so much rejected as ignored.

Riesman's view of materialism in American life was largely paralleled in *The Organization Man*. Whyte noted that heroes of recent American fiction did not covet great riches, but rather were "positively greedy for the good life," which involved no "renunciation of materialism." Instead, Whyte saw what he called "sanctimonious materialism," in which heroes (like Tom Rath of *The Man in the Gray Flannel Suit*) walked away from the risks and lures of Dreiserian drivenness and ambition — and made out better anyway! The Organization let them have their cake and eat it too. Such a hero's "precipitous flight from the bitch goddess success will enable him to live a lot more comfortably than the ulcerated colleagues left behind" — and it was the latter group anyway, Whyte argued, who were actually the less materialistic, if such a quality is to be measured by one's quixotic willingness to sacrifice comfort for the sake of great ambitions and intangible goals. In the past, novels had to be built around the conflict of the individual with society — but no more, since now "society is so benevolent that there is no conflict left in it for anyone to be rebellious about" (Whyte 1956, 278-79).

---

7. Riesman is linked with Nietzsche, via Erich Fromm, by Bloom in *The Closing of the American Mind* (1987, 144-55). The most charitable thing to say about this account is that it does not appear to have been based upon a reading of *The Lonely Crowd*.

As for the meaning of "the good life" in Whyte's understanding, it was inseparable from the cohesiveness of the Organization and the special kind of social solidarity inherent in the new suburban lifestyle. In the latter environment, the regnant ideology of consumption had become, *contra* Veblen, one of *in*conspicuous consumption (a phrase that Whyte used as a chapter title) and marginal, non-invidious distinctions. When Whyte's suburbanites repeatedly professed that there was no compulsion to "keep up with the Joneses" in their neighborhood, their protestations took on, to him, the force of an ethical precept, "a social compact" which assured that all who wished to be accepted in the social life of the community could be, so long as they stayed within a certain range of visible consumption — not more, and not less. "The job . . . is not to keep up with the Joneses," Whyte averred. "It's to keep *down* with them" (345-64, especially 345-46). The force of group taste and group judgment determined what levels of consumption were acceptable; and one ignored the group's judgment at the risk of social ostracism.

In general, then, Whyte, like Riesman, suggested that the problem with American materialism was less one of rampant anarchic greed and naked egoism than one of a pervasive, almost suffocating socialization of desire inherent in the organized, other-directed order of things. Far from expressing individual wants and urges, acts of material consumption in postwar America instantly took on social meaning, becoming linked to an all-embracing system of social signs and status indicators, whose ultimate purpose was not individual gratification but rather the promotion of social cohesion and the maintenance of group identity. The selection and display of consumer goods inevitably involved one in an act of self-presentation, but in a rather different way than Veblen had envisioned: one bought "status symbols" not to stand out but to fit in.

Nor did Whyte give any credence to the notion that religion might be needed to act as a check on materialistic impulses. Looking at the example of the metadenominational United Protestant Church in Park Forest, led by its practical-minded minister Hugo Leinberger, all Whyte saw was that the desire for social belonging in "the church of suburbia" was so intense as to overwhelm all concerns about doctrinal and denominational distinctions. Religion has always been a powerful force behind the construction of human communities; but in Whyte's eyes it seemed that religion's power came less from its creedal and doctrinal content than from its status as yet another desirable, shared consumer good. And, unlike Herberg, Whyte was not unwilling to praise such churches for at least meeting the social needs of their congregations — the clear implication being that the churches would have little else to offer anyway (421-22). In the end, it seemed, the great juggernaut of Social Organization had made even the church bow its knee to the Social Ethic as Lord and Savior.

5

Under such circumstances the pursuit of individuation, of "idiosyncratic" pleasure and uncoerced gratification, represented an act of radical rebellion. Riesman's book was particularly alive to that possibility, and it attempted to elevate dramatically the cultural status of fantasy and play in a culture of affluence for which the Protestant ethic no longer seemed viable. Play, it argued,

> far from having to be the residual sphere left over from work-time and work-feeling, can increasingly become the sphere for the development of skill and competence in the art of living. Play may prove to be the sphere in which there is still some room left for the would-be autonomous man to reclaim his individual character from the pervasive demands of his social character. (276)

Riesman urged that researchers reorient their thinking away from the tendency to give cultural priority to work; and he sought to liberate consumption from its community-building responsibilities and other social constraints. He spoke with disdain of hidebound "neotraditionalists," whose critiques of contemporary life boiled down to an assumption that "people have not too little freedom but too much." Such critics (some of whom spoke "from a religious platform," others of a concern with "urban anomie") wanted to prescribe a kind of premodern social order and "freeze people into communities in which friendship will be based largely on propinquity" — even though their "own friends were scattered over two continents"! Better, he argued, to embrace and maximize the freedoms we already enjoy, and reconceptualize consumership and play as avenues toward autonomy, essential tools in the modern art of living. Indeed, he argued, the findings of market researchers could be used not to manipulate consumers but to "find out not so much what people want but what with liberated fantasy they might want" (302-3).

There was a feeling of boundlessness and openness in this benign vision of material consumption, a feeling of implicit trust in the dignity and trustworthiness of human desire, and a sense that modern American society was cohesive in some relatively simple fashion — feelings that Riesman himself now labels, in retrospect, a form of innocence (Riesman 1990, 78). But if it was innocence, it was hardly his or *The Lonely Crowd*'s alone. Americans, of course, have an inordinate fascination with the loss of innocence; and if all the assertions that historians, journalists, and others have ever made about "the end of American innocence" could somehow be laid end to end, they could surely pave the road to perdition several times over. Yet the postwar era is especially susceptible to this treatment, since it has been so often rendered in nostalgic hues as an era of rosy and sturdy innocence, a portrait of social solidity that is reflected in the imagery of the popular culture of the time. This has long made the fifties an attractive target for social critics, and the scholarly industry thereby generated shows no sign of abating. Yet it has become clear in the intervening four decades that the quest for autonomy that *The Lonely Crowd* and *The Organization Man* expressed and underwrote actually represented two of the most venerable of American traditions: antinomianism and anti-institutionalism. If the fifties was an unusual decade, not the least unusual of its features was Americans' willingness to lend conscious support to a more corporate social ideal, a willingness that, as subsequent years made clear, has clearly been the exception, not the rule, in the American past.

The critics of the fifties offered nothing to counter that social ethic except a more unabashedly individualistic ideal of consumership and play, which, whether or not they meant it to, recalled and revived elements of the heroic Emersonian antinomianism (and laissez-faire economics) of the nineteenth century. The great cultural revolt against the "conformity" of the fifties, a revolt that became widespread in the sixties, and whose effects are still readily visible in the "culture wars" of our own time, was made in the name of ideals offered by the critics of the fifties. That such a revolt, when it came, shocked many of those same critics, notably Riesman himself, perhaps indicates how easy it had been for them to overestimate the cohesiveness and durability of what was, in retrospect, a rather fragile, shallow, and incompletely assimilated American social ethos. In any event, the ensuing years have seen an intensification of anti-institutional sentiment, a weakening of national cohesion, and the emergence of fundamentally incompatible under-standings of the nation's legitimating principles (Wuthnow 1988a). The fifties model of a homogeneous middle-class culture whose individual-istic and materialistic tendencies were held in check by a pervasive social order legitimated by a consensual civil-religious faith could not stand, and begins to look like an episode or interlude. Small wonder that the most influential social and cultural histories of the sixties and seventies bear titles like *Coming Apart* and *The Unraveling of America*.

Such titles, and the characterizations that went with them, suggest the rise of a strikingly different literature of social criticism, fueled by an entirely different set of concerns: concerns over the fragmentation of American society, the dangers of unchecked self-seeking and acquisi-tive individualism, and the consequent evaporation of widely agreed-upon normative standards of behavior and morally binding notions of the common good. I will be examining several of the most important expressions of this new social-character literature below; but I should hasten to add, at the outset, that one must be cautious about adopting these generalizations too broadly. However intellectually neat it might be, it would be misleading to rest content with a simple contrast between the fifties and the sixties as eras of, respectively, conformism and anti-nomianism. As Tocqueville well understood, individualism and social conformism are not necessarily diametric opposites; and the very fact that the appeals to individualism made by Riesman and Whyte were so resonant indicated that their writings could confidently appeal to some-thing already present in the culture of the time.

One does not have to look very hard to notice that individualistic, anti-institutional, and sometimes angrily antinomian impulses of those years had already been bubbling to the surface of the popular culture of the fifties. If *Father Knows Best* offered reassurance of the reliability and solidity of the "traditional" family, the troubled figure of youthful rebel *maudit* James Dean (around whom a cult crystallized after his death in 1955 in an auto accident) conveyed very different sentiments. One of the paradigmatic moments of the decade occurred at the very end of the great Western film *High Noon* (1952), in which a marshall played by Gary Cooper has just defended his despicably cowardly townspeople against an assault launched by a vicious criminal and his henchmen. Once the bitter job is done, Cooper strips off his badge with disgust, casts it in the dust, and stalks away from the town to start a new life with his new Quaker wife, played by Grace Kelly. Whether one understands *High Noon* as a parable of Hollywood McCarthyism, of Cold War conformism, or of the Korean War — and it can accommodate all those meanings — its larger message is one of profound disaffection with the *nomoi* and angry withdrawal from the responsibilities and constrictions of conventional social and institutional life. Such a message is not unlike that conveyed by Beat writers like Jack Kerouac and Allen Ginsberg; and at the same time it recalls the specter of privatization and withdrawal that had haunted Tocqueville.

One could endlessly multiply examples — touching on, for example, the rise of rock 'n roll music, or the devastating portrait of other-direction presented in Arthur Miller's play *Death of a Salesman* — but I trust the general point is clear: the success enjoyed by works like *The Lonely Crowd* and *The Organization Man* indicates that they may have reflected American culture as much as (if not more than) they opposed it. What is not quite so clear, however, is the precise relationship between these modes of expression or fantasy and the actual conditions out of which they arose. Or, to put the question more generally, what was the relationship between the "new" expressive individualism of the postwar years and the increasingly organized conditions of American social life in those same years? Was the relationship one of psychological compensation or complementarity, a kind of safety valve? Or was it more interactive and dialectical? Did the vogue of the Western in the postwar years seek to preserve the individualism of the frontier in safe fantasy, establishing it as a liminal state whose existence paradoxically confirmed the triumph of organization (Turner 1967 and 1969)? Or was that fantasy itself a powerful alternative source of energy and moral direction — as in John F. Kennedy's invocation of the "New Frontier" — leavening and transforming the inertness of corporate life? And what are the implications for the role of acquisitive materialism in American life? Did organization actually liberate consumption, permit it to become an act of genuine self-expression? Or did it merely offer the illusion of autonomy in an administered world where all important decisions have already been made?

6

In any event, concerns about the meaning and effects of expressive individualism in postwar American culture, and about the recovery of legitimate grounds for social cohesion and for commitments outside of the self, have become the issues at the heart of much of the social-character work done in the last fifteen years. It will sharpen the issues further and bring us up to the present to look at three examples of this literature, all of which have appeared since 1979: Christopher Lasch's *The Culture of Narcissism* (1979), the collaborative effort, led by Robert N. Bellah, entitled *Habits of the Heart* (1985), and Paul Leinberger and Bruce Tucker's *The New Individualists: The Generation after the Organization Man* (1991). Each offers an intriguing piece of the puzzle of evolving American social-character interpretation.

Lasch's book has often been read as a jeremiad against the selfish indulgence of what Tom Wolfe called "The Me Decade." It is that; but it is also more than that. The first thing one should notice about it is its subtitle: *American Life in an Age of Diminishing Expectations.* If the genial temper of *The Lonely Crowd* offered projections of smooth-sailing affluence as far as the eye could see, *The Culture of Narcissism* reflected the shipwreck of that material optimism. In other respects, too, Lasch's tone and view could not have been more different; far from fearing the excessive socialization of the self, Lasch expressed contempt, in his preface, for America's "culture of competitive individualism, which in its decadence has carried the logic of individualism to the extreme of a war of all against all, the pursuit of happiness to the dead end of a narcissistic preoccupation with the self." Cultural radicalism came under particularly heavy fire from Lasch, because its fashionable notions, which "present themselves as emancipation from the repressive conditions of the past," were actually part and parcel of the status quo; indeed, by extolling the uninhibited expressive freedom of the unencumbered self, they reproduce "the worst features of the collapsing civilization [they claim] to criticize" (Lasch 1979, 21).

At the bottom of all these pathologies, Lasch argued, was the modern American political economy, a seamless nexus of corporate capitalism and the paternalistic bureaucratic state, which systematically degraded work and undermined the integrity of domestic life. Consumer capitalism stooped to conquer, endorsing an ethos of unrestrained acquisitive materialism merely in order to transform independent citizens into supine subjects. It served as a mechanism for the manufacture first of endless desires and then of the endless flow of commodities that alone could (however partially) gratify those desires. Meanwhile, the paternalistic state, in alliance with the accredited experts of the "knowledge industry," had effectively negated all possibility of genuine self-reliance, transforming politics into administration in the name of Progress. Religion had been replaced by therapy, salvation by "mental health"; and the narcissistic personality, though a preciously unique individual in its own eyes, was only too happy to submit to the expensive self-manipulations of psychotherapists if peace of mind were the end result. The therapeutic ethos also penetrated politics; bureaucratic agencies transformed legitimate political grievances into "personal problems amenable to therapeutic intervention" (43). Just as the producer had become a consumer, so the citizen had become a client. Lasch's solution, to the extent he offered one, was neo-populist, neo-republican, and — by Riesman's standard — neo-traditional. The welfare state had badly eroded traditions of self-help and localism; and these would have to be recovered. Indeed, it was vital to recognize that the "moral discipline formerly associated with the work ethic still retains a value independent of the role it once played in the defense of property rights. That discipline [is] indispensable to the task of building a new order." Citizens would have to find ways to wrest their lives away from the bureaucrats and experts and "take their problems into their own hands." Only then could a decent society that served the interests of humanity begin to be built (396-97).

How this neo-populist revolt could occur, and avoid the ugly excesses of intolerance and retribution that so often come with populist insurgency, was another question; and indeed, Lasch's powerful and passionate analysis was far longer on critique than on specific prescription. But several points about that analysis are of particular interest in this context. First is the fact that *The Culture of Narcissism*'s vision does not stand in quite such sharp distinction to that of *The Lonely Crowd* as might appear at first sight. While the former is indeed a critique of individualism, the individualism it criticizes is an especially degraded individualism: the debased, infantilized, insecure, and voraciously dependent individualism of narcissists, whose psychological underdevelopment causes them to vacillate unprofitably between grandiose illusions of omnipotence and a profound inner emptiness. The Laschian narcissists are not rampaging egoists in the nineteenth-century inner-directed mold, nor are they strictly other-directed. Instead, their pathology incorporates negative features of each, melding petty self-centeredness to abject dependence upon the "positive strokes" of others. It is a pathology that in extreme form resembles nothing so much as an addiction to masturbatory fantasy; and it would be logical to imagine that, if Lasch is correct, the coming revolution of "virtual reality" — the sophisticated computerized simulation of all manner of sensory experience — will end up flooding our culture with such crippled personality types, who will exhibit a strange combination of monumental self-centeredness and characterological weakness.

In any event, the connection to an acquisitive-materialist ethos is unmistakable, since that ethos is characterized by a hunger to possess, even if only in imagination, and an inability to make durable commitments outside of the self. Moreover, Lasch insisted upon situating his social-character thesis within a particular understanding of American political and economic institutions, to a far greater extent than Riesman, or even Tocqueville, had done. Lasch's bitterly critical analysis of these institutions, which came out of a tradition of Freudian-Marxian social thought pioneered and epitomized by the Frankfurt School, was indispensable to his critique of the contemporary brand of American individualism and of the consumption-oriented materialism that accompanied it. Lasch refused to buy into what he saw as false dichotomies between expressive individualism and social submission posed by the existing system; for by fostering narcissism, he argued, the system actually encouraged both sides of that dichotomy simultaneously. Hence, too, his neo-populism, which flowed from his insistence that a restoration of a genuine, mature, and fully formed individuality was unimaginable unless accompanied by the restoration of political and economic institutions that would reinstate the possibility of meaningful collective action.

Here the contrast with *The Lonely Crowd* is illuminating, since

Riesman's liberal-pluralist-equilibrist view of politics, which largely eschewed the introduction of moralism into the public sphere, and his highly favorable attitude toward consumption as a form of liberated self-expression, could not have been more different. Lasch had begun a rethinking of materialism, one that led him to look back to older models of citizenship. To be sure, his populist sentiments came partly out of his sympathy with the radical-participatory elements in the early New Left. But they also clearly showed the influence of a more general appreciation among scholars of civic-humanist and republican political theory — a way of understanding political society that not only closely connected individual identity to participation in the commonweal but measured the health of the polity by the virtue of its citizens. (See Lasch 1991, especially 168-225.) This had implications for the role of materialism, for in standard republican discourse, as well as in the Puritan-Protestant moral tradition, no force served to corrupt the individual soul and poison the wellsprings of civic virtue more readily than "luxury."

The Culture of Narcissism, then, was at once radical and neo-traditional, a social-character study that did not hesitate to reveal its hortatory, moralistic, even jeremiadical intentions. But its relationship to the Protestant-republican virtues it so greatly esteemed was problematic. If there were elements of Calvinism embedded in its outlook, it was a Calvinism without Calvin or, for that matter, without any other specific gestures toward religious authority. If there was great esteem for an old-fashioned work ethic and self-denial, still there seemed little reason to believe that these quintessentially Protestant qualities could live anything more than an artificial existence under the social and economic conditions Lasch described. If there was an implicit endorsement of republican virtue as a proper object of political society, there was little discussion of the specific content of that virtue and how its moral ascendancy might be accomplished in a liberal and pluralistic social order — or even how we might find the moral grounds upon which to agree about what a "decent" society is. Tocqueville's contention that American society needed religion *and* civil religion to restrain its tendencies toward materialism and individualism received powerful support, albeit indirectly, from *The Culture of Narcissism.*

7

Touching upon many of the same themes and encountering some of the same problems was the collaborative study entitled *Habits of the Heart: Individualism and Commitment in American Life* (1985), written by a team of scholars headed by Robert Bellah. If Lasch's book was an idiosyncratic tour de force energized by a kind of sacred rage, the team-written *Habits* adopted a kinder, gentler tone, perhaps reflecting the sensitive and inclusive liberal Protestantism of its principal author, as well as its collaborative origins, and its heavy reliance upon extensive excerpts from interviews, generally presented in a sympathetic way. Whether or not the authors had anything to do with it, even the advertisements for the book (which was extensively promoted by its publisher) seemed implicitly to hold the book itself up as an exemplar of social cooperation and commitment by invariably including a picture of Bellah and his four attractive, smiling, casually dressed co-authors, posing together in a moment of warm and relaxed collegial solidarity — the very figure of a cozy little commonwealth.

Although *Habits* attempted to distance itself from Lasch's tone and analysis, the similarities between the two books were many and obvious. (See, for example, Bellah et al. 1985, 290, 318.) *Habits*, like *The Culture of Narcissism*, concerned itself with problems of an individualism "grown cancerous" and with a correspondingly atrophied sense of the public sphere and of social obligation in contemporary American life. Both books also dwelt at length upon the pernicious features of consumerism, of the managerial ethos, and of the therapeutic worldview as a source of moral support for egoism and self-seeking. Both related characterological changes to changes in political and social structure. Yet *Habits* situated its concerns far more squarely in a Tocquevillean consensus-seeking tradition, a decision evident even in its title, a potent phrase drawn from the *Democracy*. Although, unlike the *Democracy*, it saw individualism rather than equality as the inexorable constant of American life, *Habits* was dedicated above all else to the revival of "those cultural traditions and practices that . . . serve to limit and restrain the destructive side of individualism and provide alternative models for how Americans might live" (viii). In short, the *Habits* authors accepted the need that Tocqueville envisioned for religion (or the functional equivalent of religion) to serve as a check upon the American tendency toward acquisitiveness. Indeed, the most vivid and compelling aspect of their book was its demonstration that many contemporary Americans simply lacked the available language (and therefore, the intellectual and moral framework) needed to speak convincingly of obligations and commitments outside of the self. Even the Tocquevillean notion of "self-interest rightly understood" presumed notions of virtue to which self-interest paid tribute; without them, Americans were in trouble.

But it is one thing to declare a need for a consensual framework of values to forge a cohesive society in which men and women are willing to transcend their material appetites and work for the common good. It is quite another thing to begin identifying those values. What made *Habits* such an extraordinarily frustrating book was its steady insistence upon the former and its studied lack of clarity about the latter. *Habits* saw American culture as a "conversation" between the three "central strands *[sic]* of our culture — biblical, republican, and modern individualist"; and it sought to rehabilitate the first two "strands" in order to counteract the overbearing predominance of the third. Yet by merely suggesting that Americans need to place these "strands" in "conversation" as a way of enriching their moral discourse by the infusion of additional "languages," *Habits* made no case for the validity (or even the coherence) of those other traditions. In a way that recalls Lasch's hope that the Protestant work ethic might somehow survive in a post-Protestant age, Bellah and his collaborators seemed to hope that these restored "languages" might continue to have some measure of cultural authority, even if no one any longer believed in a particle of what they stood for.

Nor was *Habits* very clear about what they did stand for. It had remarkably little to say about the specific content of either of these traditions; and when, in the chapter on "Religion," it did say something about biblical Christianity, it showed how easily the credibility of this "language" was revoked and routed from the field in favor of essentially secular desiderata. For example, in a description of a conservative evangelical church where men and women practice a "biblical Christianity" that "provides an alternative to the utilitarian individualist values of this world" and learn to "put the needs of others before their own," *Habits*'s analysis nevertheless concluded on a note of breathtaking condescension: the church's alternative "does not go very far in helping [its people] understand their connection to the world or the society in which they live." Yes, it promotes honesty and decency in personal and family relations, and promotes a "special loving community" built around the shared love of Christ; but in so doing it "separates its members off from attachment to the wider society" and is therefore unacceptable. In such a church, "morality becomes personal, not social; private, not public" (231).

Such dismissal suggests how little real authority the "language" of the biblical tradition was actually likely to be accorded in the conversation of *Habits*. One could make a case that, on the contrary, such demanding but loving communities promote self-transcendence far better than do more liberal and inclusive Protestant churches that endorse expressive individualism and a therapeutic worldview.[8] One could point out that the ideal of "separation from attachment to the wider society" has always been central to a faith whose adherents strive to be "in the world but not of it," because "[their] commonwealth is in heaven" (Phil. 3:20, RSV). One could also question the validity of the hard-and-fast distinction that *Habits* made between private and public morality; but the larger point is, I think, clear enough. The biblical tradition carries weight only if it is invoked in the "right" way: a narrow gate monitored by liberal Protestants coming out of a social-gospel tradition who place a high value upon the institutional accommodation of a diversity of beliefs and practices and who see commitment to the wholesale reform of "the wider society" as a sine qua non.

This emphasis says a great deal about the cultural work that *Habits* wanted religion to do. The Grail that Bellah and Company sought was the recovery of a civil-religious vision of the meaning of America, a ground of national cohesion and consensus, a common faith, a moral modus vivendi for the post-Protestant era. The kind of church *Habits* sought, but found actually existing churches, whether liberal or conservative, repeatedly failing to embody, was a "public church." Such a church would not only serve as a moral monitor and check upon the workings of secular political, social, and economic institutions, but would draw its congregants out of their American tendency toward "religious individualism," toward the fullest possible realization of a common life. Many of these emphases became clearer in the sequel of

---

8. In fairness, however, it should be pointed out that the authors were well aware of the problems of these churches; see, for example, p. 232.

Habits entitled *The Good Society* (1991), whose very chapter titles and subheadings ("We Live Through Institutions," "Seeking Common Ground," and "The Public Church") telegraphed its orientation. The neo-republicanism of *Habits* was also further amplified in *The Good Society,* in the latter's emphasis upon an active citizenry ("Democracy Means Paying Attention") and the cultivation of public virtue ("The Limits of Moral Individualism" and "A Renewed Public"). Its agenda, to a great extent, was the Tocquevillean agenda, the quality of faith being less important than its public effects. And the specter in the background resembles what Tocqueville had feared: a society given over to individualism, particularism, privatism, and acquisitive materialism.

8

The concerns animating *Habits of the Heart* and *The Culture of Narcissism* were similar, then, in that both wished to revive those elements of the Protestant and republican moral traditions that had enduring value, over and above the particular ideological and institutional structures in which they had historically been embedded. They were reminiscent of Tocqueville in their emphasis upon the way that larger political and economic structures mold social character, in their concern for the health and vitality of the public realm, and in their insistence on the need for a "religious" check on acquisitive materialism. All political and social thought is a movement away from something as much as toward something, and both works reacted against similar characterological negatives: a self-indulgent ethos of expressive individualism that fed upon the junk food of consumerism and cheap thrills precisely because the administered life of managerial paternalism had denied it all access to more substantial and satisfying notions of participating citizenship and had crushed the very possibility of civic virtue. Although each offered a vision of American society that, at first sight, seemed to reverse the concerns of Riesman, Whyte, and the postwar critics, closer examination shows the truth to be more complex. The fear of social tyranny was still present; for it was the dominance of just such oppressive institutions that had given rise to the debased individualism and acquisitive materialism that Lasch and Bellah et al. lamented. In their view, the danger of such materialism was not just its relationship with individualism but its tendency to support the status quo by ensuring that narcissistic consumers did not turn into energetic citizens.

Philosopher Alasdair MacIntyre, whose *After Virtue: A Study in Moral Theory* (1981) left its mark on *Habits,* offered a compelling account of this condition. Men and women in modern Western societies were now guided in their personal moral judgments by what MacIntyre called "emotivism," the doctrine that moral evaluation ultimately represents nothing more than expression of one's personal preference, attitude, or feeling. This would seem to lead inexorably to a chronically disordered and anarchic society. Yet it turns out, he argues, that the modern organizational world can easily accommodate such potentially disruptive moral subjectivism. Modern society is divided into a "realm of the organizational" and a "realm of the personal," each of which operates by a different moral calculus. In the former realm, "ends are taken to be given, and are not available for rational scrutiny"; in the latter, "judgment and debate about values" occurs, but is not amenable to rational resolution. There are constant debates in such bifurcated societies about "a supposed opposition between individualism and collectivism"; but in fact, such debates are superficial and empty. The crucial fact is one upon which the opposing parties agree — "namely that there are only two alternative modes of social life open to us, one in which the free and arbitrary choices of individuals are sovereign and one in which the bureaucracy is sovereign, precisely so that it may limit the free and arbitrary choices of individuals."

In light of this "deep cultural agreement," the policy debates dominating the politics of modern societies tend to alternate between "a freedom which is nothing but a lack of regulation of individual behavior" and "forms of collectivist control designed only to limit the anarchy of self-interest." But these are fruitless debates. Bureaucracy and individualism are "partners as well as antagonists," for "it is in the cultural climate of this bureaucratic individualism that the emotivist self is naturally at home" (MacIntyre 1981, 32-33). The organization man and the emotivist individualist are brothers — mutually defined, mutually enabling. Perhaps even the practice of primal screaming can claim a padded place for itself in the organizational chart.

Yet if *Habits* shared this analysis (and it did so only partially), it did not follow MacIntyre's own foray into projective social thought, which invoked an unsettling, if familiar, parallel. In the declining years of the Roman Empire, he explained, "men and women of good will turned aside from the task of shoring up the Roman *imperium*," preferring instead to construct "new forms of community within which the moral life could be sustained" despite the surrounding darkness and barbarism. "We too have reached that turning point," he declared; the task at hand was "the construction of local forms of community within which civility and the intellectual and moral life can be sustained through the new dark ages which are already upon us." The reconstruction of "community," of the possibility of social bodies mediating between the radical individual and the vast megastructures in which he is embedded, bodies in which genuine connectedness and genuine moral responsibility would be once again possible, had now become paramount in importance. Under such circumstances, with the aggrandizing and proliferating nation-state itself having become the sworn enemy of moral community, there would be no more appeal to "civil religion" or "common ground." If even the bare possibility of moral community were to be sustained, it would have to be done by clusters of similarly committed individuals, who somehow found ways to protect their enterprise from the clutches of the state (244-45).

Such a vision endorsed, in effect, much that Bellah and other proponents of "civil religion" and a "public church" were struggling against; and indeed, MacIntyre's description bears a striking resemblance to the unsympathetic view in *Habits*, cited above, of the stance taken by members of a conservative "biblical" church. Fundamentalists in America had always been especially drawn to the option of cultural withdrawal; but MacIntyre's argument signaled that such moral self-separation, taken as an imperative rather than an indulgence, was now becoming a more general option (Marsden 1980). One of the most remarkable expressions of this inclination was the book entitled *Resident Aliens: Life in the Christian Colony* (1989), by Stanley Hauerwas and William H. Willimon of Duke University, a feisty manifesto that appeared to complete American Protestantism's journey from complacent hegemon to risk-taking counterculture. Emphasizing the Pauline language of apartness and firmly rejecting the imperatives of a "public church," the authors saw Christianity's cultural deposition as a blessing, a great liberation from the corrupting duty to "underwrite American democracy" and serve as a moral prop for an indefensible secular order. Instead, the community of the church now had a marginal status: it "exists today as resident aliens, an adventurous colony in a society of unbelief" which "asserts that God, not the nations, rules the world" (Hauerwas and Willimon 1989, 32, 48-49). Such an understanding was not intended as a license for complacent or hermetic withdrawal; far from it. But the defiant tone of *Resident Aliens* signified a profound withdrawal of affect not only from the civil religion but also from the nation itself, and its organizational and institutional life — a gesture that was full of portent.

9

What *Resident Aliens* offered to the community of American Christians was, in a strictly sociological sense, not unlike the messages increasingly sent by, and to, countless other subgroups and communities making up an increasingly diverse and self-consciously pluralistic American culture. Such a development has made the cultivation of a binding civil religion seem almost quixotic, if not covertly hegemonic. We seem to be living through an era of disaggregation and decentering, in America and in the world, in which the idea of the nation as a principle for the organization of moral community carries less weight or prestige than at any time since the Second World War. As I have already indicated, this fact helps explain why the very concept of a broad national or social character has become so controversial in our time. It also helps explain why cognitive, political, and legal affirmations of group identity — exemplified most recently by the influential discourses of "multiculturalism" and "difference" — have become so central a feature of our intellectual, political, and popular cultures in recent years. As political scientist Michael Sandel has argued, it seems that the nation-state, if only because of its scale (and that is not the only reason), simply no longer can provide the kinds of "shared self-understanding" necessary for community (Sandel 1984, 1989).

Images of disaggregation and decentering, along with the rise of a new generation marked by its disdain for the large-scale organization, also dominated the most recent contribution to the social-character genre we will consider here: Leinberger and Tucker's *The New Individualists: The Generation after the Organization Man* (1991). Although business and management-consulting types, rather than academics, have so far accounted for most of the interest generated by *The New Individualists,* that is not for any lack of ambitious scope and intellectual sophistication in it. The book was, in fact, a self-conscious successor both to *The Organization Man* (as its subtitle indicated) and to *The Lonely Crowd* (as quickly became evident in its argument). And its sense of generational timing could not have been more acute, as immediately became clear from its opening sentence. "An unprecedented transfer of power is about to take place in American life," it began, as "the organization men" gave way to "the baby boomers, male and female" (Leinberger and Tucker 1991, 1). The authors could not have known how richly their prediction would be confirmed in the presidential election of 1992 — by the new president's age, by his marriage, and, in some respects too, even by his political vision.

There was a personal connection between *The New Individualists* and *The Organization Man* that made for a great journalistic hook: Paul Leinberger was the son of Hugo Leinberger, pastor of the United Protestant Church in Park Forest. But the authors actually made surprisingly little use of that personal connection; instead, they preferred to reflect more generally and abstractly upon the social character and psychological profile of baby boomers who had, like themselves, grown up swaddled in the comforts and constraints of the organizational world that Whyte had described. The result was an offbeat, lengthy, wide-ranging, sometimes brilliant, sometimes pretentious, and frequently confused and frustrating book that projected the social character of a group even more narrow and peculiar than the one addressed by its illustrious predecessors. Yet the focus was eminently justified. Whyte and Riesman had never given much thought to what the younger generation growing up under the regime of other-direction and the social ethic would look like — and what the world would look like to them. Leinberger and Tucker sought to describe "the organization offspring," tell their story, and thereby give a convincing and useful account of what really made this new generation tick.

To Riesman's typology of tradition-direction, inner-direction, and other-direction as modes of conformity, they added a fourth to describe their target group: *subject-direction.* Those who are subject-directed are "emotionally controlled" by the emotion of *mourning* — mourning for the "death" of their "authentic self," which general affluence and the warm family life of the organizational suburb had encouraged them to cultivate, but which the decline of the American economy and the unpredictable demands of the postindustrial world have rendered impracticable. The rise of "a genuinely global marketplace linked by instantaneous communications," they argued, "has accelerated the diffusive processes of modernity, further destabilizing the self" (16). The new character type is *subject*-directed because it is acutely aware not only of its subjectivity but also of the ways in which it is subjected to artificial forces beyond its reach. Cut off from the cherished modernist dream of "authenticity," which has been both economically and philosophically destroyed beyond recall, such a subject-directed self copes with its mourning by developing a new conception of what it means to be an individual: it fashions itself into "an artificial person" whose "ensembled individualism" is nothing more than the aggregation of the roles it performs. "Artificial," Leinberger and Tucker insisted, is not a pejorative term; it does not mean "phony or insincere," though it might well be "ironic." It refers to a whole new postmodern way of understanding what it means to be an individual, one which emphasizes the fact that it is the particular forms of one's unique connectedness to the world — one's personae — and not the chimera of the "authentic self" that really matters. What is dying is the dichotomy betweeen the manifest and the latent, the surface and the depth — the notion that there is some "real self" hidden behind the facade of one's "social selves."

Such a vague and abstract formulation, which the authors sometimes make even more ineffable by using the opaque jargon of academic postmodernism, is far less compelling and plausible than any of Riesman's typologies, and seems to describe precious few people. Indeed, one sometimes has the distinct impression that the authors of *The New Individualists* are really writing about themselves and their circle of friends, working out the psychological kinks and disappointments of their corner of baby-boomerdom in public anonymity. But the book begins to gain credibility as it moves into more empirically grounded social analysis, where one sees, in sector after sector of American life, the decentering principle vividly demonstrated, with the resulting emergence of new, vital, and unprecedented forms. To pick but two of the most compelling examples, Leinberger and Tucker demonstrate the radical transformation of American suburban life and the radical restructuring of American business corporations — both of them intimately related, each representing a profound shift away from the pat-

terns of the Organization Man's generation. The rise of "postmetropoli-
tan suburbs" like Irvine, California, defies the conventional industrial-
city geography of a central business area surrounded by increasingly
affluent residential suburban rings; it has no center and no established
relational grid, but is rather a complex and fluid network that has
evolved in response to the dynamic and ever-shifting forces of the
postindustrial service economy (300-331). And the hierarchical, verti-
cally stepped organizational structure of the 1950s has given way to a
more horizontal network-like structure, characterized by ad hoc, task-
oriented work teams — a structure derived not from the rigidities of a
bureaucratic chain of command but from the decentralizing imperatives
of new information technologies (332-51).

Leinberger and Tucker attempt little or no evaluative or moralistic
judgment about these developments. Ethnographers of the new order,
they simply ask that the things they observe be recognized as *patterns,*
integral parts of a large-scale systemic change rather than random or
haphazard developments; and that the cultivation of "artificial persons"
be understood as part of a larger patterning. They also suggest that those
who have to deal with baby boomers in the workforce, such as corporate
managers, would be well advised to understand their peculiar makeup.
Their tenuous and provisional relationship to the organizations for
which they work, for example, may seem like rank disloyalty and self-
indulgent opportunism to an old-fashioned Orgman, who would never
have dreamed of job-hopping. But, the authors argue, to one who knows
the psychology of that generation, and who understands the kind of
disappointments it has had to cope with and the uncertain organizational world in which it has had to make its way, such behavior is rational
and realistic.

The New Individualists is, then, very much the book of a particular
generation — even, in its own cool and diffident way, an apologia. For
that reason, the subjects it does *not* discuss may be as revealing as those
it does discuss; and some of its silences are startling. It has nothing
whatever to say, for example, about what the brave new uncentered
world it describes might mean to the children who must grow up in it.
This is an especially strange omission, given the fact that their study
itself argues that the environment in which the organizational offspring
grew up was very different from the one their parents thought they were
creating. There are other such missing subjects. Other than a discon-

nected assault on "radical materialist" Yuppies of the 1980s, the subject of materialism and its dangers is simply not part of the book's agenda. Nor is religion, which is summarily consigned to the past, while the neo-traditional vision of *Habits of the Heart* is subjected to ridicule (387). Nor is politics, least of all participatory politics, a part of its vision. Nor, finally, is the problem of national cohesion — and not only because it is simply presumed that the nation will cohere. The authors assert that the bitter experience of the Vietnam War left many of the organizational offspring with "an ineradicable suspicion of institutions" — about their legitimacy, their benevolence, and even their rationality. Most suspect of all in their eyes, and least likely to command their loyalty, is the nation-state. If only Sylvester Stallone's character John Rambo had been a Park Forest baby boomer, he could be taken as a perfect figure of their discontent, the ultimate anti-institutionalist — betrayed by the nation, lied to by the politicians, used by the military, and harassed by the police.

10

But, despite its weaknesses, *The New Individualists* tells us much about the present state of social-character analysis, and the general decentering the authors insist upon seeing is undeniable. Partly as a result of the American nation-state's having lost some of its aura of legitimacy (not to mention effectiveness), the social landscape has seen the exfoliation of new or renewed forms of community, affiliations based upon a fairly narrow but intensely felt range of shared characteristics, identities, consumption preferences, or "lifestyle" choices. Despite their intensity, it is hard to know or to generalize about whether such forms of association represent a restoration of community or its antithesis — whether they are a counter to emotivist individualism, or an intensification and amplication of it into a form of what might be called "group individualism," the self-segregation of all who share the same opinions and desires. When such identification is freely chosen and may therefore be freely revoked or exchanged like any consumer article, it hardly constitutes much of a challenge to the primacy of the autonomous self. It does, however, reflect a growing unwillingness to rest one's identity on the idea of the nation.

One can endorse, and even revel in, the complexity and freedom of such social diversity — and yet at the same time wonder how long a nation can sustain a basis for consensual moral discourse and democratic public life under such circumstances. Indeed, the operative principle of the present order increasingly appears to be a kind of "dissensus consensus," a form of cultural pluralism that agrees in advance to bracket most, if not all, questions of ultimate ends and the right ordering of life, regarding these as essentially private matters subject only to the legal rights and emotivist choices of the individual self. Mary Ann Glendon has recently argued that American public discourse since the Second World War has been conquered by a peculiarly disabling brand of absolutist "rights talk" that is noisy about demanding its perquisites, aggressive about expanding its empire — but silent about assuming "personal, civic, and collective responsibilities." Such "hyper-individualism" trivializes "core democratic values," she believes, and has made it virtually impossible to have a "genuine exchange of ideas about matters of high public importance" (Glendon 1991, x-xi). It has become particularly well-entrenched in the American legal subculture, transforming what once was an agency of social cohesion into a combative arena tailor-made for the war of all against all — a juridical mirror of the emotivist self's unwillingness to accept civil limits and of the consumerist's ceaseless multiplication of (often insatiable) desires.

Perhaps it will be said that this account exaggerates the problem; but hard questions remain. What *is* the basis of American cohesion? Are we knit together by the limited procedural freedoms of liberal democracy and by the complex network of involvements — what Durkheim called "organic solidarity" — in which a complex political economy has enmeshed us? Or do Americans have to share some things in common and agree about some substantive beliefs? If so, what are they? Is the country held together by a creed, as Arthur M. Schlesinger Jr. has argued in responding to the challenge of multiculturalism? If so, what is the content of that creed, beyond a respect for individual rights? (See Schlesinger 1992, 27, 136). Are we left with the notion of American society as a "values" marketplace ("values" being interchangeable commodities, the proper objects of emotivist attentions), since the market is the only available institution compatible with a radical commitment to self-definition and independent personhood, and to open-ended social and cultural heterogeneity? Remembering Daniel Boorstin's suggestion that consumption is an American way of constituting communities, one wonders if moral communities can be similarly constituted — by independent sovereign selves who have freely chosen to "buy into" the same package of values. If Americans' sole reliable source of social cohesion is a shared belief in the inviolability of individual choice, then what does that tell us about the task of "rethinking materialism"? What of Tocqueville's insistence upon the need for a religious check on self-assertion and for an acknowledged standard of public virtue that permits self-interestedness to be "rightly understood"?

But perhaps a fresh reconsideration of the place of materialism in the American social character might lead one to put moralism aside and argue that acquisitive materialism, far from being a cause of fragmentation, is itself the single most reliable source of cohesion. The case is not without its strengths. For one thing, it should not be forgotten that, ever since colonial times, many more immigrants have come to the United States in search of "the good life" than have come in obedience to the Puritan mission, a fact which suggests that acquisitive materialism may deserve a prominent place in the national creed (Greene 1988). It may not be quite true that, as the old adage had it, a man is never more innocent than when about the business of making money. But it is certainly true that the hot pursuit of prosperity can encourage him to set aside the cauldron of religious, ethnic, class, and personal hatreds seething in his breast, purely in the interest of doing business. The most successful forms of multicultural association have been those found in entrepôts and other great metropolitan centers of international trade, in which the conduct of commerce stands as the city's principal reason for being. Atlanta's slogan that it is a city "too busy to hate" appeals to this conviction that in a place where the full-throttle pursuit of business success is celebrated, social problems cease to exist.

But whatever "Atlanta" may feel, Atlantans will probably always find time to hate, even working at it during their leisure hours if necessary; and by the same token, Americans will continue to feel uneasy about fully endorsing materialism as a sufficient basis for their collective lives. It seems unlikely that this is merely a quirk of social-character analysts or a vestige of old-time hypocritical moralism. Tocqueville insisted that Americans are not philosophical materialists; and it is doubtful whether even a direct encounter with Michael Milken or Ivan

Boesky would have changed his mind. Polling data consistently indicates that Americans continue to be, as Richard John Neuhaus often phrases it, an incorrigibly religious people. This is not incompatible with their being terribly materialistic. The social-character studies of the 1950s repeatedly suggested that for Americans, material things are constantly being made to serve as tokens for immaterial ones. In this connection, one might do well to think carefully about the meaning of a peculiar bumper sticker often seen during the 1980s and perhaps still glimpsed occasionally today. It read: "Whoever dies with the most toys, wins." It is an ugly and pathetic slogan, but illustrative of an important point about even the most self-consciously hard-boiled American material-ism. After all, "winning" is different from "having" or "consuming," for it is fundamentally hinged upon the question of status; others must lose. But *what* does one win? And who is left to admire one's victory? This hard-boiled dictum, in its childish naiveté, assumes that the artificial rules and closure of gamesmanship actually have cosmic meaning; and it assumes the enduring possibility of something like justification and salvation — or, at the very least, a wildly applauding crowd on the other side of the finish line rather than the silence of the grave. As Santayana once observed, American materialism is often really a strange form of idealism in which the things of this world, rather than being savored for their intrinsic worth, are regarded as spiritual trophies.

Somehow, then, the ghosts of an older soteriology still powerfully haunt American attitudes toward material success. Perhaps this is one important respect in which Americans dwell in a culture that, for all its secularism and diversity, is still decisively shaped by the legacy of Prot-estant Christianity. Because of its incarnational and sacramental theol-ogy, Christianity lends itself to the confusion or conflation of the flesh with the spirit, the material with the ideal, wealth with salvation, the nation with the Kingdom. Hence the place of material things has a perplexing and unresolvable ambiguity about it. The righteous man who obeys God's laws will prosper, we are repeatedly told; but we are also told that it is easier for a camel to pass through the eye of a needle than for that same prosperous man to enter into the Kingdom of God. More importantly, the line of division between higher and lower is shifting and indistinct. Paul told the Christians at Rome that the invisible things of God have been made visible in the things he has made (Rom. 1:20). The story of the Bible, too, is the story of God breaking into human history, not to condemn it wholly but to restore and redeem it and draw it to himself. The Spirit was made flesh so that flesh might be reborn as spirit. Such images point us out of the world, but they also point us into the world.

That ambivalence persists in a post-Protestant, post-Christian culture — if that is what we are living in — even though the terms of analysis have been largely abandoned or deeply submerged. But without the theological contexts that created this temper, it becomes ever more difficult to find the line that separates healthy affirmation of the things of the world from what Ignatius called a "disordered attachment" to them. In a recent survey of employed Americans, Robert Wuthnow discovered that his subjects consistently expressed extraordinarily contradictory attitudes about money, proclaiming in one breath that Americans are too materialistic, and in the next breath unashamedly affirming the great importance of money and openly wishing they had more of it (Wuthnow 1993). This may, as Wuthnow suggests, have something to do with the present national mood; but it probably also reflects a deeper, more hard-wired national characteristic.

It is visible, for example, in some of the characteristic themes of American literature. What makes *The Great Gatsby* perhaps the most resonant and most enduring of all American novels is the elegance with which it captured precisely the same ambivalence about materialism. F. Scott Fitzgerald fashioned the book as a tragic morality play and parable of the hazards of new fortune, as demonstrated in the destruction of a self-invented man. Yet it is equally clear that Fitzgerald himself adored and lusted after the very material prosperity that Jay Gatsby had achieved. At the same time, Fitzgerald's tale nicely exemplifies Santayana's observation, for Gatsby's corrupt materialism is entirely in service to his colossal, disproportionate idealism — an idealism that finds its consummatory object in his old flame, Daisy Buchanan, but is even more purely and memorably expressed by his yearning for "the green light," that emblem of "the orgiastic future that year by year recedes before us."

It is also of no small significance that Daisy turns out, in the end, to be an utterly vain, selfish, and contemptible woman, completely unworthy of Gatsby's frenzied pursuit. The larger significance of that fact, for us, arises out of the disparity between the depth of Gatsby's needy emotion and the shallowness of its object. It is an example of the more general peril that arises when people use worldly things to stand in for spiritual needs. It is no coincidence that the single most impressive spiritual development of recent times — Alcoholics Anonymous and the twelve-step movements based upon it — has focused upon problems relating to the chronic misuse of, and disordered attachment to, material substances. These movements therefore offer a potentially important contribution to the effort to rethink materialism, precisely because they have shown that the single most effective solution to a horrendous medical condition may lie in the search for transcendence. Such spiritual disciplines have succeeded partly because they have addressed themselves to many of the essential concerns entailed by the tangled relationship between soul and matter in an affluent but spiritually troubled post-Christian culture. In twelve-step spirituality, the two meanings of "materialism" meet and merge; for these movements contend that permanent release from a disordered attachment to some *thing* can take place only after one fully acknowledges one's helplessness and yields to the authority of a "higher power." If these movements are any guide, the effort to control acquisitive materialism may also have to address itself to the issues of philosophical materialism.

Such an assertion would appear to bring us back to Tocqueville's insistence that philosophical materialism simply will not do in America. But some features of the Tocquevillean agenda are largely missing here. In particular, one sees little mention of the hope that spirituality can support the peace and cohesiveness of the body politic, promote social justice by its countervailing force, and inhibit the effects of individualism and privatism. It is hard to see such a dynamic emerging from these spiritual disciplines, particularly in their more self-indulgent and popularized "recovery" modes. True, among the many other things the twelve-step movements do, they are in the business of building community — building it not on the shared consumption of things but on a shared recognition of disordered attachment to them (and to some one thing in particular). Yet the communities built thereby may be highly provisional and instrumental in character; and, as the trailing modifier "Anonymous" clearly implies, they are, by design, closed vessels. This is not to criticize them for failing to do things they were never meant to do. It is merely to point out that they too fit into the more general pattern, articulated by Leinberger and Tucker, of a fragmented and decentered public culture. And their very success is yet more confirmation that a serious rethinking of materialism, if it is undertaken in earnest, will not take place in the public square and will not involve the reaffirmation of a civil religion, old or new. Such is the distance that, for better or worse, we have come since the 1950s.

Economic Rationality
as a Religious System

NEIL J. SMELSER

IT HAS LONG BEEN A COMMONPLACE in sociology that nonreligious cultural productions may have religious components.[1] Economic thought has not escaped this kind of observation. Stark referred to the synthesis of Menger, Jevons, and Walras as "the dominant dogma" (1944, 57) and Blaug criticized the postulate of economic rationality as "sacrosanct" (1992, 230). The resemblances between the two bodies of thought have also been underscored recently in the small burst of literature dealing with economics and other social sciences as discourse, dialogue, rhetoric, and metaphor (see Klamer, McCloskey, and Solow 1988; McCloskey 1990; Mulkay 1985). In this literature, economics is characterized as resting on persuasion, analogies, "stories," and pre-emptive metaphors. Religious imagery is among these. Goodwin (1988), for example, characterized economic discourse as depicting the economist as "philosopher, priest, and hired gun," and with respect to the second of these, he identified a certain conception of sin in the rhetoric of economists (see also Stigler 1982). McCloskey identified the "Ten Commandments and Golden Rule of modernism in economics and other sciences" (1985, 7-8), and specified sacred commitments to

---

1. Almost a century ago, Simmel mentioned the religious element in the following settings: "the relation of a devoted child to its parent, of an enthusiastic patriot to his country, of the fervent cosmopolite toward humanity; the relation of the laboring-man to his struggling fellows, or the proud feudal lord to his class; the relation of the subject to the ruler under whose control he is, and of the true soldier to his army" (Simmel 1906, 361-62).

such ideas as prediction, objectivity, quantification, and value-neutrality. I can only report, as my reactions to this kind of effort, a mixture of fascination, amusement, and vague dissatisfaction with the thinly disguised ridicule and the limited analytic potential contained in these somewhat random, out-of-context parallelisms.

If one wishes to avoid the pitfalls of ad hoc and tumultuous analogies, one must become somewhat more formal. Part of that formality involves deciding on a definition of religion that permits appropriate and systematic comparisons. The definitional task is not an easy one. Max Weber shunned it, saying that "[the] essence of religion is not even our concern" (1968, 2:399), and ceding only that definition is possible at the conclusion, not the beginning, of study. In practice, moreover, scholars have advanced a variety of definitions, each consequential in different ways for the present exercise. Consider the following:

• *Substantive definitions.* Examples would be those that include explicit reference to the supernatural or trans-empirical, as well as specific religious forces, gods, demons, and so on. (See Johnstone 1975, 20.) Commonly criticized as ethnocentric in that they rely on distinctively Western notions of supernature, nature, and "the empirical," such definitions are of limited use in drawing parallels with avowedly secular bodies of thought such as economics, because the latter find their origin in an explicit rejection of the supernatural and spiritual. Moreover, to search for functional symbolic equivalents of gods, supernature, and so forth in these bodies of thought often results in somewhat wild symbolic searches, the usefulness of which is uncertain.

• *Psychological definitions.* Under this heading I include characterizations that call attention to the special mental or emotional states attained in the religious experience — for example, the ascetic, the mystical, the prophetic (Yinger 1971, 146-47). I would also include the classic definitions of Otto, stressing the "holy" or "wholly other" (1936 [1926], 8-41), and Durkheim, stressing the "sacred" (1951 [1915], 47) — whether natural or supernatural. Making such an inclusion may be controversial, but I do so because the ultimate criterion for what is sacred depends on a certain *attitude* (separateness, distance, awe) toward that which is defined as holy or sacred. Such a definition, which escapes specific substantive content (*any* object or symbol can be regarded as holy or sacred), will prove helpful in understanding some elements of economic thought, though it often gives rise to the fruitless exercise of attributing certain economic perspectives to economists or making guesses about what those perspectives might be.

• *Functional definitions.* These ask what religion does for individuals (psychological functionalism) or society (social functionalism). The definitions of Malinowski (1955) and Yinger ("a system of beliefs and practices by means of which a group of people struggle with . . . the ultimate problems of human life" — 1971, 7) are examples of the former. The statements of Radcliffe-Brown (1952) and Davis (1949), which stress the socially integrative functions of religion, are examples of the latter. Such definitions may be applied to economic thought because it presumably deals with "ultimate problems of human life" (though such an assertion reveals the arbitrariness and difficulty of specification of the notion of "ultimate"), and because economic thought provides explicit guidelines for the integration and coordination of economies in societies. Once again, however, the conceptual and explanatory payoff in noting such parallels is not evident.

• Finally, it is possible to define religion in a weakish way by listing its common characteristics — it displays a certain kind of belief system, contains a myth of origin, has rituals and ceremonies, is always a group phenomenon, and so on (e.g., Wilson 1978, 12-27; Johnstone 1975, 12-20). To do this is actually to define — for what is a definition if not the specification of essential characteristics? — but not to demand the fixity or exclusiveness of a formal definition. Armed with such a list, one can find parallels in secular systems of thought — for example, the high priests, sacred first principles, myths of origin, and rituals of Marxism-Leninism — but, once again, in doing this one appears to have arrived back at the beginning — that is, making ad hoc and somewhat inconsequential analogies.

Faced with this array of conceptual limitations deriving from definitional ambiguities, it seems prudent to beat a kind of Weberian retreat and decline to offer a formal definition, even though one seems to be called for if systematic comparisons are to be undertaken. On the other hand, it seems advisable to avoid scattered analogies. What I will pursue, instead, is a kind of intermediate strategy that I will develop in three steps: (1) I will identify a utopia, with the frankly religious characteristics of simplicity and perfection, that emerged in classical and neoclassical economic thought,[2] a utopia that has provided a guiding beacon for economists, even those who have assumed a heterodox stance in relation to it; (2) I will specify the central tensions associated with utopian visions — religious and others — tensions discernible both in their fundamental assumptions and in criticisms of those assumptions; and (3) I will indicate how these tensions are addressed, through scholastic exegesis and theoretical adaptation, in various strands of economic thought. The common goal of these attempted resolutions of tension has been to preserve the core articles of faith (specifically, rational calculation and maximization in a situation of choice) while acknowledging the imperfections of the "real world" that threaten to impinge on it.

I conclude this introductory section with a few disclaimers about the analysis that follows — disclaimers which I can only hope readers will believe, given what I have just said about other, similar exercises. My intent is to contribute to our understanding of the dynamics of disciplinary development in economic thought. I make no claim for *exclusivity;* similar analyses could be applied to other bodies of thought, including the disciplines of the natural sciences. I advance no claim that such an exercise "reduces" economic knowledge to something else — that is, rejects the relevance of assessing it by *other* criteria, such as its theoretical adequacy and empirical validity (see Thaler 1991). Finally, in pointing to religious themes and parallels in religious thought, I do not intend to *discredit* economic thought in any way. (Is it not ironic that such a disclaimer is necessary? We are still so much in the grip of scientific rationalism that one must apologize for finding religious [presumably nonrational] elements in a body of thought; in another age such an exercise might have been regarded as ennobling.) Described best, my intent is to identify certain common characteristics and dynamics of utopian thinking — including both religious and nonreligious instances.

2. Some may object to the amalgamation of classical and neoclassical economics in this exercise, since there are differences among them that are circumstantial for many purposes. However, I do not regard these differences as decisive for my effort to identify generalized characteristics of the economic situation in these bodies of thought.

The Utopia Emerging in Classical and Neoclassical Economics

Elsewhere (Smelser 1992) I have argued that the fundamental ingredients of classical economic thought emerged from a range of historically specific institutional dissatisfactions experienced by merchants, industrialists, politicians, and intellectuals in late eighteenth-century Britain. These agents were actively engaged in promoting the revolutionary shift from a society based on paternalistic deference and state regulation to a society based on contractual economic relations and market capitalism. Among the major dissatisfactions were these: constraints on the contractual wage labor and labor mobility found in ascriptively based labor arrangements (such as apprenticeship and slavery) and in existing systems of poor relief; the unavailability of capital and a rationalized monetary system; economically disruptive political protest, such as bread riots and destruction of machinery; the fetters of economic monopoly and privilege found in mercantilist economic policies.

The belief system enunciated in utilitarianism and classical political economy constituted "solutions" to these obstacles by removing them and creating an imaginary world without them, a world that was perfect. This world was elaborated in neoclassical economic formulations and, seen as a product of nineteenth-century economic thought, possessed the following characteristics:

• A number of *actors,* households and firms originally, with governments as economic actors entering the picture only later. While each of these actors is in fact a *collectivity,* each has motives, tastes, and behavior that are, from a psychological point of view, those of individual persons (hence the appropriateness of the term "methodological individualism": the basic units of analysis are individual actors).

• The *dispositional* characteristics of the actors. Individuals are assumed to have a hierarchy of stable preferences, or tastes. These preferences are not influenced by others (another meaning of "methodological individualism"). Agents are also assumed to have perfect information about their tastes, their own economic resources (income), the availability and cost of economically significant goods and services that gratify these tastes, and the market intentions of other actors. Finally, actors are motivated in such a way as to maximize their material well-being (utility). In this pursuit, moreover, actors calculate and behave rationally; they do not make errors, they do not forget what they know, they do not act on impulse, and they do not act irrationally — that is, in ways that run counter to the principle of the maximization of utility. This is the famous postulate of economic rationality, which is, as we will see, properly regarded as the most important first principle of economic analysis.

• A set of *relations* between actors. Actors are regarded as interdependent, in that each actor has something to offer (labor, consumer goods, money payments) that the others desire, and, by virtue of this, they enter into exchanges. Actors are equal in that neither partner to the exchange can, by coercion or fraud, influence the exchange. By the same token, the actors are free to choose whether or not to exchange.

• A frictionless *setting* for exchange. This is specified in the assumption of the perfect mobility of resources (labor, capital, goods, services), and the absence of any institutional or political restraints on this mobility. By virtue of this special assumption, moreover, all economic agents (buyers and sellers) are in unfettered competition with one another — that is, all have complete and instantaneous access to all alternative possibilities in the market.

Such is the constructed world of economic exchange. It envisions individuals with a certain internal environment — tastes, information, mental capacities for calculating and making decisions — and a certain external environment — goods and services, costs and prices, income (Simon 1982). What strikes one as remarkable about this construction is how much is given (i.e., stable, parametric) and how little is variable. Actors' internal environments are regarded as stable and unvarying, and outcomes of exchanges are, in the last analysis, regarded as a product of variations in the availability of goods and services, their cost or price, and the capacity of economic actors to initiate exchanges for those goods or services. In this sense action is, paradoxically, based on free choice but is determined in the end by external factors. (The crucial analytic significance of the notion of "givens" will be reconsidered presently.)

There is a second — separate and identifiable — external environment in nineteenth-century economic analysis as well, sometimes mentioned but largely implicit. This is the institutional and political environment that permits and assures the conditions necessary for the constructed economic world to exist and function. Consider the following illustrations:

• John Stuart Mill explicitly noted that exchange by gift and "industrial operations" that are "effected by force" (1965-73, 4:331) lie outside the realm of economic exchange and thus beyond economic analysis. The assertion excluding force involves more than an analytically convenient decision. It assumes the presence of an active force that would *control* cheating, bread riots, and criminal theft (appropriation by force) and permit peaceful economic exchange.

• Economic exchange presupposes, in all cases other than barter, the existence of generalized media such as money and credit. It presupposes, furthermore, that those media are legitimate and acceptable, and that they have a certain stability of value over time. It is the banking-government establishment which assures those qualities, and that establishment is also assumed.

• Economic exchange presupposes mutual trust and predictability. The mechanisms assuring these are not only individual dispositions but also institutional arrangements, in the form of contracts that guarantee the terms and conditions of exchange as well as avenues of redress if these are violated. The governmental establishment is also responsible for sustaining, through laws, private property and rights over its use, control, and disposal.

These assumptions about the second environment give the lie to any literal interpretation of laissez-faire (governmental passivity) as a realistic characterization of the political doctrine that accompanied classical political economy. The illustrations reveal a preference for a very *active* state that protects and guarantees the constructed world of markets, as well as the processes of exchange, earning, and profit making in them. Like so many components of ideologies, the principle of laissez-faire was overgeneralized; it properly refers to certain *selected* restraints that governments should place on themselves (e.g., restraints on monopolistic control of production, government ownership, tariffs, and market-clogging policies for relief of the poor).

The Edenic qualities of the constructed economic world are apparent. There is a kind of perfection for the individual — orderly tastes, a world free of ignorance and error (one ingredient of sin in the Judeo-Christian tradition), and a predictable environment. The negative assumptions that eliminate power, force, fraud, and open conflict and the positive assumptions that assure trust and predictability also make that world one of freedom, equality, and absence of exploitation. (The ideal element of equality is clearly apparent in the construction of economic exchange. Inequality appears, however, in the unequal distribution of returns [wages, profits, rent], even in the perfectly competitive economy, and this kind of inequality, while certainly advertisable as the most efficient means of allocation, was the component of the classical political economy that made it most vulnerable to attacks from the left [including Marx and other socialists] on grounds of social injustice.) Even more precise religious echoes from ascetic Protestantism can also be identified — in particular, the idea that asceticism (saving, or nonexpenditure) and investment (deferred gratification) are means to reward (profit), though one hesitates to press toward too great detail in such comparisons.

There are utopian elements at the social level as well. Political economy presented its own advocacy of social justice through its linkage with Bentham's utilitarianism, arguing that the existence of a free economy was the mechanism for realizing the greatest good for the greatest number. (The Pareto optimum, a policy strategy for assuring winners but no losers, was a subsequent variant of the same linkage.) But above all the social utopia was one of perfection through stability. Various notions of this appeared. The most vivid example is Adam Smith's "invisible hand" of more or less automatic if unconscious maximization of collective welfare and social stability through the individual pursuit of self-interest. The mechanism of "clearing the market" through the assumption of perfect mobility and marginalist solutions yielded a view of a smoothly functioning world without shortages and derived forms of deviance (black markets), delays and waiting, and unemployment of resources. Finally, the ideas of equilibrium, both partial (Marshall 1880) and general (Walras 1954 [1874]), provided economists with an idealized notion that the constructed economic world was always *tending* toward stability, a notion which, if reified, implies the existence of stability.[3]

3. The idealized and possibly misleading features of the notion of equilibrium have been noted in another field — organizational theory — that has also been preoccupied with rationality and efficiency: "[The] equilibrium orientation obscures the constant change that organizations and their environments are always undergoing. We

At the cultural level, the nineteenth-century economic vision was firmly rooted in a range of cultural values that were put forward as legitimate, universal, and utopian. One set of these values is to be found in Newtonian science, after which the political economists closely modeled their notions of laws, principles, and causality (Halevy 1928). Another set were those values that emanated jointly from the eighteenth-century French enlightenment and the British utilitarian reaction against a society based on organized religion's claims on moral and spiritual monopoly and on class privilege — the values of freedom, individualism, rationality, democracy, progress, and materialism (Dumont 1977). Coleman, in characterizing the fundamental assumptions of rational-choice theory (of which nineteenth-century economics is the progenitor), argued that these assumptions are "grounded in a humanistically congenial image of man." By this he meant the classical liberal image — "the freedom of individuals to act as they will" and a concern of "constraints that social interdependence places on that freedom" (Coleman 1990, 4).

The constructed economic paradigm contained all the major elements of a religious system: a worldview or cosmology; a system of legitimizing values, orderliness, and coherence as a belief system; more or less derivable moral implications; and factual claims about the empirical world.[4] The political economists separated the scientific and moral-political aspects of their theory by the distinction between positive economics and normative economics — a distinction that retains life up to the present day. In light of the above characterization of the nineteenth-century economists' system, however, the effort to separate the empirical from the evaluative seems somewhat hopeless; for example, to describe empirically how a system has deviated from its tendency toward equilibrium is patently an evaluation of that system in relation to an adhered-to principle of the constructed economic world.

---

contend that neither firms nor their environments are ever in a state of equilibrium" (Nohria, Gulati, and Eccles, forthcoming).

4. Consider Geertz's definition of religion in this connection: "a system of symbols which acts to establish powerful, pervasive, and long-lasting moods and motivations in men by formulating conceptions of a general order of existence and clothing these conceptions with such an aura of factuality that the moods and motivations seem uniquely realistic" (1973, 90).

Economists have also constructed various kinds of negative utopias in relation to their preferred economic system. For Adam Smith and his followers, the vast array of arrangements encompassed by the mercantilist economic system constituted such a negative utopia. More generally, a core of economic evils is found under the heading of "market failures," of which two principal types were identified — imperfections such as monopoly, entry barriers, restrictive practices, and tariffs on the one hand, and externalities such as public goods, pollution, and national defense on the other (Hartley 1992). Over the years specific controversies have revolved around the market-poisoning effects of phenomena such as the "Corn Laws, Imperial Preference, the Zollverein, the Common Market, and Smoot-Hawley" (Goodwin 1988, 211). In the past half-century the principal negative utopia has been the politically administered price systems of the Communist regimes of the former Soviet Union and Eastern Europe, which constitute imperfections in the extreme. The trumpeting of the market principle — both as ideology and as mode of social integration — and the corresponding denigration of administered economies and their inefficiencies reached almost manic proportions in the immediate aftermath of the revolutions of the East in 1989-90. In general, the idea that "the price system or market is taken to be an effective and desirable social choice mechanism" appears to remain the tenet of greatest consensus among economists (Frey et al. 1984, 994).

Regarding the constructed economic world of the nineteenth century, we might ask: From where is imperfection — or sin, if you will — likely to arise? The answers to this question appear to be of two kinds: denial and externalization. The first is that, if one endows the constructed world with either an actual or a promised empirical existence, then one would have to conclude that the world is truly utopian, that imperfection does not exist. The second answer is that imperfection is likely to arise from *outside* the constructed world, especially in the second external environment — the world of institutions, law, and politics that were frozen into parameters. As indicated, one sort of imperfection arises in the form of "externalities" — a clear and literal reference to "the outside." The other form is meddlesomeness on the part of the polity that creates friction, trade barriers, artificial prices, or whatever else in the market.

John Stuart Mill formalized this distinction analytically in his distinction between "immediate causes" of economic behavior and what he called "disturbing causes" of it. (The use of the term "disturbing" itself suggests a kind of unwanted, foreign quality.) For the economy, the "immediate causes" are within the economic world — that is, "those which act through the desire of wealth; and in which the psychological law *mainly* concerned is the familiar one, that a greater gain is preferred to a smaller" (Mill 1965-73, 4:331). "Disturbing" causes are those which belong to "some other science" (331). In the language I have been employing, they are the external "givens" or "parameters" of economic analysis. The investigation of the effects of the immediate causes constitutes the central enterprise for formal economics, though it is apparent that the "disturbing" influences do have some kind of causal status, because they are in fact labeled as "causes" by Mill and can intrude on the economy and "disturb" it.

To regard this issue more generally: the distinction between the constructed economic world (the world of immediate causes or "operative variables") and the world external to it (the world of disturbing causes or "givens") constitutes an interesting economic variation on the distinction between the sacred and the profane, which is a near-universal in religious systems (Durkheim 1951 [1915]). The distinction is between an inside, ideal world and an outside, disturbing — perhaps even polluting — world. In the main, economists have employed two analytic strategies to deal with disturbing causes: first, they have excluded them from consideration (as in the case of James Mill's treatment of force, fraud, and gift-giving); and second, they have rendered them inoperative by freezing them analytically into the status of "givens." Yet the latter operation reveals a fundamental ambivalence. On the one hand, "given" means that a potential cause — a change in tastes, institutional change, a breakdown of civil order — is neutralized and does not matter for purposes of analysis. On the other hand, it is acknowledged that it is a *potential* cause (or else it would not have to be confronted and neutralized) and might change its status and become "disturbing" at any time. In many religious systems, believers and practitioners maintain an ambivalent and suspicious attitude toward the profane, and the analytic status of the notion of a "given" reflects a similar ambivalent disposition in the corpus of economic analysis.

Sources of Imperfection

Mill drew an indistinct line between immediate and disturbing causes, a line capable of being crossed. Some external causes "might be brought within the pale of the abstract science" (Mill 1965-73, 4:331). These would supplement and correct the analytically distinct science of economics; they might even work in directions different from the principle of the maximization of wealth. He mentioned population in particular:

> In a few of the most striking cases (such as the important one of the principle of population) [these corrections] are . . . interpolated into the expositions of Political Economy itself; the strictness of purely scientific arrangement being thereby somewhat departed from, for the sake of practical utility. (323)

Mill surely could not have realized the prophetic nature of that enunciation. In it, however, he provided a kernel of the account of a great deal of the future evolution of economic thought. In fact, much of the history of economics can be regarded as a repeated process, each repetition involving several steps: (1) a recognition, deriving either from internal perceptions by economists or from external criticisms by others, of the inadequacies of the assumptions about "givens" and the consequent imperfection — or, to continue the running analogy, a recognition of the intrusion of the profane as something variable, not fixed and controllable; (2) an attempt to accommodate this recognition in one way or another, including modification or adaptation of parts of economic theory and investigation; (3) a simultaneous attempt to preserve the core analytic assumptions — or articles of faith, if you will — of economic theory. I will devote the remainder of the essay to demonstrating this dynamic selectively.

Before I proceed to that demonstration, it should be noted that such a dynamic is strikingly similar to the theological account of the secularization of Christianity, as this was characterized by Ernst Troeltsch, the historian and sociologist of religion. For Troeltsch, Christianity consists of a core of theological assumptions (e.g., personalistic theism, divine love, and charity) that consistently leads believing Christians to portray the "world" as outside (Troeltsch 1931, 1:100). In the last analysis they come to regard "the world and all its ordinances" as "a solid and unchangeable mass of evil" (101). At the same time, Troeltsch noticed a continuing and growing mundaneness of the churches, which was his recognition of the process of secularization. For him, however, secularization involves not the *replacement* of the sacred by the profane but rather a process of compromise on the part of the churches in order to preserve their centrality in the face of complexity. Troeltsch regarded secularization as a kind of conversation between the continuing religious attitude and the world:

> Nowhere does there exist an absolute Christian ethic, which only awaits discovery; all that we can do is to learn to control the world situation in its successive phases just as the earlier Christian ethic did in its own way. There is also no absolute ethical transformation of material nature or human nature; all that does exist is a constant wrestling with the problems which they raise. Thus the Christian ethic of the present day and of the future will also only be an adjustment to the world situation, and it will only desire to achieve that which is practically possible. (2:1013)

Whether or not one shares Troeltsch's precise analyses and predictions, his account of the theological dynamics of secularization remains a persuasive one.

What, then, are the sources of imperfection in what Mill called "the abstract science" and what I have called "the constructed economic world"? As indicated, these are to be found in the array of "givens" which surround that world. I have mentioned a few instances. To proceed somewhat more systematically, we might link those "givens" in the form of a number of critical assertions about them and, in so doing, develop a catalog of the major criticisms of the dominant nineteenth-century economic model:

- Actors' tastes are not ordered and stable over time.
- The tastes of individual actors are not independent of (i.e., are influenced by) the tastes and actions of others.
- The information available to actors is incomplete and/or uncertain; more specifically, the market strategies and behavior of others may be disguised or otherwise unknown.

- Actors do not maximize, or they maximize in ways different from the ways characterized in marginalist analysis or indifference curve analysis.
- Actors do not always calculate, but rely on habits, rules of thumb, and impulses of the moment.
- Actors behave in ways contrary to rational maximization — that is, irrationally.
- Actors pursue goals other than their material well-being — for example, they perform altruistic actions, or they pursue spiritual or military goals.
- Resources (e.g., labor and capital) are not perfectly mobile, with the consequence that chronic market frictions and disequilibria develop.
- Power or political considerations intrude on market exchange, whether in the form of deceit, coercion, exploitation, monopolistic control of the market, or government regulation and intervention.
- As a result of the last two considerations, the markets do not "clear" through the price mechanism, and phenomena such as underemployment and unemployment may become regular features of economic life.
- Derivatively, the equation that maximum social welfare is achieved through the rational pursuit of self-interest on the part of individuals does not hold.
- The institutional "givens" characteristic of the industrial-market economy of the West are historically specific and cannot be generalized to other periods of history or to other societies in the contemporary world.

Elsewhere (Smelser 1992), I have identified two observable responses to these kinds of criticisms in the economics literature: denial (ignoring or reasserting an orthodox position) and generalization (sometimes called imperialism). The more creative reactions are those that attempt to accommodate or to incorporate the profane imperfections but at the same time preserve the essential core (rationality, maximization, the market). In doing this, they express a parallel with the process of religious secularization. I now consider a few of these cases.

Elaboration of the Constructed World in the Face of Imperfection

Materialism

To begin, let us consider an item central to the theme of this volume. The history of nineteenth-century economic thought — including and especially that of Karl Marx — has been closely associated with materialism. According to Dumont's account (1977), the development of the ideologies of utilitarianism and political economy marked a struggle between the hierarchical-deferential and spiritual emphases of the pre-industrial world on the one hand and the ideology of materialism on the other. The latter came to triumph over a long period of time. That triumph reached a climax in the historical materialism of Marx, in which the materialist principle attained the status of a first axiom in a general theory of society and evolution.

It is true that the language of economics still contains certain materialist references — "material well-being," "material satisfactions," and so on. However, economic thinking early began to experience something of a dissociation between the idea of self-interest and the idea of material acquisition. There are good logical and historical reasons why this should have happened. For one thing, to specify precise referents of "material" is extremely difficult, and the effort to do so involves the user of that term in ambiguities if it is thought to be identical with the "physical" as conceived by the natural sciences. And if "material" is identified with anything that satisfies, it involves the user of the term in a system of circular reasoning. And finally, the monetization of the market process itself comes to include services and symbols that are clearly not "material" in any sense of the word, thus creating even more difficulties for the consistent identification of "the material" with "the economic."

In any event, Bentham himself developed a large and generally unsatisfactory classification of types of gratification (utilities), many of which were not "material." Mill's definition of the central economic postulate was the "desire of wealth" (1965-73, 4:331), which is sufficiently general to avoid any identification with "the material." Marshall defined "the economic" as dealing with phenomena that are subject to measurement in terms of money. However flawed that definition, it also broke the connection between the economic and any strictly material connotations. By 1932, Robbins was completely explicit in his assertion that "Whatever Economics is concerned with, it is *not* concerned with the cause of material welfare as such" (1952 [1932]). More recently, Becker extended the principle and went beyond Marshall:

> The economic approach is not restricted to *material goods and wants or to markets with monetary transactions,* and conceptually does not distinguish between major and minor decisions, or between "emotional" or other decisions. Indeed . . . the economic approach provides a framework applicable to all human behavior — to all types of decisions and to persons from all walks of life. (1981, iv; emphasis added)

As a result of this split, "the economic" comes to connote choice in a context of scarcity of things of value, the connotation of "things" being left entirely open.

What does such a dissociation accomplish? From a philosophical point of view, it permits an escape from the maze of difficulties that arise in defining and specifying "the material." From an ethical point of view, it permits economists to sidestep criticisms that they themselves are "profane" in a traditional religious sense — that is, that they deal only with "the world" or "matters of the flesh." From an empirical point of view, it constitutes a more realistic specification of what is exchanged in market economies. And from an analytical point of view — if we consider Becker's extension of the economic beyond "market transactions" — it generalizes and transforms economics into a completely general psychology, separated from any institutional context.[5]

One might argue, with reason, that economists' dissociation of their subject matter from "the material" is really beside the point, and that the decisive theoretical and ideological — indeed, religious — import of utilitarianism and political economy had to do with the *rational* pursuit of *self-interest,* because these two elements marked the most significant departure from the traditional Christian emphasis on sin,

---

5. This operation, which simultaneously extends the inclusiveness of a concept or symbol and reduces the specificity of its references, is akin to what Parsons referred to as "value-generalization" in the cultural sphere (see Parsons 1971).

self-denial, and altruism. What is certain, moreover, is that the conceptual shedding of "the material" as the basis of economic science does *not* imply a simultaneous desertion of the fundamental core constituted by the ideas of rationality and self-interest. In a word, the dissociation might be regarded as an adaptation on the part of economics to its outside "world," a concession but not a true compromise of orthodoxy.

Information Economics

Nearly three-quarters of a century ago, Knight (1921) pointedly raised the question of the problematics of economic behavior under conditions of risk and uncertainty. Shackle (1957) later put the question in salient form:

> The prices of all goods could be decided if we knew with sufficient detail for each person in the market the answers to the questions, "What does he like?" and "What does he possess?" It did not occur to most of those who built the beautiful neo-classical structure of static value theory to put upon the same footing a third kind of question: "What does he know?" or "What does he believe?" (198)

Both Kenneth Arrow (1984) and Herbert Simon (1982) built their contributions to economic theory on modifications of the perfect-information postulate.

The modifications of the postulate of perfect knowledge that information economics have made are too numerous to detail in short compass, but in general they deal with changes in economic calculation and behavior when risks of unknown dimensions are present in the actor's environment, when the consequences of a given choice are uncertain, or when incomplete information makes calculation difficult. One of the most important theoretical outgrowths of the latter situation has been to treat the gathering of information as a transaction cost, with various models built on the idea that before making an economic decision an actor will dedicate his or her resources to the gathering of information up to the point where the further search for information becomes too costly (see Lamberton 1992). One might also consider the development of game theory in economics — a major tradition in the past decades — to be based on a modification of the perfect-information postulate: the knowledge of the utility functions and maximization strategies of *other actors* are unknown to an actor, and that actor must guess about and consider the possibility of various strategies, bluffs, reactions to counter-strategies, and so on in calculating his or her own sequence of behaviors.

The key question for purposes of this essay is this: To what degree does the economics of information constitute a qualitative break with the neoclassical model based on perfect information? In one sense it is a clear break, because a key "given" is turned into an operative variable. But at the same time, the fundamental elements of calculation and maximization do not appear to have undergone qualitative change. As Lamberton argues,

> The likes and possessions *and* the knowledge and beliefs . . . find their place in the information model of the economy which is needed to complete the traditional production/consumption mode. . . . An information-theoretical approach that endogenizes information processes is not destructive of economic theory, although it will inevitably weaken and hopefully destroy some of the rigidities and associated vested interests. By pushing back the boundaries of the *economic*, the new approach permits a richer analysis that fuses together the continuing processes of resource allocation, learning, and development. (1992, 122)

A more succinct statement of the theoretical harmlessness — indeed, the benefits — of secularization for the basic fundamentals would be difficult to produce.

Alteration of Preference Schedules

Keynesian economics marked a departure from the neoclassical tradition in two major respects. The first involved a modification of the marginalist utility assumptions, and the substitution of a number of alternatives in the form of the marginal propensity to consume, the involuntary withdrawal of labor, the liquidity preference function, and the assumption of the marginal efficiency of capital. It was by virtue of the systematic incorporation of these modifications of the utility functions of the key actors (consumers, laborers, lenders, and investors) that Keynes was able to demonstrate that the economy could generate more or less permanent market disequilibria, especially systematic unemployment of labor (Keynes 1936) and, later, inflation. Keynes's second innovation was the introduction of government as an active economic agent, particularly in the pursuit of monetary and fiscal policies designed to relieve or correct those disequilibria. Moreover, the effectiveness of government policies (e.g., redistribution of income through taxation or welfare) also rested on the presumed validity of the utility functions posited by Keynes (e.g., the marginal propensity to consume in the redistributional examples given).

These innovations have been labeled the "Keynesian revolution," but it should be clear that, revolutionary as they were from the vantage point of marginalist economics and the laissez-faire ideology, they preserved the fundamentals of calculation and maximization on the part of the major actors. The novel arguments were that these actors maximized *in different ways* than had previously been imagined. Even the government as economic agent could be conceived as economic utility in its interventions — that is, as re-establishing market equilibria that were problematic and not normally assured by the operation of the market. In that respect the Keynesian revolution was more continuous than revolutionary.

In a very different micro-economic arena, much of the work of behavioral economists has been to modify assumptions regarding both information and utility assumptions of neoclassical economists to account for anomalous choice behavior in experimental and uncontrolled situations of economic choice (see Kahneman and Tversky 1986). At the same time, most of the work in this area retains the ideas that actors are aware of their economic options, that they assess their choices, and that they opt for those choices which they feel are best for them in those situations.

Concluding Remarks

Additional examples of the innovation/preservation process could be generated — for example, the analysis of monopoly and oligopoly and its regulation as the systematic relaxation of the assumption of absence of power in the market — but enough illustrations have been given to demonstrate the typicality of that process. It only remains to note that this kind of "secularization cycle," as it might be called, is usually where the action is in economics. According to a compilation of most-cited sources in the social sciences over the past decades, the economics literature is dominated by those areas of "significant parametric modifications of classical and neoclassical economics: modifications stressing variations in information, decision-making, organizational strategies and structures, economic motivation, and institutional behavior" (Smelser 1987, xxii). Many of the recipients of the Nobel prize in economics have been those noted for innovations at the parametric edges of the discipline.

At the same time, innovations often generate concerns with heterodoxy and orthodoxy and heated internal debates in the field — a final element that finds parallels in the dynamics of religion and theology as well. On the one hand, those who achieve breakthroughs by relaxing the orthodox assumptions are ultimately rewarded. On the other hand, anxious concerns are given voice by those in the mainstream. In his classic exposition entitled *Value and Capital*, Hicks warned of the consequences of the "general abandonment of the assumption of perfect competition" and "the threatened wreckage" of "the greater part of economic theory" unless it was assumed that "the markets confronting most of the firms . . . do not differ greatly from perfectly competitive markets" (cited in Lamberton 1992, 119).

The general picture of the discipline that emerges from this dynamic is that of a cultural enterprise which — like enduring religions — is notably innovative in its adaptation to the realities of an increasingly complex world, but at the same time is continuously looking over its shoulder at the consequences for its own theoretical integrity and unity, worried about possible "theoretical wreckage," and continuously assuring the world that it retains a fundamental, enduring, and legitimate core.

The Economic Absorption
of the Sacred

JOHN BOLI

Introduction

FOR BETTER AND FOR WORSE, the moral dimension of social life is particularly pronounced in Western culture. Life is not something simply to be lived, as in some Asian philosophies; life must have a purpose, a meaning. What qualifies as adequate purpose and meaning is quite demanding. Veneration of ancestors (Japanese Shinto) is not enough, nor is faithful reproduction of the social order (the Indian caste system), nor is complete submission to the will of Allah (Islam). In the West, with its peculiarly individualistic cultural style, *principled* purpose and meaning are a social imperative (Meyer et al. 1987; cf. Wuthnow 1987).

What this means is quite simple. In the West, individual life is oriented around a complex set of goals that are to be attained via rational principles of action. The pursuit of these goals is itself morally virtuous and existentially meaningful; the goodness and sense of our lives are derived from the pursuit, even though we inevitably fail to attain the goals fully. What makes the pursuit virtuous and meaningful is the fact that the goals to be pursued are derived from the sacred order of Western

---

This essay was originally presented at the conference entitled "Rethinking Materialism," sponsored by the Center for the Study of American Religion, Princeton University, June 11-13, 1993. Michael Rainey and Tom Loya provided welcome research assistance.

culture. By aligning our action with the sacred order, we convince ourselves that our individual lives are consonant with the "nature of things" and therefore proper and sensible. We avoid the interpretive difficulties that inhere in contradicting the cosmic order. We avoid having to cope with a view of ourselves as seriously anomalous vis-à-vis the classificatory system that shapes our consciousness (cf. Douglas 1966).

The argument I will make in this essay is that the sacred order which structures individual action in American, Western, and, increasingly, world culture is primarily "represented" in the economic realm. I see the sacred order as the "deep structure" of culture, comprising the fundamental ontological, epistemological, and procedural assumptions that ground social behavior. As such, it is not "contained" in any particular societal sector but operates at a more abstract and generalized level. But the sacred order is expressed in and shaped by the development of the various institutional sectors that collectively make up the social order. Because the economic realm is the dominant sector of our age, the sacred order of our culture is now peculiarly "economic" in nature.

The sacred order is no less moral, purposive, or meaning-oriented for that. What we must recognize is that, like modern society itself, the content of the modern sacred order is differentiated and highly complex, with much internal inconsistency. The principles we are supposed to actualize cannot all be enacted at the same time, and compartmentalization (of the social order, the self, the psyche . . .) is the only generally available means of maintaining cosmic consonance in our interpretive schemes.

It is here, I will argue, that the source of much of our anguish about materialism has its root. The anguish may be justified, but I submit that it is improperly focused because of several failings in our conception of economic life:

1. We fail to recognize that a moral order grounded in the sacred operates in the economic realm. This failure leads us to underestimate the difficulties of aligning economic behavior in accordance with other moral orders (notably, traditional religious morality).

2. We fail to understand that the materialism which troubles us is not materialistic. Materialism is above all a way of constructing and expressing meaning symbolically. The failure to recognize this fact leads us to underestimate the spirituality of economic behavior — hence the

difficulties of reducing our devotion to acquisition, consumption, and display.

3. We fail to recognize that the monetarization of social life is not essentially an economic process. The attachment of monetary value to objects and processes is driven more by the institutionalized quest for rationality, which requires a standard metric comparable across all social settings, than by the venal motive of profit accumulation. This third failure reflects the larger mistake we make in supposing that capitalism is essentially a system of production and exchange rather than a model of value creation through the rationalization of activity by rational actors. We therefore infer quite erroneously that bounding capitalism will reduce materialism.

I share the anguish over materialism. Meaning and purpose can be generated in abundance outside the realm of rationalized value. The pursuit of meaning and purpose via monetarized rationalization poses a serious threat to the possibilities of substantive freedom, justice, and rationality, even to life itself. But we must come to terms with the depth of the problem: we are dealing with a highly institutionalized economic religion that must be confronted on its own terms, and many of the cultural underpinnings of that religion are, I believe, truly sacred to us all. Whether we can desacralize economic religion without at the same time destroying the foundations for the "good society" we perpetual millenarians carry around in our heads is a question we must confront at every moment.

This essay has four main sections and a concluding section. In the first section I provide a brief historical background for considering the issue of economic morality. In the second section I describe the moral order of the economy as a specification of the cultural sacred order; a key process that I identify here is the sacralization of desacralizing forces. In the third section I analyze the sacredness of the economic realm directly, paying particular attention to rituals and symbols in economic life, while in the fourth section I explore the economic religion of contemporary society. In the fifth and final section I elaborate on the implications of the analysis for the problem of materialism.

The Autonomous Economy
and the Rational Individual

The first issue is the source of the problem of materialism. I locate it in the emergence of autonomous economic morality.

As long as the West was dominated by Christendom, a monolithic (albeit internally contentious) ideological structure, and as long as the only significant institutional cleavage was that between the religiously defined realms of the sacred and the profane — the church and the state — traditional religious morality was infused throughout the cultural framework. (Proto-)states were minor actors, particularly on the moral stage; they were for a very long time simply the "police departments" of the church (Strayer 1970).

An autonomous basis for action emerged when new loci of purpose and meaning could be established. The first attempt came in the political realm, which was the primary domain of societal "self-thematization" (Luhmann 1982) throughout most of history. Machiavelli attempted to legitimate political autonomy from religiously based moral considerations not simply on behalf of the Prince but for the welfare of the polity; the critical response to his argument demonstrated the inseparability of church and state in his time (Hinsley 1986, 110ff.). *Raison d'état* became an acceptable basis for state action only when the troubling question *"L'état de qui?"* was given a universalistic answer by the institutionalization of the democratic theory of the state in the nineteenth century.

Luhmann insists that the definitive breakthrough came earlier, with the differentiation of the economic sphere from the eighteenth century onward. Based first on the rationalization of agriculture, later on the application of rational technique to manufacturing methods, the differentiation of the economy introduced material criteria of value and purpose that we summarize in the concept of efficiency. The justification for human action could then be formulated in terms of instrumental rationality: the good was that which contributed to the improvement of mundane welfare via increases in productive efficiency, which in turn resulted from the task specialization engendered by economic exchange.

From a more institutional perspective, the differentiated economy can be characterized as the moral autonomy of humanity; or, the enthronement of (human) Reason; or, a human project successful enough to make a convincing argument that the sin of the Fall — the striving for autonomy from the will of God — was self-justificatory. Human autonomy acquired legitimacy via the emergence of the doctrine of progress, an intellectual distillation of evident and widespread improvements in technique, production, and organization (cf. Nisbet 1980). Durkheim (1951) teaches us that society's image of God is its image of itself. What the autonomous project accomplished was the reverse: society became God, while the Christian God was confined to a spiritual corner of existence and turned into a subjective matter of faith or even, more recently, opinion.

The differentiated economy was not freed from traditional moral considerations, only from irrational impediments to rationalization. Early writings in political economy were as much the work of moralists as those of any other branch of scholarship in the eighteenth century. Adam Smith offers us more a defense than an analysis of unbridled capitalism, but it is a defense that brings the sacred inside society. The invisible hand is a mystical god, working in mysterious (or at least unexplained) ways with more than a touch of miracle to produce a holistic beneficence that is not predictable from the unholy motivations of the self-interested actors subject to its intervention. Utilitarian liberalism thus theorized and legitimated the secular society on a non-deistic basis, thereby promoting (and reflecting) the view that the economy could yield "the greatest good" in the absence of moral actors. The glory of God was no longer the point; rationalized economic strivings achieved the glory of humanity.

But the subjective, moralistic individual was a product of the same developments that liberated the economy from religious morality (Durkheim 1933; Simmel 1971a). Rationalized differentiation proceeded by way of dialectical processes involving the state and civil society on the one hand and the individual on the other. The state undermined intermediate groups and identities in its nation-building activities (Bendix 1964; Tilly 1975), shaking out the individual from above; civil society generated a realm of public discourse (Habermas 1962) in which the nascent subjectivity of the individual was fostered from below. This universalistic individual became, as it were, the "sovereign representative" of the symbolic universe of Western culture — each person representing both the abstract concept of the individual and the authority lodged in the national polity. In short, subjects became citizens, endowed with rights and obligations and empowered, to varying degrees, to take the fashioning of progress and justice into their own hands.

The combination of an autonomous humanity, a societal project of progress, and a universalistic, rational-by-presumption, morally purposive individual made the monetarization of social life an aggressively expansive process. Naturally enough, monetarization was quite uniformly categorized as an "economic" process in the take-off period, since most of the activity incorporated into the realm of rationalized accounting involved the production of basic material goods. Illogically, however, monetarization has continued to be conceived as fundamentally economic even to the present day, despite the primarily symbolic nature of most of the "goods" that are "produced" in highly monetarized societies. I will return to this issue subsequently.

Sacred Order in the Economy

To speak of the absorption of the sacred by the economic realm is to raise the issue of the meaning and identification of the sacred. For Durkheim (1951) the sacred is the inviolable, the powerful; for Douglas (1966) it is the ordering principles of culture and the symbols of danger that surround these principles; for Ellul (1973) it is at once the powerful promise and the destructive potential of the transcendent. Let it be all of these; we know it when we "see" it. But do we?

Perceiving historical Christianity through our poorly focused lenses, we identify the sacred rather easily. It was religious, bound up with symbols of divinity in various forms and a plethora of representations linked to those symbols (saints, icons, relics, and the like). We forget about the "folk religion" of those converted pagans, about their stubborn devotion to animism and their capacity to discover immanent spiritual forces in every niche of their habitat. Be that as it may; they lived in natural and spiritual worlds drenched with sacred imagery.

But we err in our analysis. The sacred was never located in the natural or spiritual world. If we take Durkheim's claim seriously, along with the main thrust of the sociological analysis of culture since Durkheim's day, the sacred is social (cf. Bellah 1970; Geertz 1973). The sacred is externalized and dramatized representations of social structure. Not just any elements of social structure chosen at random, but fundamental elements — elements that are constitutive of the cultural complex, elements that form the ontological and epistemological foundation of social structure. Arunta society was built on the clan as a fundamental element; the clan was a highly reified assumption deeply embedded in Arunta culture; the clan provided the most basic source of structure and identity for members of Arunta society. Ergo, totems emerged as sacred representations of the clans. Totems were created and maintained as elements of the sacred through their dramatization in extraordinary interaction events (cf. Collins 1988).

Think in these terms about contemporary Western culture. The fundamental elements of culture, the assumptions that ground social structure, are liable to sacralization. What are they? This is tantamount to asking, What are the fundamental social units, processes, and purposes that ground the contemporary West? We know them well. The individual, the state, the national polity, the ethnic group — these are some of the basic units, highly reified as the building blocks of social organization. Technical rationalization, monetarization, formal organization, voluntaristic association, reflexive social monitoring, revolution — these are some of the self-evident mechanisms for treating human problems. Progress, equality, justice, self-actualization, liberation — these are some of the institutionalized purposes that are to be realized in the Western project (Thomas et al. 1987).

We quarrel endlessly about what these constructs mean and how they are to be operationalized. We recognize the many contradictions inherent in their relations with one another. But that they constitute the platform upon which the Western edifice is built is, from within the Western frame, almost true by definition.

If these are the foundations of Western culture, they are subject to sacralization. And they have been sacralized. Durkheim's model can be applied quite mechanically, and it works. The individual is sacred, surrounded by notions of ultimate worth and inviolability (Boli 1989) and the giver and receiver of ritualistic affirmations of the venerability of the bounded self (Goffman 1956; Durkheim 1933). The nation (in Hegelian variants, the state) is sacred, an all-powerful but threatening being that may demand the ultimate sacrifice but rewards the faithful with a fixed identity and physical security (cf. Kertzer 1988; Lane 1981). Technology reigns over the material world, a potent god whose power must be properly harnessed to contain its inimical tendency to run out of control. Equality prevails: who can explicitly favor its opposite? Inequality poses a perplexing legitimation problem for the rich and powerful, putting them incessantly on the defensive.

Apply the model mechanically and it works, but with the vibrancy of a droning Lutheran sermon. Add the dynamic of Ellul's analysis in *Les nouveaux possédés* (1973), and the model at once becomes more specific, hazardous, and convincing. Ellul insists on the dialectical nature of the changing content of the sacred order in Western history: *the forces of desacralization are themselves sacralized in and through the desacralization process.* By disenchanting the world, desacralizing forces acquire the spiritual aura stripped away from the formerly sacred; they are themselves constructed as loci of ultimate power, danger, truth. The desacralizing force of primitive Christianity (challenging the sacredness of nature and of political power as such) was sacralized after Constantine; the desacralizing Protestantism of the sixteenth century was sacralized in the seventeenth and eighteenth centuries (Ellul 1973).

In the standard accounts, the sacred order of medieval society was overthrown by rationalization (Weber's disenchantment); capitalism (Marx's commodification); differentiation (Simmel's objectification); technique (Ellul).[1] More generally, the natural and spiritual worlds were desacralized via reflexive processes of analysis and control developed in new institutional spheres whose distinctiveness was justified via logics orthogonal to those of the religious realm. Each of these processes was in turn sacralized, generating a new and more complex structure of the sacred order.

We then come back to the economy. The economy is the realm of rationalized action to which the metric of money is applied — not the realm of production, distribution, and consumption but the realm of Marx's cash nexus, of Weber's double-entry bookkeeping. Unmone-

---

1. The major desacralizers of our time, in Ellul's view, are the two great forces of order and restraint in the modern era, the state and technique; each is accompanied by its transgressing counterpart, revolution and sex, respectively. Thus, twin axes of contradictory but mutually reinforcing forces are at the heart of the sacred order: the state/revolution and technique/sex. While Ellul's analysis is extremely insightful, it is restrictive (most glaringly, it leaves out the individual) and a bit too neat. The sacred order in differentiated cultures is complex, messy, and elastic enough to be stretched to fit a wide range of enacting institutional realms.

tarized production is anomalous from the economic point of view. Its value cannot be determined but can only be estimated by analogy with monetarized realms; it can hardly be rationalized, as rationalization in the absence of a universalistic metric is nonsensical. Even rationalization in terms of technical efficiency is no trademark of economic action; as Collins (1986) shows, the technical innovation is not an innovation unless conditions are right for its incorporation into the sphere of monetary value.

The economic realm is, then, the sector par excellence of universalistic rationalization. It is also a sector of highly elaborated individualism, at least in the West, and, less paradoxically than at first appears, of broad and intense state control (Evans et al. 1985). In short, the economy is constructed from key elements of the sacred order that are themselves key aspects of the great desacralizing forces of the early modern period.

By most accounts, the economy is now the dominant institutional sphere, eclipsing even the political realm. The global economy is typically depicted as larger and more powerful, albeit less centralized, than the interstate system (Chase-Dunn 1989); national economies are depicted as having broader reach and scope than the "arbitrary" territorial boundaries associated with their particular states; complaints arise on all sides that the economy's appetite for unmonetarized social activities is insatiable. The economy is, therefore, the dominant modern moral order.

What confuses analyses of the sacred and moral orders in modern "secular" society is the differentiation of the sacred order in recent centuries. The sacred is discovered in science, technology, medicine, politics, sex, sports, music, even religion; priesthoods of all sorts are identified; icons and sacraments are espied on all sides; the shopping mall, the hospital, the sports arena are all depicted as temples (cf. Belk et al. 1989; Berman 1984). How can any of this be taken seriously? But the analysis is entirely correct: sacralization goes on in each differentiated sector, with each sector oriented to different aspects of the sacred order and arriving at a more or less coherent moral vision that may be at odds with the moral orders of other sectors (on the role of purification rituals, cf. Douglas 1966, 69).

Occupational differentiation implies, in turn, that contemporary culture has generated a differentiated clerical estate made up of various professions intimately linked to sacralized social elements. The sacred body has its clergy of physicians and sex therapists, technology its scientists and engineers, the nation its lawyers and judges. In a rationally instrumental ("expert") way they mediate between the lay public, normally faithful but not infrequently troubled by doubt, and the modern deities whose esoteric truths are not directly accessible to the public. A paradox of individualism, the structure is more Catholic than Protestant.

In sum, the moral order is highly differentiated, with differentiated, limited, specialized moral orders emerging in distinct realms overseen by specialized priesthoods. Interconnections among the various realms are normally weak and intermittent. Integration is provided, often little more than nominally, by the religious sacred: God is a backup device when the gods of medicine, therapy, or science fail. Most of the differentiated moral orders retain the universalism of the Christian tradition — among sacred entities, only the nation is explicitly particularistic — but this universalism is partitioned in distinct but partially overlapping social spheres.

Sacred Properties of the Economic Realm

I do not offer the sacredness of the economy as an analogy or a metaphor. The economy *is* sacred. Let us explore this theme.

1. Power and Danger

The economy is conceived in radically ambivalent terms, in several dimensions (Parry and Bloch 1989; Parsons 1979; Barton 1989). Cognitively, the economy is reified as the source of both great power and great danger. Economic action is the sole means of harnessing the resources required to meet human needs; the rationalized economy is capable of production essentially without limit. The economy is also a dangerous manic-depressive neurotic whose alternating outbursts of exuberance and numbed passivity must be rigorously regulated. The economy promises prosperity but can collapse into misery. The economy is a changeling, growing and shrinking in fits and spurts. The economy is mysterious, unknowable, intransigent, despite the best managerial efforts of its associated clergy.

In the aesthetic dimension, the rationalized economy is held accountable for both extraordinary elegance and unmitigated ugliness. The synthesis of function and beauty achieved in a wide range of goods and structures and spaces is adulated with just as much fervor as the repulsive blight of garish commercialism and pure functionalism is decried. Our ambivalence knows no bounds. The economy attracts and repels with tremendous force.

As a moral force, the economy is a primary source of good and evil. The good is the very essence of the economy; it produces "goods" that have "value," and the expansion of the sum total of that value is perhaps the ultimate purpose of the political system. Various voices may question the goodness of economic growth, but they are entirely ineffective; the desirability of a "rising standard of living" is taken for granted in most social sectors. And with good reason, given that the expanding economy is credited with prolonging life, making us healthier, giving us diverse leisure activities, enriching our lives.

The evils of the economy need not be rehearsed here. The West has condemned the heartless rationality of the cash nexus for more than two thousand years; moral resistance to its expansion has been endemic even in American culture, as Zelizer (1983, 1987) illustrates in her studies of the monetarization of the human life and the child. Wuthnow's (1993) finding of "pious materialism" in the U.S. population only confirms the persistence of extreme moral ambivalence toward the economy; the Marxist critique of capitalism is but the most prominent political expression of this ambivalence. Marxism's religiosity (Boli 1981; Lane 1981) affirms the sacredness of capitalist exchange — indeed, reinforces it by reifying capitalist exchange as the satanic source of all evil in the world.

2. Rituals

Despite all that has been said, money is ritual, not rationality. "Money can only perform its role of intensifying economic interaction if the public has faith in it. If faith in it is shaken, the currency is useless" (Douglas 1966, 69). Faith lies not in money itself, of course, but in the institutions that stand behind it. The passing of money from hand to hand (even more, from data bank to data bank) is in every instance the

ritual affirmation of our faith in those elements of the sacred order —
the nation, the rational individual, rationalized public and private organization — that give money its value. Lose that faith, and a bushel of
apples can be acquired only with a bushel of money.

Money is a symptom, an indicator, a reflection of economic conditions. Economic conditions must be managed; managing the economy
is, indeed, the dominant "infrastructural" concern of the state. Interest
rates, the money supply, taxation, investment, employment, competitive
conditions — all must be regulated to steer the economy between the
twin perils of deep freeze and overheating. Policy formulation and im-
plementation is the ritual process employed. Economic policy is rational
ritual, pinning its hopes not on fixed formulae but on one or another
rationalized analysis of where the dangers and opportunities lie at the
moment. Its ritualism inheres in its imperative nature: political and
economic managers must continually reformulate economic policy if
they are properly to enact the moral order, regardless of the persistent
tendency of the economy to behave at variance with the model employed
to manage it. To paraphrase, it's always broke, so keep on pretendin' to
fix it.

A third prominent ritual, bearing strong resemblance to economic
management, is advertising. Both adored and reviled, advertising is the
obligatory propitiation and manipulation of the consumer. Advertising
draws upon such sacred elements as self-actualization, autonomous
identity formation, and individual rationality to forge links between the
consumer (a derivative of the sacred individual) and the values embodied in goods. Tellingly, advertising emphasizes not so much rationalized (monetary) value as qualities whose value has not been metricized (cf. Lears 1983). Consumer participants in advertising rituals
interpret advertised goods primarily in symbolic terms (cf. Douglas and
Isherwood 1979), trying on alternative images of their various selves
that may never in fact be realized. Advertising thus gives both advertisers
and consumers a mechanism for settling on temporarily dominant
modes (fashions) for the enactment of the sacred in everyday life. Both
parties are seen as beneficiaries of this mutual interplay, although the
manipulative rationality of the advertiser is a continual irritant to the
principle of individual autonomy.

3. Symbols

Durkheim insists on the sacralization of social elements through symbols. Money is surely a sacred symbol: we hesitate to deface it, we endow it with great power, we fear the destruction it can wreak on society or our own selves (corruption). But what symbols represent the economy as a whole?

The question as posed is misleading. The totem can symbolize the clan as a whole because the clan operates under a theory of unity and comprehensiveness in a relatively undifferentiated structure. The economy is fragmented, partitioned, diverse; its totemic representations should have these properties as well. And so it is. Economic actors and commodities have unique totems: the consumer's checkbook and credit card, the product's brand name and trademark (Martel-Van Doorne 1977), the company's logo and stock-exchange symbol. Some of these symbols are more sacred than others, depending on the relative weight of the symbolic and the instrumental associated with their referents (cf. Jeppersen and Meyer 1991). The credit card, a direct extension of the sacred individual, is jealously guarded; the stock-exchange symbol, whose referent is a weakly sacralized rational organization, is more a label of convenience for instrumental purposes (though struggles over stock-exchange designators are not unknown).

More comprehensive economic symbols are rare and, typically, extremely abstract. Such measures as the GNP, unemployment, and national income symbolize aspects of the economy as a whole, but as raw indicators they are virtually meaningless. Standardized by the appropriate populations — that is, translated into measures that bring the sacred individual into the equation (GNP per capita, unemployment rates) — they are suitable subjects for economic management rituals. But they still are not easily made the focus of the sort of intense interaction experiences that Durkheim found so crucial for the reification of the sacred. Their reification depends on more banal settings, such as economic summit meetings, television news reports, and conferences of economists.

We thus find that the sacrality of the economy is generated less by the ritualization of the economy as a whole than by that of its constituent parts — companies, products, consumers, styles, sometimes particular technologies (the computer, the automobile) or economic sectors. For the parts, intense interaction rituals are common, certainly in the form of electronic advertising but even more in industry trade shows, product fairs, retail sales events, home marketing parties, swap meets, and so on. Belk et al. (1989) describe a wide range of everyday processes whereby material goods, experiences, and special occasions are sacralized.

Only one symbol has effectively come to embody the economy as a whole, and it is both highly abstract and larger in connotation than any single national economy: "capitalism." (Its more individualistically flavored equivalent, "free enterprise," can hardly be used to signify the economy anywhere but the U.S.) Capitalism is a well-established symbol for the political left, but its symbolic power pales in comparison with that of many more specialized symbols: consider the "customer loyalty" that attaches to the IBM logo, the Cheerios product name, or the American Express credit card.

A Note on Value

The sacred order identifies, among other things, the cultural sources of value or worth. If God is the only sacred, everything of value comes from God; if the individual is sacred, value is presumed to flow from individual action. The sacredness of the economy implies, with only slight exaggeration, that only economic value has any reality. That is, only the value of economic goods is specifiable; comparisons of economic value are the only ones that can be made; the money metric is universal, readily understood and assessed. Non-economic entities — non-commodities such as peace, personal relationships, and a star-filled sky — have no value because they cannot be exchanged (cf. Simmel 1978). They are, indeed, priceless; but pricelessness is neither here nor there, neither high nor low. The lack of a metric for priceless entities exposes them to the risk of being constructed as "mere desiderata," too vague to enter cost-benefit calculations. Increasingly, they are liable to being irrationalized out of consideration; they have, indeed, no value.

Such is the logic underlying the primacy of participation in the monetarized economy (having a job) as the indicator of social worth. The housewife is now suspect because she does not earn money; she is therefore a slave of her husband, only half a person at best (proposals to include the "value" of housework in the GNP are justified by the correct claim that this would raise the status of the homemaker). Gender, racial, and ethnic equality translate above all into equal partici- pation rates at equal pay (compared with that of white males) at all levels of the economy. The division of labor in the household is more egalitarian as the income of the woman relative to that of the man rises. Thus, participation in the economy is almost a prerequisite for a sense of social worth (Lane 1991) and the key institutional factor behind the increase in working hours in the U.S. in recent decades (Schor 1992). Values that are not monetarized carry little weight. Value has been virtually monopolized by one sacred domain: the economy.

Economic Religion

Marxism illustrates another aspect of the sacred order that is crucial to completing this analysis of the meaning of the economic realm in con- temporary society. The sacred order forms the mythical core around which religion develops — "religion" taken here to mean any system of symbols that provides explanations of such puzzles as life's origins, mean- ing, and purpose, and guidelines for behavior that will suitably enact those explanations in everyday life (cf. Wuthnow 1988b). These explanations and guidelines (the latter ranging from automated ritual prescriptions to much-analyzed ethical systems) are themselves sacralized by their deriva- tion from or association with the sacred order. By enacting them, we establish a parallelism between our individual lives and ultimate reality, thereby translating abstract Meaning and Purpose and Order into the meaning and purpose and order of our specific existence (cf. Lears 1989). By failing to enact them, we risk plunging into the abyss of uninterpreta- bility: our actions make no sense because they are at variance with the prevailing cultural classificatory system (Douglas 1966). Even more, our failure is morally reprehensible: we cannot maintain a positive image of our selves or of the roles and collectivities we enact.

It will come as no surprise when I claim that we now guide our lives primarily in terms of economic religiosity. If you will, this is only an elaboration of Bellah's concept of civil religion (see Bellah and Ham- mond 1980). What Bellah and his followers stressed, however, was the shared *commonalities* of secular, mostly national political, religion; in the economic realm, deep-structure commonality (of the sacred order and its derivatives) serves as a foundation for distinctiveness (à la Bourdieu 1984). Distinctiveness of a peculiar form, of course — that of radically conformist individualism, as perceptively analyzed by Simmel (1971b) in his discussion of fashion (see also Kaiser et al. 1991). Further, the civil religion argument seemed troubled by the obstinate unwillingness of church religion to fade quietly away. I suggest here that multiple religions are not only possible but inevitable in differentiated cultures. They may conflict, but they also reinforce each other, as I will argue below regarding church and economic religion.

1. Materialism as Symbolic Order and Expression

Economic religion has very little to do with materialism. As Veblen (1899) insisted, economic goods, even when they are physical objects that have use functions, are not first and foremost material. Believe Douglas and Isherwood (1979) when they say that goods constitute a system which establishes the meaning of the self, social position, trustworthiness, or future intentions (to name a few aspects). For the most part, we do not consume the goods we buy. We display them, flaunt them, hoard them; we incorporate them into the self, liberate ourselves with their aid, use them to confirm our understanding of reality, build our personal relationships around them (Daun 1983; Hacker 1967; Boorstin 1973). Even such literal consumables as food are selected and consumed in part for their ordering capacity and communicative capacity, the more so as the publicness of the consumption increases. Guests cannot be served the same meals as one's children; Americans do not eat dogs.

Although applicable to a wide range of human societies (Appadurai 1986), this perspective should be easiest to accept in an economy that is dominated by the "consumption" of intangibles or near-intangibles. A great proportion of monetarized activity now involves "cultural" products in the realms of film, advertising, video, publishing, art, games, and the like (see Lash 1990); experiential products, such as visits to amusement parks and vacation sites, wilderness adventures, bungie jumping, and paintball wars; personal enhancement industries, including education, therapy, exercising, and body care; and a host of other domains that are typically referred to as the services or tertiary sector.

This is not materialism; it is the use of material and non-material objects and processes to generate and maintain meaning, order, and purpose (cf. Sahlins 1976; Miller 1987; Zelizer 1988; Hummon 1988). We may decry it, but we must recognize how fundamental a dimension of everyday life it has become.

2. Economic Religion

If there is an economic religion, it should provide solutions to the basic puzzles of life and guidelines to the proper enactment of the sacred order. I believe that it does, as long as we remember that economic religion is compartmentalized and specialized rather than comprehensive.

What are the origins of (economic) life? For the lay parishioner, the Industrial Revolution and, perhaps, modern science. For the esoterically initiated, the bourgeoisie, Calvinism, or (as in Collins's 1980 distillation of Weber's later work) a combination of broad, long-term historical developments. What is the meaning of life? Full participation in the exchange economy, as both producer of value and consumer of goods. What is the purpose of life? The full development of the individual, both through value production (work should be enhancing, not alienating) and rational, voluntary consumption (Lears 1983; cf. Campbell [1987] on the "other Protestant ethic" of Romantic subjectivism as the basis for modern "hedonism"); and the pursuit of collective progress and justice via the same mechanisms (Meyer et al. 1987).

Naturally, many variants on the answers to these questions are possible; justifying the version given here is unnecessary as long as we recognize that well-institutionalized answers are available and that they all build upon the sacred cultural elements that ground the rationalized economy. What is most important about them is that they provide meaning and moral justification to participants in the economic order (Rainwater 1974).

It should not be necessary to elaborate on the guidelines for behavior ensconced in economic religion. I want only to note that, unlike Douglas's primitive rituals, ritual performance in the modern system is supposed to have rather direct effects for the actor: the more faithfully one enacts the model of the rational individual, the larger one's rewards will be (hard, disciplined work is the path to success). Ritual enactment is rational behavior, and vice versa. The distinction between the rational and the irrational is preserved elsewhere, in the recognition that rational conformity is not a guarantor of success because of the imperfect rationality of the economic realm. But the irrationalities are also rationalizable: success requires that one also master such activities as networking, political maneuvering, organizational empire building, and so on. A host of techniques, courses, books, and other formalized guides are available as aids in acquiring these skills.

3. Experience

"The money question is so strong not because money is ultimately real but because our experiences with it have become — for most of us — the most vivid and intense experiences of our lives" (Needleman 1991, 165). We live in an exchange economy. We hesitate to leave home without our wallets. Rare is the day that we do not engage in money rituals. Some of us love to shop, others abhor it, but we all do it. We spend a larger portion of our time working for money (and for much else, to be sure, but still for money) than doing anything else. Our major holidays have gift-giving as a central component. Vacations are periods of extraordinary consumption. Everyday leisure activities normally carry a price tag.

The monetary rationalization of social activity means that our lived experiences are increasingly economic. This does not mean, however, that our behavior is necessarily more impersonal, more instrumental, more manipulative, more acquisitive, than in other times and places. Here I think Simmel and Marx are simply wrong. The subjectivity fostered by differentiation and rationalization enables — indeed, compels — the individual to set exchange activity in frameworks of meaning in which *homo economicus* is conspicuously absent. Consider some mundane examples:

Apparel. "This jacket is just *you*," the salesperson asserts, and the customer assesses the accuracy of that claim. Is it really me? No, I don't wear black leather (I'm not a motorcycle moll, please!); I look best in pastels (I have a refined, subtle personality). Apparel (re-)presents the self; price serves mainly to set upper and lower limits to the range of options that can be considered. Collective selves are also at issue, since every individual is a member of collectivities; my clothing makes symbolic statements about my family, my ethnic group, my profession, my employer, and so on.

Gifts. Gifts represent the giver, the giver's conception of the recipient, the giver's conception of the recipient's conception of the giver, ad infinitum. Gifts represent past and future reciprocities and obligations. Gifts are evaluated before and after the giving for their appropriateness in light of the complex relationship between the giver and the receiver, including the relationships among the collectivities to which the two parties belong (Mauss 1976; Gregory 1982). For gifts, "it's the thought that counts" — quite literally.

The coupon. The marvel of the discount coupon lies in its ability to strengthen the coupon user's self-image as an economically rational actor despite its marginal effect on expenditures. "Every penny counts," we assure ourselves, even though we are most often penny-wise and pound-foolish. The meaning potential of the coupon is vividly illustrated by the remarkable phenomenon of the coupon club, in which dedicated rationalists have coffee and cakes at pleasant evening get-togethers sharing coupons and coupon lore. The coupon clubber, armed with her multipocket coupon organizer and a detailed shopping plan, may shave her grocery bill substantially — but not as much as if she simply bought generic products rather than the more highly reified (and therefore more valuable) major brands.

Grandparenting. The grandparent is truly liberated. At long last, rational economic constraints on expenditures may safely be ignored: value may, indeed should, be showered upon the grandchild. As a symbol of the triumph of the family over individual mortality, the grandchild is infinitely worthy. We sometimes cluck our tongues about such indulgence, but our moral disapprobation is minimal because grandparental largesse is deemed to have little potential to "spoil" the child (i.e., to distort the child's capacity for rational value assessment). Instead, our hearts are warmed by the joy we see our parents experiencing when they give uninhibitedly to our children. The release from rationality is itself a source of much meaning, as long as it occurs under proper conditions.

4. Economic and Traditional Religion

Finally, we cannot help noticing the fusion of traditional and economic religion, particularly in the United States. On one side, television evangelists are bemoaned as cynical marketeers who use the Word as a path to the Dollar (Hughey 1990; Hadden and Shupe 1988); more generally, religion is big business these days. On the other side, numerous businesses (Mary Kay Cosmetics, Shaklee, Amway, Herbalife) are more revivalist movements than rationalized enterprises (Biggart 1989). Some operations so thoroughly merge church and economic religion as to defy classification — for example, the gospel of money, preached by charismatics from Russell Conwell in the 1870s (Barton 1989) to the contemporary Reverend Ike ("Pray to the Lord: money l-o-v-e-s to come into my wallet!").

The enormous attention given to "corporate culture" in the 1980s suggests that relatively coherent subworlds of religious meaning and purpose are routinely based in particular organizational forms. Apple Computer is renowned for its championing of the subjective, holistic individual ("PC culture"), IBM (in recent years, at least) for its necktied "organization man" image ("mainframe culture"). Corporate cultures are, we might say, particularistic specifications of the "production" side of economic religion, like so many proselytizing sects selling varied interpretations of the economic moral order to both their employee members and the lay public.

Implications: The Dilemma of Desacralization

Moralizing against the supposed materialism of the late twentieth-century world is unlikely to be a fruitful endeavor. Contemporary culture, especially in the West, consists of a large number of differentiated moral orders that are based on a more or less common sacred order but that interpret the sacred order in quite disparate ways. The realm of rationalized exchange is not amoral; as I have tried to argue, it is thoroughly infused with moral meaning and purpose. Its morality is certainly at variance with traditional religious morality in some respects, but the two moral orders are quite consonant with each other in other respects, as Weber (1946) clearly perceived in his travels in the United States in 1904.[2]

The problems with moralizing about the economic order are basically two. First, traditional morality no longer provides a firm "place to stand" from which to critique the economic order. Ours is an island

2. See his essay entitled "The Protestant Sects and the Spirit of Capitalism" in Weber (1946 [1906]).

culture, not a continental one; religion is isolated, something for Sundays and the soul, separated by a tempestuous sea from other social islands. More importantly, the island of traditional religion has shrunk in importance and cultural power, while the island of monetarized relations has grown imperiously. Religion may help us save our souls or understand the agony of life and death, but it cannot help us obtain the vast array of goodnesses, meanings, and purposes that is proffered in the economic realm. Working at a distance and at cross-purposes, religion cannot successfully critique the economy. Religion wants to apply the wooden yardstick of the past to assess good and evil; how can that compete with the laser-beam metrometer of the future-oriented technicized economy?

Second, in its critique of materialism, religious morality draws on the same sacred order that economic morality uses to defend materialism (bearing in mind, of course, the symbolic nature of materialism!). Individual responsibility, the search for authenticity, self-actualization, submission to the will of a greater power — these features are not peculiar to religion. Hence, religious morality is not only weaker than economic morality. It also, it seems to me, has less to offer with respect to opportunities to enact the sacred order. It is the implicit recognition of this fact that has led so many churches to emulate the "secular" realms by bringing folk music, social causes, and the electronic media into the sanctuary.

As I see it, if materialism is to be challenged, there are three possible routes of approach. One route, the easiest, is to work in the direction of history (Ellul 1971): promote the trends that are already firmly entrenched, push the sphere of rationalized exchange to as fully an immaterial level as possible. Aim, in other words, for a thoroughly postmodern society, an entirely virtual reality in which the electronic simulation of material consumption and the consumption of symbolic tangibles replace materialism as such. Life inside the totalizing computer game: any takers?

A second route is to attempt to break the links between economic goods and the sacred order. Decouple, in other words, the sacred order from exchange-mediated rituals. This means diminishing the reality of the economy, recasting it as being only what the economists have always mistakenly claimed it to be: structures for the allocation of scarce resources to meet the needs of a population. It might help to abolish advertising, trademarks, logos, credit cards; without symbols, the sacred tends to wilt. It might help to impose severe restrictions on the inequality of income and wealth and on the variety of products available for purchase, so that status striving could not be accomplished through consumption. One might argue that these and similar measures would deal only with symptoms, but a defusion of the power of the symptoms can also ameliorate the disease. One might also argue, quite correctly, that these measures are completely unrealistic as long as the sacred order remains unchanged.

The third route is far more perilous; it is also both impossible and necessary. If we seriously wish to diminish the importance of possessions in the ordering of everyday life; if we believe that a contraction of the sphere of monetarized exchange would improve the quality of human existence; if we see the culture of consumerism as a source of major social problems — then the sacred order itself must be desacralized. But we deceive ourselves if we believe we can desacralize the economic order alone. At stake is the desacralization of the individual, the disenchantment of rationality, the questioning of the primacy and value of the nation, the rejection of self-development as an inevitable desideratum, and so on. We cannot desacralize only the economic aspects of these elements, or metricized rationalization will simply be displaced to another realm. The sacred order has to be taken on in toto.

Currently fashionable deconstructionism and postmodernist criticism move in this direction but are quite lopsided. While they challenge various status orders and some aspects of instrumental rationality, they only increase the sacredness of the individual, subjectivity, the body, and many other underpinnings of the economic moral order. More radical challenge is called for if we are to escape the realm of necessity constituted by the sacred order.

Two questions must be faced. The first: Can we desacralize the modern order and still retain our commitment to the worth and intrinsic value of every person, to the use of reason in the resolution of conflict, and to the other aspects of the sacred order that we do in fact hold near and dear? The answer here is surprising: *Only* by desacralization can we in fact value people concretely, put genuine reason to work, and make democracy meaningful. The sacred order is abstract, universalistic, disembodied; by its very nature it prevents us from dealing with the complexities of specific persons, processes, and problems. It is the sacred order that makes it possible to sacrifice millions of individuals for the sake of individualism (or democracy, or the nation, or ethnic identity . . .). On this score there is no problem: our ideals can be realized only if they are not sacred.

The second question: Can the sacred order be desacralized without simply replacing it by new forms of the sacred derived from the desacralizing forces? On this score I am less sanguine. Whether Ellul's desacralization/sacralization dialectic is a "law" of social change or only an empirical generalization, it seems to hold remarkably well across many times and places. The real issue here is whether human society is possible at all without some sacred order providing unquestioned structure to the chaos of life, and I am inclined to believe that it is not. A life lived perpetually at the edge of uncertainty is intolerable for almost all of us. In desacralizing the sacred order, then, we would have to be aware that the new sacred would generate its own peculiar problems. There would be no final destination in such a sequence, only a kind of criticism/self-criticism process that could never be relaxed.

Finally, a word about one frequently favored route that is apt to lead to a blind alley. Socialism, if it means the collectivization of capital under the control of national states or a world state, is unlikely to diminish modern materialism. The state is one of the great rationalizing forces of our age, promoting monetarization as necessary for the control and regulation of social life. Hence, state dominance can shift materialism from the individual to a more collective and generalized level, but it cannot reduce materialism. A socialism that also rejects the state by operating at the local level and explicitly rejecting the notion of a master project for sweeping social change has some prospects of fundamentally reorienting contemporary culture. A socialism that essentially trades one sort of domination for another has none.

"Where Your Treasure Is": Popular Evangelical Views of Work, Money, and Materialism

MARSHA G. WITTEN

[Some Christian workers] say, "I will have nothing what-soever to do with moral compromise [at the job site] in any form. And neither should any other Christian." . . . [But] I believe . . . we can be principled people and still function in the world as it is.

Stanley Baldwin, Take This Job and Love It

When Jesus uses the Aramaic term *mammon* to refer to wealth, he is giving it a personal and spiritual character. When he declares, "You cannot serve God and mammon" (Matt. 6:24), he is personifying mammon as a rival god. Jesus is [saying that] . . . mammon is a power that seeks to dominate us.

Richard Foster, The Challenge of the Disciplined Life

Since the world is God's creation and since God placed us in such a close relationship to the material world, the creation and use of wealth is a perfectly proper activity.

Ronald Nash, Poverty and Wealth

> A good reason for simpler living is the reward God promises us if we lay up treasures in heaven rather than [on] earth. . . . If I choose a smaller house now, investing the difference in cost in God's kingdom, God will give me a bigger house in heaven.
>
> Randy Alcorn, *Money, Possessions, and Eternity*

THESE QUOTATIONS from popular Christian books suggest some of the range in contemporary Protestant evangelical attitudes toward Christian behavior in the marketplace. At issue in these books is how, in late twentieth-century America, religious faith and practice might respond to the norms of secular culture as they pertain to work, money, and the ownership of material possessions. That secularity might pose concerns for practitioners of conservative American Protestantism is signaled, among other things, by the considerable output of popular evangelical writings on these topics. Lining the shelves of Christian bookstores under such headings as "Christian life" and "Christian psychology," and featured as selections of Christian book clubs, these books offer laypeople the guidance of evangelical psychologists, management theorists, entrepreneurs, and pastors, all of whom purport to explore the dilemmas of faith in a secular society from the vantage point of Christian principles.

But how exactly, in these books, does Christian thought interact with the norms of secularity? Worldly conduct has always posed difficulties for Protestants, whose faith has dispatched them into commerce with secular society. But these difficulties are intensified by cultural forces in contemporary America. Pluralism creates a bazaar of ideologies and creeds in which Christianity encounters numerous competitors. Secular ideologies of individualism, empiricism, and relativism sometimes challenge the very grounds on which conservative Protestantism rests.

How has popular evangelicalism in America confronted the challenges of living an appropriate Christian life in the contemporary world? What guidance do evangelical writers offer believers? In this essay I examine the language of eighteen recently published popular evangelical books about work, money, and possessions in an attempt to discover how and to what extent secularity leaves its mark on these religious pronouncements. All of the books I chose for analysis were written by professed evangelicals or by authors widely read in evangelical circles; they appeal to popular rather than academic audiences; they are currently (in mid-1993) on the shelves of trade or Christian bookstores, or are carried by large Christian book clubs; and their titles and/or shelving locations make it obvious that they deal with issues of work, money, and materialism. My goal was to draw on books that the evangelical layperson or pastor might seek out for guidance about behavior in response to these issues.[1]

The Nature of Work

Many of the books in my sample explicitly set out to legitimate work as a properly Christian activity. Work is presented as the fulfillment of God's plan for the world and, more immediately and concretely, for the individual worker. Since God made the universe and called Adam to tend it, work is a necessary element in God's design for human beings and is thus mandated as a central obligation of human life. According to the books, work correctly includes activities of producing, creating, preserving, cultivating, and managing (all named in Genesis 1–2, the passage from which proof texts for this proposition are most often taken). Some authors additionally read the Genesis accounts as establishing one's God-given "right" to accumulate the products of labor, an interpretation that undergirds arguments for a biblical defense of capitalism. As these authors see it, all work that is ethical and legal — not just church work — is fundamentally and equally justified. While Christians might believe that the ministry is more valuable to God than work

---

1. Publication information for the books in the sample appear in the bibliography. I analyzed the contents of each one. I selected the books on the basis of the criteria I mentioned in the text, criteria drawn from the following sources: the summer 1993 catalog of Christian Book Distributors (the largest Christian book jobber in the United States, with the widest selection); stocks of the Mustard Seed and Whole Works Book Shops, both of which are regional (Pennsylvania) Christian bookstore chains; stocks of the Barnes and Noble and Borders bookstores in Bryn Mawr, Pennsylvania, both trade-book "superstores"; and the 1992-93 publishers' catalogs from InterVarsity, Navpress, Word, and Moody.

in the secular world, this assumption is in error. God sanctifies ordinary work by participating in it. The authors underscore this point with various job-related images: God is a supervisor for human labor; Christ is the boss of human employees; people are Christ's junior partners. Work lends dignity to human life because of God's plan and involvement.

In addition to conferring dignity and self-esteem, work also molds character. A naturally occurring benefit of work, some authors argue, is that it teaches individuals responsibility for managing time and effort. Through the regularity and orderliness of work, laborers learn the virtues of punctuality, conscientious performance, efficiency, and accountability to superiors. Thus they are formed into "mature adults" who accept the consequences of their actions. One author, a pastor, explains, "Those on staff at my church know how I feel about promptness. We begin our day at the office at 9:00, not 9:02 or even 9:01. Am I a tyrant? No, I simply believe that I can serve those under my supervision best by teaching them responsibility with regard to their schedules . . . helping them develop a habit and a consciousness of value to them as long as they live" (Hybels 1982, 14). Of course, the workers are also internalizing and responding to the attributes of capitalism, with its discipline of time and routinization of activities.

But work is not mere dry obligation or dutiful character formation; according to these authors, it should also offer a sense of personal fulfillment, excitement, and passion. They view work as a calling from God that is different for each unique human being. They hold work to be centrally important to human life because it provides the psychological fulfillment of pleasant activity and meaningfulness. Through their jobs, men and women not only participate in God's design for the universe but also develop their own capabilities, reach the height of their potential. Work, say the authors, should "enhance creativity," be a source of "enjoyment," and be experienced as "purposeful." The essentialist language they use to describe human nature and the biblical scripts they employ to argue that human beings have an obligation to work are mingled freely with the psychological language of the secular human resources movement.

The authors thus reaffirm traditional Calvinist principles in their portrayal of work as a biblical obligation, a calling, a service to God in fulfillment of his plan for the universe, and a forge on which mature personality (according to the discipline of capitalism) is hammered out. But they also assert more contemporary norms when they describe work as a vehicle for self-expression, personal realization, enjoyment, and "growth" — goods that more easily serve as incentives in the contemporary secular context.

Moral Order in the Work World

In many of the books I analyzed, the moral order at work is above all signified through appropriate interpersonal relationships — that is, those marked by honesty, openness, and trust. For example, in *Christians in the Marketplace*, Hybels asserts that "people were Jesus' business" (1982, 28), and he urges Christians in the workplace to take action to affirm relationships, share problems, and make themselves freely available to give and receive psychological advice and reassurance.

These books teach that the conscientious fulfillment of production tasks makes up only a part of one's obligation in the workplace; an equally important function of Christian workers is to uphold their relational duty to colleagues and superiors. Establishing appropriate relationships is a complex and delicate matter which demands that Christian workers know psychological principles and follow God's example in their behavior.

When the authors apply models of divine conduct in Scripture to human behavior in the workplace, they stress truthtelling, loyalty, fair play, and respect for others as qualities that God exhibits and that he demands of his creatures. In addition, the authors use God's biblical interactions with men and women — in which he both facilitates human self-disclosure and lays bare his own needs — to present paradigms of appropriate "open communication" in the workplace.

One author uses the biblical account of the flight of Elijah from Ahab and Jezebel (1 Kings) to demonstrate Yahweh's role as the prophet's therapeutic work partner. In this rendition, God's sole function is to help his employee Elijah cope with his work difficulties (for it appears that Elijah has turned heel and run because he is suffering from job burnout). To accomplish his cure, God urges Elijah "to ventilate his intense feelings, to get rid of negative feelings, . . . patiently prompting him three times to open up" (Minirth et al. 1986, 44). The prophet's

opportunity for self-disclosure is deemed essential for his eventual recovery, the first step in God's "wellness program." Like Elijah, the author
suggests, many Christian workers, at risk for burnout because of their
high standards and well-tuned consciences, require interpersonal relationships with work colleagues and supervisors that offer them unconditional support.

Similarly, Jesus' behavior gives workers a model of how to communicate openly with others. When these authors exhort readers to
imitate Jesus in his relationships with others during his ministry, they
present a portrait of Christ that apotheosizes interpersonal openness
and vulnerability. The Christ who chucks the moneylenders out of the
temple or withers a fig tree in anger is supplanted by a sensitive and
vulnerable Lord who uses open communication to ask his "co-workers"
— his disciples — to meet his psychological needs. One author offers,
as a model of appropriate self-disclosure, a Jesus who reveals his most
intimate emotional longings: "We read that Jesus took with Him Peter
and the two sons of Zebedee . . . and said to them, 'My soul is deeply
grieved, to the point of death; remain here and keep watch with Me.'"
The author interprets the text this way: "In this passage, [Jesus, as leader,
is saying,] 'Please listen to Me. I need to have someone understand how
I feel. . . . Will you support Me?'" (Hybels 1982, 52).

Christians are thus urged to employ the techniques of empathic
listening and to invite other employees to express themselves and offer
input; this will help maintain an essential part of the moral order of the
workplace. That these authors stress the principles of openness and
self-disclosure might seem to suggest that they are supporting norms
of egalitarianism; however, because the frank sharing of feelings in the
workplace tends to level differences in rank, the books I assessed place
distinct limits on these principles. The authors mark these limits with
a strenuous justification of hierarchy, bolstered by proof text.

In these books, the attitude toward workplace authority almost
invariably is that workers should obey superiors and maintain the status
quo with respect to power. Citing Paul (Col. 3:22: "Slaves, in all things
obey those who are your masters on earth"), the authors assert an
analogy between the scriptural relationship of servant to master and the
workplace obligations of subordinate to employer. It is appropriate to
engage in discussions with superiors, and sometimes even negotiate with
them, say the authors, but only in egregious cases of unethical behavior

are they to be disobeyed. Likewise, the authors deem as legitimate the impersonal rules of modern business because they help stem the tide of sinfulness in a fallen world. The errancy of humankind is checked by bureaucracy's rationality and regulation (Dayton 1992, 51).

Because the principle of obedience is central to the moral order of business, the authors suggest that it is the obligation of Christian employees to keep the workplace on an even keel. Implicit in this pre-scription is the need for Christian workers to control their own emotional states. They must constantly evaluate their attitudes and behavior to make sure that they are appropriate to the goal of workplace harmony. Thus, while the authors encourage the open articulation of feelings, they also teach that such expression must never degenerate to the level of grumbling or, in a more biblical construction, of murmuring against authority (e.g., Exod. 15:24). Even more, workers must be certain to maintain a positive attitude, the optimism and confidence of the saved, preferably displayed to the world at large through cheerfulness.

That Christian workers are to express positive emotions clearly signals the fact that these authors place limits on the demands that workers should make of their employers. In gratitude for their oppor-tunity to serve God and develop their own potential, and out of respect for the legitimacy of authority, workers should cheerfully accept the order of the workplace. As one author puts it, "[When] God told Adam to cultivate and care for the Garden of Eden. . . . Adam didn't complain. He didn't ask for a negotiation table, for greater benefits, for higher pay. He accepted the responsibility joyfully as a meaningful assignment from God" (Hybels 1982, 10).

The authors also say that Christian workers must likewise strive to subdue the potential passions of anger and bitterness. Because it destroys the harmony of interpersonal relationships and acts as a toxic poison (Sherman 1991, 13) on the inner core of the self, the misplaced experience or expression of anger is held to be calamitous both to the orderliness of the workplace (rending the social fabric) and to one's psychological balance (leading to stress and burnout). The authors ad-vise that Christian workers instead use a variety of therapeutic behaviors — venting anger and bitterness through prayer, for example, and choos-ing to feel emotions of thanks or goodwill (Baldwin 1988, 112). When conflict arises with superiors or colleagues, the authors exhort Christian workers to put their anger aside, choose to forgive, or, when necessary (in some books, only in extremis), lovingly confront the offending party using carefully restrained techniques of affirmation and concession such as those of Rogerian argumentation (Sherman 1991, 126).

Control over the display of passion is likewise implicit in the authors' treatment of the issue of witnessing. Although many authors underscore the urgency of evangelizing unbelievers in a general context, they suggest constraint with respect to giving testimony at the workplace. No matter how compelling one's love of Christ, no matter how ardent the desire to share the Good News, the Christian worker must cautiously search out appropriate opportunities and approach the potential convert with a calculated plan of action. A lack of interest or receptivity should signal the need for temporary withdrawal. Above all, the witness should not thrust his or her ardor uninvited into the path of the unsaved; the temptation to stridency is a tool of the devil and should be rejected by believing Christians. "Be a French horn," one author advises, "not a clanging cymbal" (Sherman 1991, 131).

In fact, some authors suggest, Christians bear most eloquent witness through the way they present themselves in the daily affairs of the workplace. They communicate the gospel not only through the moral behavior they exhibit but also through their cheerful faces, their display of quiet confidence, and their moderation of passion and intensity. "You are the only commercial of Jesus Christ that most people will ever see," counsels one book. "Your co-workers can't see Jesus' face, but they can see yours" (Sherman 1991, 30). Just as the flight attendant's smile or the warmth of the telemarketer's voice functions to lend a positive quality to the service they are providing, so the Christian's quiet joy advertises the benefits of a relationship with Christ.[2]

But, of course, Christian workers cannot strive to preserve the moral economy of work without confronting challenges. The authors assert that the structures and systems of modern work do pose problems for the proper realization of Christian faith. What are these difficulties, and how are evangelicals advised to overcome them?

2. Descriptions of the commercial and ideological functions of the control of emotional displays in secular contexts are given in Hochschild (1983), Mumby and Putnam (1992), and Rafaeli and Sutton (1989).

Christian Dilemmas in the Marketplace

Many of the books I analyzed contend that a major problem with the secular world of work is that it sends out myriad invitations to sin — understood, in this context, as violations of the Decalogue. These invitations are issued through the ordinary practices of business life. Norms of unbridled acquisition appear to justify covetousness. Lax attitudes about appropriation of workplace materials seem to inspire stealing. Pragmatic concessions to truthfulness with competitors and creditors ("The check is in the mail") seem to condone situation ethics. Business trips taken together by male and female colleagues are irresistible opportunities for adultery. "It's a jungle out there," one book says (Sherman and Hendricks 1987), referring not to the bestiality of competition but to the disorderliness of a sinful life. Because some of the daily routines of business life involve temptations to sin, they are seen as snares for the unguarded Christian.

Of course, the authors declare, Christian workers cannot allow their conduct to be dishonest or adulterous. God's Word is paramount in these cases and must not be broken. But there are other areas of behavior at work which call for decisions that may not be so straightforward. Participating in work that is illegal is clearly out of the question. But working to produce goods that, while legal, are nevertheless harmful physically (e.g., tobacco) or ethically (e.g., radar detectors) are deemed gray areas, since one is able to achieve approved goals of supporting oneself and one's family through these endeavors.

Likewise, the worker may find himself or herself expected to participate indirectly in a task of questionable morality (such as in the case of a public librarian asked to catalog a book on witchcraft for inclusion in the collection). Here, the worker must consider all the options: selling out, compromising, negotiating, and quitting (Baldwin 1988, 45). He or she must also ponder the risks of self-assertion, of disobedience, and of whistle-blowing, and also seriously reflect on God's Word and the dictates of conscience. Ultimately the individual must make his or her own choices.

In addition to the lure of sin and the necessity of making sometimes perplexing decisions, the authors accentuate another set of difficulties for the Christian in the secular workplace. Consonant with their emphasis on the importance of meeting personal needs and maintaining good interpersonal relationships at the workplace, the authors assert that the secular world of work presents risks to one's psychological health. As they see it, the role of religion is to offer Christians the rewards of expert therapeutic advice.

The potential psychological hazards of the workplace are legion, and the authors dramatize them in detail. For one thing, engaging in the world of work may engender all sorts of unpleasant emotions. The inherent competitiveness of business is likely to endanger one's self-esteem. Its demands for performance may lead to feelings of anxiety. The endless rounds of repetitive labor involved in some jobs may promote a feeling of futility. Unfair treatment by bosses might cause one to release in his or her heart the corrosive poison of anger, bitterness, or resentment.

As evidenced by the amount of space the authors devote to a discussion of these issues, the potential for "bad feelings" in the workplace is seen as posing real and serious difficulties for Christians. But although these negative emotions are said to be almost universally experienced in the modern workplace, the authors examine their root causes and offer solutions for them by using language that is utterly privatized. Never do they view competition or mindless labor or efficiency demands or power inequities as systemic — as, say, inherent injustices of capitalism. Just as the authors portray these problems solely as effects on the individual's psychological apparatus, so the solutions they offer are to be sought in psychological adjustment.

What to do about threats to self-esteem? "Remember that your worth comes from being God's special creation, in his image," advises one author. How to handle feelings of anxiety? "Know that God loves you unconditionally, no matter what you do," counsels another. How should one endure boredom? "Use the opportunity of monotonous tasks to pray or meditate on Scripture," one author suggests. Dealing with an oppressive boss? "Try to put yourself in his shoes and understand his point of view" is the advice given. Keeping a faith diary, monitoring one's feelings with the aid of a psychological checklist, meeting regularly with a mentor who is "mature in Christ" to ventilate ill feelings, establishing a thirty-day program for inspirational Scripture reading — all these are suggested as more methodical ways of exploring the self and altering one's emotions. The task for the Christian lies in tinkering with his or her psycho-spiritual mechanism rather than in challenging the structures of the business world.

As hurtful as "bad feelings" are for Christians, however, the difficulties they pose pale in comparison with another dilemma for Christians on the job: the temptation to "workaholism." The majority of the books I studied in my sample addressed this problem; for many of these authors, workaholism pinpoints the dangers of the secular workplace for believers.

The Christian worker is particularly susceptible to workaholism, the authors assert. (These authors usually feature male characters in their examples of workaholism. Females may suffer from an analogous disorder, "shopaholism," which is deemed to have similar causes and can be cured through similar techniques. See K. O'Connor 1992.) The Christian worker's high degree of conscientiousness and refined sense of accountability, as well as his possible misinterpretation of the traditional Protestant work ethic as total commitment, are already risk factors for the disease and addiction of overwork. But on top of this, the setting of the workplace may give the Christian the misguided impression that he can cope with difficulties of self-esteem by striving to earn his worth. Or he may be masking inadequacies in interpersonal relationships by immuring himself in the office. Or he may indeed be "sick," suffering from one or more of the 42 personality traits that are described by one author as indicators of obsessive-compulsive syndrome, driving him to exaggerated perfectionism (Minirth et al. 1986, 61-66).

The authors raise two sets of issues with respect to workaholism that account for their portraying it as a serious problem for Christians. First, as some of the authors see it, the causes that are attributed to behaviors of overwork constitute central understandings of sin. They believe that just as violations of the Ten Commandments are serious transgressions, so workaholism is sinful because it marks a grave misunderstanding of one's relationship with God. According to some authors, workaholics are attempting to substitute justification by works for faith. They are mistaking the source of self-esteem, demanding it from the marketplace instead of accepting it as a free gift from God. They are creating an idol out of work, forgetting that allegiance is owed only to the Lord. They are thus committing key theological errors that lead to sin in the biblical sense of separation from God.

In addition to identifying workaholism as sin, many authors elaborate disincentives to workaholism that dwell on its pragmatic, "this-worldly" costs to adherents. In its construal as an emotional disease or addiction, it can be seen to unbalance the psychological health deemed to be a reward of Christian faith. Workaholism is to be shunned because it re-establishes the endless rounds of guilt over the insufficiency of one's efforts that the guarantee of salvation is supposed to erase. It makes one feel bored and cynical about life. If one's efforts go unappreciated, it leads to bitterness, resentment, and outright anger. It undoes "God's will for the Christian," which is "the experience of tranquility, contentment, the absence of inner strife, and completeness" (Minirth et al. 1986, 36).

In addition, excessive work robs the Christian of the balanced pleasures of life that are appropriate to faith. One's relationship with one's spouse and children and the enjoyment of hobbies and leisure time are seen not only as obligations of Christian life but also as vehicles for ensuring one's proper perspective on work.

How, then, do the authors explain the sources of workaholism and suggest eradicating it? Once again, they seek the sources of the problem and its solutions in the bounded context of the individual psyche and the privatized arrangements of family and friends, not in the larger social context.[3] If a Christian is driven to overwork, the problem is not the production expectations of the market but the inadequacy of his personal relationship with God. If he views his obligations as fully contained by his profession, it is not that he has absorbed capitalist lessons of efficiency and accountability but that he is terrified of intimacy with his wife. If he puts in a seventy- or eighty-hour workweek, it is not that downsizing demands he be ever more fruitful in order to keep his job, but that his parents were too critical of him as a child and he is still trying to earn their love. And so on. Occasionally an author will make an observation like "Workaholism is selling out the soul to the marketplace" (Baldwin 1988, 121), but the subsequent analysis makes it clear that workaholism is not viewed as a structural issue.

The conception of workaholism as a private matter and, further, as a psycho-spiritual disease invites some authors to offer solutions that employ the full contemporary know-how of Christianity as therapy. In a chapter entitled "Jesus Treats Twelve Tired Men," one author discusses Christ's program for healing job burnout through such prescriptions as

---

3. Deetz (1991) has written about the ideological function of the characterization of "workaholism" as a psychiatric disease in the secular work world.

positive self-imagery, quiet self-reflection, dwelling in the present, and sharing feelings with others (Minirth et al. 1986, 97-102). Sufferers are advised to seek self-exploration through "faith journaling," pastoral counseling, and meeting with those similarly afflicted in twelve-step recovery groups.

For other authors, however, remediating workaholism calls more for an application of biblical principles to one's behavior and an altera-tion of one's conduct by using the methodical techniques of time man-agement. For example, since God created the world in six days, some books suggest that a Christian ought to work no more, no less. To track one's expenditure of time and to maximize control over one's work effort, one should keep systematic records. One should also carefully schedule time spent with one's family and in leisure activities and keep an account of such activities.

The Nature of Money and Possessions

Work in the marketplace, of course, yields money, and money can be used to purchase goods, can be saved, and/or can be given to others. Accordingly, consumption, saving, and charitable giving become issues for Christians in the world. How do the books I analyzed advise readers on these matters?

Most of the authors do not see money and possessions as prob-lematic in themselves, but only insofar as they threaten the correct spiritual attitudes that Christians are enjoined to achieve. Just as NRA members argue that "guns don't kill people, people do," so these authors claim that money doesn't promote evil behavior, but rather people's choices regarding money do.

When used properly, money can serve justifiable human needs; one can fulfill the biblical mandate to provide for self and family (1 Tim. 5:8). God created resources so that human beings could sustain them-selves, implying the right of workers to be paid for their labor. Indeed, in the view of some authors, Christians are obliged both to earn and then to spend money. Money is also necessary in order to provide for the needs of other people and for God's "kingdom purposes." For some authors, the proper allocation of money for self and for others is what constitutes stewardship.

In addition, the authors tend to insist that evangelical values do not mandate asceticism; it is not necessary for Christians to renounce ownership of property in the world. The good Christian is not called to be like Mother Teresa, whose material sacrifice is not in fact biblically supported (Alcorn 1989, 42). The Christian must avoid the Gnostic error of viewing matter as evil. After all, argues one author, "Jesus was a middle-class carpenter who had middle-class businessmen as his disciples" (Dayton 1992, 161).

The problem with money and possessions, some authors argue, is that in a fallen world human yearning for them can become disproportionate. Such overwhelming desire can manifest itself in the biblical sins of greed, covetousness, and pride. Just as work can become an idol, so the desire for money and possessions can transform neutral objects into false gods. When devotion is transferred from God to money, people forget their connection with the very source of their being. But this is not the fault of money; it is a result of the innate sinfulness of humankind since the Fall.

A sharply contrasting view of money is offered by Jacques Ellul in *Money and Power* (Ellul 1984), and his view is paraphrased or quoted by two other authors (Foster 1985; Wells 1989). According to Ellul, money, far from being a neutral vehicle of exchange, is a material and spiritual power with an active, seductive force of its own (Ellul 1984, 76). As a mechanism of buying and selling, it is fundamentally alien to what Ellul calls "the God-world." In fact, Ellul says, the only commodifying act that God has ever committed is when he purchased the redemption of his Son from Satan. In using "money," he met Satan on the devil's own terms. However, when the other authors of the books I analyzed acknowledge this point of view, they informally rebut it or even mock it.

Christian Dilemmas Concerning
Money and Possessions

Whether they view money as a means to carry out God's work, as a likely tool of Satan, or as a neutral medium of exchange, all of the authors in my sample agree that money and goods can pose problems for the Christian life. Accordingly, they explore several related issues:

how money and possessions might conflict or, alternatively, be brought into harmony with the spiritual demands of Christian living; how they might present psychological benefits or dangers to believers; and how they should be managed in a way consonant with scriptural teachings.

The authors suggest that there are three general categories of concern about money and goods. How much money is it legitimate for a Christian to keep for self and family, for purposes of consumption, saving, and investment? How much should one give to God's purposes, through contributions to church, evangelism, and charity? And what is the appropriate nature and extent of the Christian's response to the poverty of others? (There are, of course, two assumptions underlying this list of questions that the authors generally accept without comment: first, that Christians should be paid and should accept money for work; and second, that they have a right to own private property and to decide voluntarily how to share it or give it away.)

In virtually all of the books, the authors raise questions about the appropriate distribution of a Christian's money with reference to the individual believer, who operates according to the dictates of his or her own conscience, biblical principles, and personal communication with God. Generally, the authors do not see as relevant to their readers' concerns the possibility that there might be structural causes of or solutions to poverty and economic inequality. When a few of the authors do raise the topic of economic systems, the discussion almost always appears as background to general discussions of work or money, usually confined to a broad, informal defense of capitalism.

In fact, it is suggested that the Christian should take the economic system of capitalism as a given in deciding on issues of money and lifestyle. As one author puts it, "The right question is not which economic system would be the closest to a biblical ideal. That's an interesting question, but it is really a problem of economic theory. . . . Most of us are trying to deal with problems at our own individual levels, in our own lifestyles. . . . Consequently, the question I think we need to ask is: How can each of us live and work as a Christ-follower in this economy . . . ?" (Sherman and Hendricks 1987, 178).

On the issue of how much money a Christian ought to keep for self and family, the authors generally agree that it is not (within certain broad limits) the amount that one spends or owns that is important, but rather one's attitude toward one's goods. One should not idolize money and possessions so that one worships them and forgets that all these goods come from God.

Criticizing, sometimes ridiculing, the premises of "prosperity theology," some of the authors take pains to assert that neither poverty nor wealth is in itself good or bad, nor should wealth be seen as a demonstration of God's blessing, an assertion that counters some generally held interpretations of certain Old Testament passages (Alcorn 1989, 103). One can engage in modest enjoyment of one's prosperity, but it is an error to suppose that it is a sign of special regard from God. Equally, poverty is not an indication of God's punishment. Should one become poor, one should not view one's state as a divine indictment.

As might be expected, the authors frequently use examples of Jesus' life to model the attitudes that Christians should have about money. Although the authors interpret these examples in different ways, they tend to converge on the same point. Some of them portray Jesus as a middle-class citizen who did not reject material goods in their own right. As one author writes, "Jesus did not see anything sinful in the ownership of houses, clothes, and other economic goods. He had wealthy friends and followers (Luke 14:1); he stayed in the homes of wealthy people; he ate at their tables (Luke 11:37)" (Nash 1986, 163). Another author suggests that when Jesus called Peter, Andrew, James, and John to be his disciples, they divested themselves of their possessions — the fishing gear they owned — not for spiritual reasons but because they were "traveling missionaries" whose nets would be too difficult to cart around (Alcorn 1989, 294).

Other authors state that Jesus and his followers not only disdained material goods for themselves but also shared whatever few possessions they had in common. Nevertheless, according to the authors, that model does not apply to the contemporary context. (They supply no reason for this assertion.) As one author puts it, "We are not called to imitate Jesus' poverty, but to follow him in his example of love and self-giving, not caring whether we be poor or rich so long as we follow him and do his will. Should God heap material riches upon us, well and good. But if our lot should be one of pain and penury, we are to laugh at our difficulties, counting them as nothing" (White 1993, 134).[4]

---

4. White (1993) issues a blistering attack on materialism in the church, terming the church a "harlot" for marketing itself shamelessly and for worshiping success based

Nevertheless, wealth can entail special risks. For one thing, the wealthy are more likely than the poor to make an idol of their money and possessions and to develop the un-Christian character traits of arrogance and self-reliance (Nash 1986, 166). In addition, the accumulation of goods can lead to a vicious cycle of increasing one's effort to acquire still more, thus cutting into the time one dedicates to one's family and one's spiritual life and leading to psychological problems of anxiety (Caywood 1989, 80). And finally, one author explains, the efforts to acquire mundane material possessions are misplaced "investments" of labor and time, because these goods are useless in eternity (Alcorn 1989, 303).

But what, exactly, constitutes wealth? How much is too much? The books in my sample offer only vague prescriptions on these matters. The general principle that is rendered concerns the need for responsibility (sometimes the word "stewardship" is used) for one's money and goods. This includes employing one's money properly for the biblically mandated functions of caring for the needs of self and family and for tithing and giving freewill offerings to the church. It also includes the notion of managing one's money methodically and prudently. But beyond these general principles, the authors offer little concrete guidance for the Christian in resolving contradictory biblical scripts about legitimate levels of wealth.

For example, one author simply rules out "living in opulence" (Alcorn 1989, 302). Several recommend related notions of the "limited lifestyle" (Sherman and Hendricks 1987, 189) and the "practical theology of enough" (Wells 1989, 97). These terms refer to a general strategy, developed in prayer with God, of ascertaining a level of consumption adequate for sustaining one's self and family, keeping the necessary funds, and giving away the rest. In one book a concrete purchasing plan is recommended: the strategy involves buying the least expensive item for the purpose at hand (Sherman and Hendricks 1987, 189).

---

on bigger church buildings and quantitative results in evangelism. The passion of his writing and the fearlessness of his charges are biblical in their intensity. But for all that, White gives little concrete advice that applies directly to the individual adherent. For this reason, I have seldom quoted or paraphrased White in this essay. It should be noted, however, that in some substantive ways he provides a voice of dissent to the discourse that prevails in the books I examine here. Shelley and Shelley (1992) also provide a (much milder) critique of church marketing practices.

The difficulty with this suggestion is that the idea of selecting items adequate for tasks or purposes is left unexplained, leading to an apparent uneasy relativism. The co-authors of one book suggest that while it is generally true that Christians shouldn't purchase fancy cars, it might be necessary, say, for a real-estate salesman — whose business relies on his image — to drive a top-of-the-line sedan (Sherman and Hendricks 1987, 190). Likewise, another author explains, "Some Christians may well need a 5,000 square foot home to accomplish what God calls them to do in their community" (Burkett 1990, 45). A third author relates his personal experience: "Working in the American business world, I must dress appropriately for my position. When I worked at a commercial bank some years ago, I was expected to wear a suit. A sport jacket was not acceptable. A positive theology of enough would say, 'Don't feel guilty about spending enough money on good clothes. They are necessary to your job'" (Wells 1989, 97).

But despite the vagueness of these guidelines, the authors explain that Christians can reach resolutions about purchasing decisions by communicating with God. Some authors hold that God will signal the propriety of individual transactions, sometimes even providing the good. One author relates his experience of denying himself an expensive car, only to receive it unexpectedly as a gift from a colleague. "I guess the Lord is not as concerned with cost as I am," he concludes (Burkett 1990, 46).

Even though there is a lack of clarity in these notions, the general principle of the limited lifestyle signals an attempt on the part of these authors to address the ethical dilemmas of consumption in an affluent society. In fact, one author includes a detailed and thoughtful chapter on teaching one's children to keep money in perspective (Alcorn 1989, 383-98). Other suggestions for controlling consumption include rational strategies for delaying gratification by postponing purchases, making do with what one has by conserving resources, curtailing use of one's credit cards, and keeping careful records of money flow.

How much of one's income is it proper for a Christian to save? Once again, the authors do not specify percentages or quantities. The act of saving in itself is neither biblical nor unbiblical, they say; its legitimacy depends on one's attitudes and reasons. If the goal of saving money is to become independent of God, then obviously this is a spiritual error. On the other hand, according to one author, the Christian should save enough so as not to presume on God.

The matter is particularly tricky with respect to saving for retirement, since this may constitute stockpiling funds that could be used more immediately for "kingdom purposes" (Alcorn 1989, 342). Saving for retirement is probably unnecessary anyway, since most people throughout human history have gotten along fine without it. Actually, one author notes, retirement itself may be an unbiblical notion (Burkett 1990, 212-14). But there are no certain rules.

A second area of expenditure addressed by these books concerns giving to one's church and related organizations. At issue for some authors is the propriety of the tithe. While some authors see tithing as a biblical mandate still binding on Christians, others suggest that it should be viewed not as a law but as a principle that should be followed anyway (Burkett 1990, 204). In any case, they say, the tithe should be supplemented by freewill offerings. In contrast, some authors argue that one commits the error of legalism when one regulates the amount given to God, and that one should give only what one can give joyously (Caywood 1989, 212). This is a matter for the individual to decide.

Since the total amount of one's gift is therefore discretionary, some authors detail incentives to generous giving. They say that funding God's work is necessary for the goals of evangelism, for personal spiritual growth, and for ridding oneself of psychological anguish over how money should be spent. In addition, however, some authors suggest that giving to God is a wise financial strategy, in that one is guaranteed an extremely favorable return on investment. Some imply that financial rewards will ensue in this life. Two of the authors, for example, quote the assertion of Christian entrepreneur R. G. LeTourneau: "'I shovel the money out [to God's works], and God shovels it back in. And God has a larger shovel than I do'" (Alcorn 1989, 241; Burkett 1990, 209). Some authors discuss specific instances of unexpected financial rewards that they personally received as a result of generous giving.

However, other authors elaborate on the material rewards in the next life that will come to those who give generously in this one. Interpreting Luke 12:33-34 ("Provide yourselves with . . . a treasure in the heavens that does not fail"), one author explains, "When Jesus talks about treasure in heaven, He's talking about money. In other words, Jesus is suggesting that you take care of your eternity. To the rich Christian He would say, 'Do not end your financial planning with your retirement. Include eternity in your plans and make yourself wealthy in heaven with lots of spending power.' We remind ourselves, 'You can't take it with you.' But yes, you can! Jesus wants you to put your cash in heaven. He's not talking about emotional riches or spiritual riches. He's talking about money" (Caywood 1989, 127-28).

Similarly, another author concludes that proper stewardship of money in this life (which includes the proper apportionment of income and resources to self and family on the one hand, and to Christian service on the other) will lead to the tangible reward of a larger home in the next life. The author explains, "We must conclude that each of us will have a specific individual location in heaven, an address of our own. . . . The size and quality of our eternal dwelling is influenced by how we live our lives now. . . . We might imagine that some of us are sending ahead sufficient materials for pup tents, some for studio apartments, some for trailer homes, some for ranch houses, and others for great mansions" (Alcorn 1989, 174-75). All of this depends on taking advantage of Christ's "investment opportunities" for one's assets. Here we see clearly used the language of monetary relationships, of commodification and exchange, of the instrumental use of charitable acts.

Finally, the authors address the issue of one's responsibility to help the poor and suffering and to alleviate economic inequality in general. Consonant with the widely held view (explicit in some works, only implicit in others) that accumulating wealth is not a zero-sum game, the authors acknowledge the existence of suffering and poverty while denying that some people's acquisition of material resources is responsible for the deprivation of others.

According to some authors, the systematic redistribution of material goods is not only unnecessary; it is also unscriptural and unworkable. They criticize on both biblical and economic grounds the ideas of those on the left who call for a reapportionment of wealth from the rich to the poor. (The ideas of Andrew Kirk and Ronald Sider come under particularly sharp attack.) They make a case for capitalism unimpeded by state intervention on the basis of Bible verses that they see as supporting the natural right of human beings to freedom of exchange and freedom from coercion, on the basis of examples from Jesus' ministry in which he produced wealth from equity (the multiplication of the loaves and fishes), and on the basis of the inherent limitations of state economic planning as a result of the innate depravity of human beings (Colson and Eckerd 1991; Nash 1986). These scriptural arguments are coupled with familiar economic arguments drawn, with or without attribution, from secular proponents of laissez-faire such as Ludwig von Mises, Friedrich Hayek, and Milton Friedman.

The authors leave no doubt, however, that Christians should, as individuals or as members of churches, attend to the needs of others, whether through tithing and freewill giving alone or through additional acts of charity. In fact, the authors frequently defend a Christian's making a substantial amount of money on the grounds that he or she will thereby have more to give away. In general, however, the authors make few specific recommendations about the extent or quality of one's charitable obligation. Most of them discuss charity as a general principle rather than offering a specific plan of action, sometimes explicitly leaving charity up to individual choice.

And according to some authors, as might be expected, alleviating the suffering of the poor should be attempted only in concert with — and, some would say, as a second priority to — the spread of the gospel. One author concludes a chapter titled "Helping the Poor and Reaching the Lost" with this anecdote: "One day a Nigerian brother and I were talking. After he shared what a privilege it was to be visiting our country, I said to him, 'It surprises me that you seem to have such a great appreciation for America. . . . Wasn't it from Nigeria that many children were bought or stolen and shipped to America and sold as slaves? I'd think you of all people would despise us for what we did.' I will never forget his measured response. 'No matter what else you did, you brought us the gospel, and that is all that matters'" (Alcorn 1989, 264). This same author sees funding evangelism as a way to invest in eternity, with its concomitant promise of material rewards (Alcorn 1989, 263).

Conclusions

Evangelicals, as many of the authors of the books I analyzed remind their readers, are called to be in the world but not of it, and that delicate position can make it difficult for Christians to put their faith into appropriate practice. The workplace is a domain where evangelicals see enacted, sometimes in particularly vivid form, what secular culture has done to Americans' values and behavior. The "ordinary" conduct of lying, stealing, cutting corners on the job, and engaging in adultery with a coworker; giving in to false values of workaholism and of placing trust in the acquisition of wealth; scrimping on time spent in achieving harmonious and supportive relationships — all these things, as the authors see it, directly contradict precepts of the Christian life.

Nevertheless, the authors are clearly confident in the ability of believers to cope with the pitfalls of the workplace and the marketplace. All assert that evangelicals can succeed in their jobs and gain financial security while doing business, as one author terms it, "by the Book" (Burkett 1990).

What is the source of this confidence, and what purpose does it fulfill? Is it the visible manifestation of the secure belief that God and his people will prevail despite the trials with which modern secularity confronts Christianity? Is the confidence analogous to the cheerfulness that Christians are enjoined to express as they go about their work tasks, simultaneously advertising the psychological benefits of faith and encouraging obedience to its authority? Or is the confidence a result of the fact that — as it turns out — the demands that evangelicalism places on believers in the workplace are not all that different from the prevailing norms of secular culture in the first place? I think it is probably an amalgam of all three.

Scholars of contemporary American religion have noted that, although religion survives and in many cases thrives as an important social institution, the secularity of the modern world takes its toll on traditional religious belief (Demerath and Williams 1992; Hunter 1983; Hunter 1987; Witten 1993). Secular norms of individualism, rationalism, relativism, and trust in psychotherapy are bound to leave their mark, to a greater or lesser degree, on the pronouncements and practices of religion. And a faith set loose in the world will invariably make a set of strategic compromises with modern life. We can see some of these adaptive strategies in the books reviewed here. The major ones can be grouped into four general categories and summarized in four basic statements:

Spiritual matters are psychologized. In an effort to mark the relevance of Christian belief in a modern world in which supernatural belief grows increasingly implausible, the authors of these books naturalize religious speech by adopting the secular language of psychology. The purpose of religion, then, becomes one of providing professional counsel to believers, of addressing their inner states and feelings. The authors stress the rewards of faith, which take on psychological significance, as they are said to alleviate feelings of anxiety or guilt. Work is legitimized partly on the basis of offering opportunities for "personal growth" and "reaching one's potential." Positive spirituality is translated as psychological health, and spiritual imbalance becomes a psychiatric disorder. Interpersonal relationships with others take on therapeutic functions for the believer, as they become the locus of "venting" and "support." God is portrayed as the humanistic therapist par excellence, as much of his purpose is to offer an unjudgmental ear and unconditional acceptance.

Procedures of spirituality are rationalized. Although many substantive issues lack prescriptive certainties, the authors emphasize and describe in detail instrumental means toward certain ends. They enumerate and order precise steps toward increased psycho-spiritual health. They elaborate "investment strategies" for heavenly rewards, as norms of exchange govern decisions about spiritual matters. Even though the individual believer is simply engaging in certain behaviors in an attempt to meet certain predetermined goals, he or she seemingly takes charge of his or her spiritual development. The orderliness of the recommended procedures not only gives the individual the sense of being in control of some aspects of faith, but also gives religious adherence an aura of rational "respectability."

Behavioral precepts are privatized and relativized. In these books, the authors indicate that decisions about many behaviors are a matter of individual discretion. The psychological mechanism of feeling (sometimes authors use the more spiritual language of "conscience") is the gauge for decision making. The authors use admonitions against legalism to justify individual preferences. Although the Christian is sometimes counseled to seek advice from friends, support-group members, or professional clergy in making difficult choices, he or she nevertheless acts independently of communities of tradition in these areas.

Christian behaviors are normalized. The prescriptions that authors give for workplace behavior stress the need for Christians to follow the guidelines for expected conduct at their place of business. (The possible exceptions are that they should distinguish themselves by their honesty and diligent work habits.) Christians should obey authority almost without exception, work on human relationships to achieve harmony, and be polite. If they engage in witnessing, it must never be obtrusive, confrontational, or insulting. In meeting these criteria, Christians adapt appropriately to the ordinary conduct of middle-class American life.

But, of course, these adaptive strategies don't tell the whole story. The books also include examples of what scholars have termed "religious resistance" to secular norms and practices. The authors clearly draw the line with respect to compromise over certain behaviors. They do not condone violation of the moral code of the Decalogue. Many of them still use the Bible as the ultimate authority (although there is enormous latitude in the way particular verses are interpreted). They do not explain away God through relativizing scientific or social-scientific discourse. They recognize that humankind is fallen and that sin still exists as a category of human behavior (although most of them do not represent sin as something that makes God particularly angry).

It is possible, of course, to draw conclusions about the appropriateness for evangelical faith of the strategies of adaptation and resistance examined here, and about what they bode for the future of evangelicalism in a secular world. But we might want to assess the books from a different perspective, too. What exactly is it that evangelical laypeople and clergy get when they purchase these volumes in search of advice about conduct at the workplace or the place of money and possessions in life? Do they find ideas, suggestions, admonitions, or reflections that might challenge — or at least make one think about — the taken-for-granted beliefs of modern, secular, middle-class America? Or do they see reflected in the books a comfortable "pious materialism," as Wuthnow (1993) has called it, a genteel affirmation of a "normal" American life?

The answer is, I think, that the message of the books is mixed. On ethical issues of interpersonal behavior — honesty, sexual conduct, respect for property, and so forth — the books do prescribe norms that are different from — or at least more categorical and explicit than — those that are found in most contemporary secular workplaces. It is clear that some of the authors went to considerable effort to try to work through a responsible applied theology of money. In emphasizing the Christian's obligation to charitable giving, they challenge the "me-first-ness" said to characterize secular culture. In insisting that wealth is not a sign of God's blessing nor poverty a sign of his disfavor, they militate against biblical interpretations that could be used to legitimate maltreatment of the poor.

But on other issues, of course, the authors of these books tacitly endorse the structures and systems of secular American life. The status quo of workplace hierarchies, with the logic of exchange that everywhere undergirds them, is not just accepted but sacralized. Incentives for spiritual behavior employ — and not just metaphorically — the language of the trading floor. The accumulation of money, except in extreme excess, is deemed just fine if only one's attitude is right. And only the vaguest limits are placed on the acquisition and consumption of goods, although the appropriate contours of many other behaviors (e.g., how long a workweek one should have, or how to keep a record of one's prayer activities) are specified in detail.

It is important to remember that the authors of these books do not always speak in harmony with one another, and that theirs are not the only voices within evangelicalism. As analysts have shown, for example, there is nothing about evangelicalism that inherently links it with political or economic conservatism (Iannaccone 1992). And evangelical scholars take positions all across the spectrum on the issue of capitalism (Gay 1991). But this diversity is apparently not reflected in the readily available selection of popular books. The evangelical in search of theological and practical answers to spiritual questions about work and money cannot know the range of possible responses from these books.

II. TOWARD A CRITIQUE
OF MATERIALISM

Has the Cloak Become a Cage? Charity, Justice, and Economic Activity

NICHOLAS WOLTERSTORFF

In Baxter's view the care for external goods should only lie on the shoulders of the "saint like a light cloak, which can be thrown aside at any moment." But fate decreed that the cloak should become an iron cage.

Max Weber

"History is irreversible," says the French socialist Lucien Goldmann in his *Philosophy of the Enlightenment,* "and it seems impossible that Christianity should ever again become the mode in which men really live and think" (Goldmann 1973, 82). The choice for humanity is now between the "bourgeois individualism" of capitalism, which Goldmann sees as spiritually empty in its devotion to morally neutral technical knowledge, and socialism, which he sees as an immanent, historical, and humanist religion committed to the creation of a new community. The choice, he observes, is a painful one, since the spiritual emptiness of capitalism is balanced by the violation of individual conscience characteristic of socialism as we know it. But the possibility of

This essay was originally prepared for a conference entitled "Rethinking Materialism: Sociological and Theological Perspectives," held at the Center for the Study of American Religion, Princeton University, June 1993.

a transcendental faith shaping history is probably over; and, in any case, "the 'judgement of history' has passed Christianity by. Diderot's argument that modern society makes it impossible for anyone to give a genuinely Christian character to his whole life is more valid than ever today. The more sincere and intense the Christian life of modern man, the more it becomes a purely inward, psychological 'private matter' deprived of all influence on life in society" (82).

In what follows I want to consider whether these haunting words of Goldmann are true. I will follow Goldmann in speaking mainly about Christianity. It is clear from Goldmann's words that he regards what he is saying as true for "any transcendental faith shaping history" — Judaism, Christianity, Islam, whatever. The day of all such faiths is over; in the modern world, "transcendental faith" is a "psychological 'private matter' deprived of all influence on life in society." But my discussion will be more focused if I concentrate on just one religion, leaving it to the reader to draw out the analogues. I shall choose that religion that I know best: Christianity. And I shall speak only about the economy. Goldmann's thesis is that Christianity is without formative impact on all spheres of public life; even from the comments quoted, however, it's clear that he himself regards the economy as central.

Goldmann is of course following in the footsteps of Max Weber. Weber is notorious for his thesis that religion, specifically Calvinism, and more specifically yet, Puritanism, made a crucial causal contribution to the emergence of capitalism. Weber assumed that for capitalism to emerge in any part of the world, a victorious struggle against the "traditionalism" already in place must occur. One characteristic feature of traditionalism is the presence of a wide variety of ethical prohibitions against a wide variety of economic transactions; for capitalism to emerge, these must be removed and be replaced by a rationalized legal system whose centerpiece is laws enforcing the sanctity of free contracts made between non-deceiving parties, and the view must gain currency that all that is ethically prohibited is deceiving or coercing one's contracting partner and breaking one's contract. A second feature of what Weber has in mind by "traditionalism" is explained by him in these words: "A man does not 'by nature' wish to earn more and more money, but simply to live as he is accustomed to live and to earn as much as is necessary for that purpose. Wherever modern capitalism has begun its work of increasing the productivity of human labour by increasing its intensity, it has encountered the immensely stubborn resistance of this leading trait of pre-capitalistic labour" (Weber 1958, 60). The structure of a capitalist economy is that of "the rational utilization of capital in a permanent enterprise and the rational capitalistic organization of labour" (58); for this structure to become operative, people must acquire the habit of working whether they have to or not, just to make (more and more) money.

The "traditionalism" from which capitalism initially emerged was the Christianized traditionalism of Western Europe. Accordingly, Weber asked how the *unnatural* character formation necessary for the workings of this virtually *amoral* system emerged from Christianity. What makes of the question a puzzle is that the traditional ethic of Christianity is an "ethic of brotherliness." Weber's famous answer was that the Puritans provided the crucial link, with respect to both the unnaturalness and the amoralism. Weber interpreted the Puritans as saying that the roles allotted us by the capitalist economy are to be seen as our divine callings; accordingly, we are to work devotedly in accord with the imperatives of the system. We serve God by working hard at making money and by investing for profit. The Puritans, on Weber's interpretation, took the roles offered them by the capitalist system and propounded the audacious claim that, no matter how "unbrotherly" one's action in these roles might be, we are nonetheless called by God to play these roles. It is God who calls us to hard work in these hard-hearted roles for the impersonal goal of making money!

Now that the system is in place, however, it reproduces itself without the aid of this or any other religious basis:

> Since asceticism undertook to remodel the world and to work out its ideals in the world, material goods have gained an increasing and finally an inexorable power over the lives of men as at no previous period in history. Today the spirit of religious asceticism — whether finally, who knows? — has escaped from the cage. But victorious capitalism, since it rests on mechanical foundations, needs its support no longer. . . . The idea of duty in one's calling prowls about in our lives like the ghost of dead religious beliefs. Where the fulfilment of the calling cannot directly be related to the highest spiritual and cultural values, or when, on the other hand, it need not be felt simply as economic compulsion, the individual generally abandons the attempt to justify it at all. In the field of its highest development, in the

United States, the pursuit of wealth, stripped of its religious and ethical meaning, tends to become associated with purely mundane passions, which often actually give it the character of sport. (Weber 1958, 181-82)

Weber's thesis about the causal contribution of Puritan religion to the emergence of capitalism in the West is much contested by historians; by contrast, his view about the nature of economic behavior within capitalism is the orthodoxy of modern economists. With more than a touch of irony in his prose, the economist Amartya Sen, in his recent book entitled *On Ethics and Economics,* gives this characterization of the view that most of his fellow economists hold of their discipline: "Perhaps the economist might be personally allowed a moderate dose of friendliness, provided in his economic models he keeps the motivations of human beings pure, simple and hard-headed, and not messed up by such things as goodwill or moral sentiments" (Sen 1987, 1).

The church and its representatives continue to pour forth pronouncements on economic life. Some of these are critical of what transpires in the economy; some are legitimating. Some are aimed at motivating people to continue doing what they are already doing; some are aimed at motivating people to change what they are doing. Materialism is condemned, charity is urged, stewardship is praised, the dignity of work is celebrated, God is thanked for blessings received and petitioned for blessings hoped for. But all of this noise makes no difference. The economy as a whole proceeds exactly as if none of these preachments had ever been made; and individual believers *do* function and *must* function within the economy just like everyone else, each pursuing his or her interests. No longer can anyone give "a genuinely Christian character" to his or her economic life.

I want to consider whether this Weberian picture is correct; and I want to consider whether it is correct on two different levels. Is it true that Christian ethical convictions have become irrelevant to our *motivations and dispositions* as we engage in economic activity in a capitalist system? And is it true that Christian ethical convictions have become irrelevant to our *appraisal of the social outcome* of our economic activity?

Christianity applauds a wide array of motivations and dispositions. But it does not regard the motives and virtues that it applauds as a mere grab bag. It sees them all as organized, in one way or another, around a core motive and virtue: that of *charity*. So we can conveniently ask one of our questions this way: Is charity irrelevant to economic activity within our modern capitalist system?

And how shall we pose our question concerning appraisal of the social outcome? Most of us who are academics in the West manage to work and play without coming into contact with impoverished people. Nonetheless, the plight of the poor has been brought to the attention of those of us who read liberation theology by their insistent presence in those works, and to the attention of all of us by our public media. So I propose balancing the extreme generality of our question about the relevance of charity to economic motivation and disposition by posing a somewhat more limited and focused question at this point. I shall retrieve from the Christian tradition a principle concerning justice to the poor, and then ask whether that principle has any relevance to appraising the social outcome of our modern capitalist economy. What is said concerning the relevance of this principle of social appraisal can be generalized to others. As it turns out, the principle I have in mind, though it emerges from principles deep in Christianity and was affirmed by prominent thinkers and influential preachers throughout most of the history of Christianity, is now almost forgotten; accordingly, we must take a few minutes to retrieve that principle.

The Rights of the Poor

Well along in the stately, unperturbed fugal discourse of his *Summa Theologica*, Aquinas, after arguing that theft and robbery are always *mortal* sins, adds this provocative clarification:

> In cases of need all things are common property, so that there would seem to be no sin in taking another's property, for need has made it common. . . . Since . . . there are many who are in need, while it is impossible for all to be succored by means of the same thing, each one is entrusted with the stewardship of his own things, so that out of them he may come to the aid of those who are in need. Nevertheless, if the need be so manifest and urgent, that it is evident that the present need must be remedied by whatever means be at hand (for instance when a person is in some imminent danger, and

there is no other possible remedy), then it is lawful for a man to succor his own need by means of another's property, by taking it either openly or secretly: nor is this properly speaking theft or robbery. (*S.Th.* II-II, q.66, a.7, *resp.*)

It is not theft, properly speaking, to take secretly and use another's property in a case of extreme need: because that which he takes for the support of his life becomes his own property by reason of that need. (II-II, q.66, a.7, *ad* 2)

The most striking point in this passage is, of course, the remedy that Aquinas permits: When no other recourse is available, it is morally permissible for the extremely impoverished person to take what he or she needs for sustenance from the person with plenty; Aquinas adds that "in a case of a like need a man may also take secretly another's property in order to succor his neighbor in need" (II-II, q.66, a.7, *ad* 3). On this occasion, however, I am less interested in Aquinas's permission of this remedy, striking though that is, and more interested in his understanding of the evil to which "taking" is a permissible remedy.

In the course of his comment, Aquinas speaks about the *duties* of the better-off toward the poor: "Each one is entrusted with the stewardship of his own things, so that out of them he may come to the aid of those who are in need." But Aquinas doesn't content himself with speaking about the duties of the better-off; in fact, it's not even his main point here. His main point is about the *rights,* the *claim-rights,* of the poor. It's true that he doesn't use the word "rights." But the thought is there nonetheless. The suggestion that one rather often hears — that the concept of rights is a modern invention, for good or ill — is patently false. If some parcel of food that you need for your survival is in the legal possession of someone else who does not need it for his survival, then it's yours, in the sense that you have a morally legitimate claim on it. And if, to exercise this right, it's necessary for you to *take it,* whether "openly or secretly," then that's permitted, for the reason that you would only be taking what is morally yours — that is, what you have a morally legitimate claim to. An implication is that should the better-off person *offer it* to you, that is not to be regarded as an act of charity on his part — not, at least, of supererogatory charity — but as an act of extending to you what you have a morally legitimate claim to — extending to you what is yours by (moral) right.

Underlying Aquinas's discussion would seem to be the conviction that we *all* have a natural right to means of sustenance — that is, to *genuine access* to means of sustenance — and then to *fair* access, lest justice be violated at that point. Perhaps it's possible to act in such a way that one forfeits this right. And no doubt the right is a *situationally conditioned* right, in the sense that if one finds oneself in a situation so appallingly bad that no means of sustenance are available, then one doesn't have a morally legitimate claim to means of sustenance. Furthermore, what a given person needs for sustenance may, though available, be so exotic and expensive that satisfying this right would infringe on more rights of others; the right may be, in that sense, *defeasible.* And of course it's not entirely clear on the face of it what is to count as a means of sustenance: food that nourishes, of course; but what degree of avoidable toxicity is allowable without rights being infringed upon? Aquinas doesn't delve into these matters, neither here nor elsewhere. Nor does he reflect on better and worse arrangements for securing our common human right to genuine and fair access to means of sustenance. Of course these issues are important. Nonetheless, on this occasion I wish to set them all off to the side and emphasize the core of what is implied by Aquinas's discussion: We human beings all have a *natural right* to genuine and fair access to means of sustenance.

In all his work, Aquinas thought of himself as *interpreting* the tradition handed on to him; there is not a touch of the modern hubris of beginning over. So too here. Aquinas cites the words of Ambrose, embodied in the Decretals: "It is the hungry man's bread that you withhold, the naked man's cloak that you store away; the money that you bury in the earth is the price of the poor man's ransom and freedom." He might also have cited these words of Ambrose: "Not from your own do you bestow upon the poor man, but you make return from what is his" (from Avila 1983, 50). And he might have cited these words from Basil of Caesarea:

> Will not one be called a thief who steals the garment of one already clothed, and is one deserving of any other title who will not clothe the naked if he is able to do so?
>
> That bread which you keep, belongs to the hungry; that coat which you preserve in your wardrobe, to the naked; those shoes which are rotting in your possession, to the shoeless; that gold which you have hidden in the ground, to the needy. Wherefore, as often as you were

able to help others, and refused, so often did you do them wrong. (from Avila 1983, 66)

As usual, however, it was John Chrysostom who stated the point most vividly — and, in this case, also with the greatest acuity:

This also is theft, not to share one's possessions. Perhaps this statement seems surprising to you, but do not be surprised. I shall bring you testimony from the divine Scriptures, saying that not only the theft of others' goods but also the failure to share one's own goods with others is theft and swindle and defraudation. . . .

Just as an official in the imperial treasury, if he neglects to distribute where he is ordered, but spends instead for his own indolence, pays the penalty and is put to death, so also the rich man is a kind of steward of the money which is owed for distribution to the poor. He is directed to distribute it to his fellow servants who are in want. So if he spends more on himself than his needs require, he will pay the harshest penalty hereafter. For his own goods are not his own, but belong to his fellow servants. . . .

The poor man has one plea, his want and his standing in need: do not require anything else from him; but even if he is the most wicked of all men and is at a loss for his necessary sustenance, let us free him from hunger. . . . The almsgiver is a harbor for those in necessity: a harbor receives all who have encountered shipwreck; and frees them from danger; whether they are bad or good or whatever they are who are in danger, it escorts them into its own shelter. So you likewise, when you see on earth the man who encountered the shipwreck of poverty, do not judge him, do not seek an account of his life, but free him from his misfortune. . . .

Need alone is the poor man's worthiness; if anyone at all ever comes to us with this recommendation, let us not meddle any further. We do not provide for the manners but for the man. We show mercy on him not because of his virtue but because of his misfortune, in order that we ourselves may receive from the Master His great mercy. . . .

I beg you remember this without fail, that not to share our own wealth with the poor is theft from the poor and deprivation of their means of life; we do not possess our own wealth but theirs. (Chrysostom 1984, 49-55)

Down through the ages, the church has often spoken to the well-to-do of their *duty* to see to it that the poor have access to means of sustenance — probably more often than it has spoken of the *right* of the poor to such access. In these passages, however, the talk is all of the rights of the poor. The talk is not about the *moral guilt* of the well-to-do who fail or refuse to make such means of sustenance available but about the *moral injury* to the poor who do not enjoy what they have a right to.

The line of thought underlying this strand of Christian ethical reflection was clearly articulated by Aquinas in the same article that I have already cited. "According to the natural order established by Divine Providence, inferior things are ordained for the purpose of succoring man's needs by their means," says Aquinas. Aquinas does not take this as implying that all private property arrangements are wrong — not even that all allotments of *means of sustenance* to persons as their private property are wrong. Instead, he takes it to imply that private property arrangements must satisfy a certain condition if they are to be in accord with natural moral law. Nothing in natural moral law specifies which property is to be assigned to whom; "the division and appropriation of property . . . proceeds from human law." But if the property arrangement we select is to be in accord with natural law, we must keep in mind that since "man's needs have to be remedied by means of [inferior things] . . . , whatever certain people have in superabundance is due, by natural law, to the purpose of succoring the poor."

The contrast with the main tradition of modern liberal thought, with its near-exclusive emphasis on negative rights and civil liberties, is of course stark. Nonetheless, the line of Christian thought to which I have pointed was still alive in John Locke, this in spite of the fact that Locke is indisputably the great founding father of modern liberalism. It's true that Locke spends no time developing the thought that there is a natural human right to genuine and fair access to means of sustenance; his attention was elsewhere. But the acknowledgment is there, unmistakably, prominently, at the very beginning of his chapter entitled "Of Property" in his *Second Treatise:*

> Whether we consider natural *reason,* which tells us that men, being once born, have a right to their preservation, and consequently to meat and drink, and such other things as nature affords for their subsistence: or *revelation,* which gives us an account of those grants

God made of the world to Adam, and to Noah, and his sons, it is very clear that God, as King David says, *Psal cxv.16. has given the earth to the children of men;* given it to mankind in common. (§25)

Taking for granted these two classic Christian themes, that we all have a natural right to means of sustenance and that God has given the world to human beings in common, the question which drew Locke's attention was how it can be that "any one should ever come to have a *property* in any thing." What he will "endeavour to shew," says Locke, is "how men might come to have a *property* in several parts of that which God gave to mankind in common, and that without any express compact of all the commoners." Most of Christian tradition before Locke would have assumed that the answer to this question would lie in the origin of the fundamental elements of a particular society's legal arrangements concerning property. From Locke's discussion it becomes clear, however, that he is assuming that property rights are not simply a matter of "human law." He is assuming that although the earth was given by God to human beings in common for their sustenance, nonetheless each normal adult human being has a *natural moral right* to certain items of property and not to others; he wants to know how that comes about.

His ingenious and influential answer, as we all know, begins with the claim that "every man has a *property* in his own *person:* this no body has any right to but himself" (§27). Although the plants and minerals of the earth have been given by God to all of us in common, *my body* has not been given to everyone in common; it belongs only to me, by natural moral right. But Locke does not linger to explicate this dark saying, that by natural right we each have exclusive title of possession to that particular human body, among all bodies, which is ours. Instead, he moves on to claim that it follows that by natural right each person also has exclusive title of possession to the *bodily labor* that he or she engages in: "The *labour* of his body, and the *work* of his hands, we may say, are properly his." And from this in turn Locke infers that each person, by natural right, has exclusive title of possession to whatever, from the common stock of nature, he or she puts the imprint of his or her labor on:

Whatsoever then he removes out of the state that nature hath provided, and left it in, he hath mixed his *labour* with, and joined to it something that is his own, and thereby makes it his *property*. It being by him removed from the common state nature hath placed it in, it hath by this *labour* something annexed to it, that excludes the common right of other men: for this *labour* being the unquestionable property of the labourer, no man but he can have a right to what that is once joined to (§27).

What is important to notice, for our purposes, is that Locke's opening affirmations lead him at once to attach two conditions to one's right to that which bears the imprint of one's labor; the metamorphosis of Locke's thought into standard modern liberal thought required forgetting these two conditions.[1] The first condition is that, in Locke's words, "there is enough, and as good, left in common for others" (§27). And the second condition is that, "of those good things which nature hath provided in common, every one had a right (as hath been said) to as much as he could use, and *property* in all that he could effect with his labour; all that his *industry* could extend to, to alter from the state nature had put it in, was his. He that *gathered* a hundred bushels of acorns or apples, had thereby a *property* in them, they were his goods as soon as gathered. He was only to look that he used them before they spoiled, else he took more than his share, and robbed others" (§46).[2] "Nothing was made by God for man to spoil or destroy" (§30; cf. §37).

In the "state of nature," if an area became heavily settled, then by compact "the several *communities* settled the bounds of their distinct territories, and by laws within themselves regulated the properties of

---

1. It might be thought that Locke himself, as his discussion proceeds, forgets this opening affirmation of our natural human right to means of sustenance. Not so. To cite just one piece of evidence: Late in his discussion, in §183, Locke says that "the fundamental law of nature being, that all, as much as may be, should be preserved. . . ."

2. The passage continues thus: "If he . . . bartered away plums, that would have rotted in a week, for nuts that would last good for his eating a whole year, he did no injury; he wasted not the common stock; destroyed no part of the portion of goods that belonged to others, so long as nothing perished uselessly in his hands. Again, if he would give his nuts for a piece of metal, pleased with its colour; or exchange his sheep for shells, or wool for a sparkling pebble or a diamond, and keep those by him all his life, he invaded not the right of others, he might heap up as much of these durable things as he pleased; the *exceeding of the bounds of* his *just property* not lying in the largeness of his possession, but the perishing of any thing uselessly in it" (§46).

the private men of their society, and so, *by compact* and agreement, *settled the property* which labour and industry began" (§45; cf. §38). In a somewhat similar way, one can contract one's labor to another (§85). But it was Locke's argument that such compacts and contracts presuppose that we each have a natural moral right to certain things — specifically, to our labor and to that which bears its imprint.

What, though, about a society in which money — that is, nonperishable items whose value is exchange rather than use — has been introduced? To such items, the proviso "No more than one can use" simply lacks application. What holds in this case is rather the following:

> Gold and silver, being little useful to the life of man in proportion to food, raiment, and carriage, has its *value* only from the consent of men, whereof *labour* yet *makes,* in great part, *the measure,* it is plain, that men have agreed to a disproportionate and unequal *possession of the earth,* they having, by a tacit and voluntary consent, found out a way how a man may fairly possess more land than he himself can use the product of, by receiving in exchange for the overplus gold and silver, which may be hoarded up without injury to any one. (§50)

The flow of Locke's argument is surprising indeed, not to mention obscure and controversial at many points. He begins with the conviction that we each have a natural right to our labor and to that which bears its imprint, subject to qualifications which flow from the conviction that God has given the world to all of us in common for our sustenance. By the end, it turns out that just by using the monetary system of our economy, and just by consenting to the property laws of our society, we have bartered and contracted away what we possess by natural right so that now, by natural right of agreement and compact, we rightly possess pretty much all and only what our economy and laws say we do. About this culmination of his argument, however, Locke is at pains to say that there are some things which no one can rightly be thought to have disposed of by agreement or contract; and among those is one's natural right to the means of self-preservation:

> [The legislative] power, in the utmost bounds of it, is *limited to the public good* of the society. It is a power, that hath no other end but preservation, and therefore can never have a right to destroy, enslave,

· 156 ·

or designedly to impoverish the subjects. The obligations of the law of nature cease not in society, but only in many cases are drawn closer, and have by human laws known penalties annexed to them, to enforce their observation. Thus the law of nature stands as an eternal rule to all men, *legislators* as well as others. The *rules* that they make for other men's actions must, as well as their own and other men's actions, be conformable to the law of nature, *i.e.* to the will of God, of which that is a declaration, and the *fundamental law of nature being the preservation of mankind,* no human sanction can be good, or valid against it. (§135)

This passage leaves no room for doubt that the long Christian tradition to which I have pointed — that there is a natural human right to means of sustenance — was still alive and well in Locke. Although Locke's account of property rights was in many ways innovative, he continued to affirm the ancient Christian teaching that a morally acceptable system of property arrangements must honor this right. The notion that the moral significance of involuntary avoidable poverty is that the poor have somehow failed in their duties, or that the well-to-do have failed fully to implement their duties of almsgiving, is not to be found in Locke.

Is Charity Irrelevant?

About ten years ago now I served — quite amazingly — as a philosophical consultant to the Herman Miller Furniture Company in Zeeland, Michigan. Max de Pree, the executive officer of the company, had invited an architect, a physician, a journalist, a furniture designer, a theologian, and me to an all-day session with him and about five of the top officers in his company. At the beginning of the day he posed ten questions that he wanted us to discuss, in whatever order we wished. He asked us not to concern ourselves with trying to say things that we thought would be useful to the company; he wanted the discussion to take whatever shape it wanted to take. I remember three of the questions. "What is the purpose of business?" he asked. Some of his younger executives were saying that the purpose of business was to make money. He himself didn't believe that; but he wanted to talk about it. Second, he wondered whether there was "a moral imperative," as he called it, for companies to produce products of good design. And third, he wanted to discuss whether it was possible to preserve what he called "intimacy" in a large company.

It became clear, in the course of the discussion, what de Pree himself regarded as the purpose of business. The purpose, as he saw it, was twofold: to produce products that serve a genuine need and are aesthetically good, and to provide meaningful work in pleasant surroundings for those employed in the company. He added that these purposes had for a long time shaped his operation of the company.

Now it seems to me that these two purposes are, or can be, an expression of charity — that is, both consist in concern to promote the welfare of the other. As a matter of fact, it became clear in the course of the discussion that it was de Pree's religious commitment — specifically, his Christian commitment — that had led him to embrace these goals. He saw his operation of the company as an exercise of charity — though he didn't use that word. His own case, at least as he presented it, was a case of "transcendental faith" shaping economic activity.

Was he prevaricating? Or deluded?

One would think that he was if one adhered to the view of human motivation which Amartya Sen, in the book I have already cited, attributes to his fellow modern economists. Let us look into that view a bit. And since the generalizations and observations by a highly skilled economist like Sen about the views of economists carry more weight than those of a non-economist like myself, let me make liberal use of Sen's helpful and pointed discussion.

Sen observes (Sen 1987, 12) that the view typical of modern economists, that human beings are motivated by the desire to maximize self-interest, is typically arrived at, or supported, by two moves: the identification of actual behavior with rational behavior, and the identification of rational behavior with the attempt to maximize self-interest. There are also some economists who give an alternative characterization of rational behavior — namely, as behavior that exhibits internal consistency of choice. But if that is how rational behavior is identified, the claim that actual behavior is rational behavior does not yield the conclusion that ethical considerations play no role in determining motivations in economic behavior; accordingly, for our purposes here, we can set this characterization of rational behavior off to the side. It may be added that the characterization of rational behavior as consistent-choice behavior isn't, as a matter of fact, at all plausible. Sen makes the relevant point: "If a person does exactly the opposite of what would help achieving what he or she would want to achieve, and does this with flawless internal consistency . . . , the person can scarcely be seen as rational, even if that dogged consistency inspires some kind of an astonished admiration on the part of the observer" (13).

As to the alternative characterization of rational behavior, why, asks Sen, "should it be *uniquely* rational to pursue one's own self-interest to the exclusion of everything else? . . . To argue that anything other than maximizing self-interest must be irrational seems altogether extraordinary. The self-interest view of rationality involves *inter alia* a firm rejection of the 'ethics-related' view of motivation. Trying to do one's best to achieve what one would like to achieve can be a part of rationality, and this can include the promotion of non-self-interest goals which we may value and wish to aim at" (15). "Universal selfishness . . . as a requirement of *rationality* is patently absurd" (16). In short, the typical economist's way of getting to the conclusion that people always try to maximize their self-interest — by identifying actual behavior with rational behavior and rational behavior with behavior aimed at maximizing self-interest — will not do.

But may it nonetheless be the case that the conclusion is correct? Or, more cautiously, may it be the case that, however human beings act in general, this is how they act in economic matters? "Does the so-called 'economic man,' pursuing his own interests, provide the best approximation to the behaviour of human beings, at least in economic matters?" (16). It appeared to Max de Pree that his motivations in the operation of his company were not confined to his attempt to maximize his self-interest. Have economists discovered something about human nature which makes it probable that de Pree was mistaken about that?

Apparently not. "While assertions of conviction are plentiful," says Sen, "factual findings are rare" (18). He adds, "Sometimes the alleged case for assuming self-interested action seems to be based on its expected results — arguing that this would lead to efficient outcomes. The success of some free-market economies, such as Japan, in producing efficiency has also been cited as some evidence in the direction of the self-interest theory. However, the success of a free market does not tell us anything at all about what *motivation* lies behind the action of economic agents in such an economy. Indeed, in the case of Japan, there is strong empirical evidence to suggest that systematic departures from self-interested behaviour in the direction of duty, loyalty and goodwill have played a substantial part in industrial success. . . . [We] are beginning to see the development of a whole range of alternative theories about economic behaviour to achieve industrial success, based on comparative studies of different societies with different prevalent value systems" (18-19).

Max Weber's reasons for holding to the view that a capitalist economy is an autonomous sphere of human action to which ethical considerations are irrelevant were more subtle than those of the modern economists that Sen has in mind. Weber was not of the view that human motivation, *by nature,* is exclusively self-interested — quite to the contrary: "The magical and religious forces, and the ethical ideas of duty based upon them, have in the past always been among the most important formative influences on conduct" (Weber 1958, 27). Instead, Weber's thought ran along the following lines: Every society can be thought of as offering to its members various roles for them to play; for example, among the roles that European feudal society offered to its members were those of lord and serf. European society no longer offers those roles. Prominent among the roles it offers instead are those of laborer and entrepreneur.

These roles of laborer and entrepreneur are different in a number of ways from the roles offered by medieval society. First of all, they are clearly *economic* roles, whereas the roles of lord and serf had, at best, an economic *dimension.* Between us and medieval Europe lies the social sectoring of which Weber makes so much.

Secondly, the roles of lord and serf were *ethically infused.* To play the role of lord or serf was not just to act in a certain typical and coherent way but was to see oneself and was to be seen as subject to a specific cluster of *requirements* with respect to one's fellow human beings, the fulfillment of these being enforced and reinforced by social expectations. To have the role of serf was to be required to spend a high proportion of one's time laboring for the lord of the manor; to have the role of lord was to be required to provide protection and security to one's serfs. These requirements were for the most part not legal requirements. But neither were they merely instrumental requirements — that is, causal conditions for achieving one's goals. They were *moral* requirements, matters of duty and right. And in good measure they were not just *general* moral requirements pertaining to all persons in all roles whatsoever; rather, to a specific role was attached a specific ethic. To occupy a certain station in life was to be subject to a specific set of duties and to enjoy a specific set of rights. By contrast, the role of entrepreneur in a capitalist society is defined not by a particular configuration of rights and duties to other members of society but instead by the goal of operating an enterprise for profit; and the role of laborer in a capitalist society is likewise defined not by a particular configuration of rights and duties to other members of society but instead by working for contracted wages. In place of person-to-person rights and duties defining one's station in life, there is the impersonal goal of making money, be it in the role of entrepreneur or in the role of worker. An *ethic* of personal relations has been replaced by a *calling* to work for that impersonal thing called "money." All that is left by way of an ethic — that is, by way of duties to one's fellow human beings — is the ethic of contract.

Thirdly, no matter what roles a society offers to its members, those members have to learn to play those roles. They have to acquire the requisite character formation, the requisite "ethos," the requisite complex of cognitions and abilities and dispositions. That was true for medieval society; it remains true for modern society. But here too Weber saw a difference: the roles of entrepreneur and laborer require vastly more discipline, more "rationalization," than the roles offered by medieval society — that of monk and nun excepted! Our capitalist economy is not the whole of our modern life, however; and the fact that such a character formation is necessary for the working of the economy does not imply that the same is needed for the totality of life in modern society, nor does it imply anything about human nature — other, of course, than that human nature is sufficiently malleable to submit to such formation.

Getting a capitalist economy to emerge out of the seedbed of traditionalism required a special impetus; supposedly the early Protestants, with their preachments about working with religious devotion in one's calling, provided that special impetus. But now that the system is in place, it perpetuates itself by rewarding disciplined pursuit of wages and profit and punishing other modes of behavior. Other behavior still occurs, of course; but over the long haul it gets snuffed out by the competition of the marketplace.

Let me quote Weber himself:

The impulse to acquisition, pursuit of gain, of money, of the greatest possible amount of money, . . . exists and has existed among waiters, physicians, coachmen, artists, prostitutes, dishonest officials, soldiers, nobles, crusaders, gamblers, and beggars. . . . Unlimited greed for gain is not in the least identical with capitalism, and is still less its spirit. Capitalism . . . is identical with the pursuit of profit, and forever *renewed* profit, by means of continuous, rational, capitalistic enterprise. . . . We will define a capitalistic economic action as one which rests on the expectation of profit by the utilization of opportunities for exchange, that is on (formally) peaceful chances of profit. (Weber 1958, 17)

The earning of money within the modern economic order is, so long as it is done legally, the result and the expression of virtue and proficiency in a calling. . . . This peculiar idea, so familiar to us today, but in reality so little a matter of course, of one's duty in a calling, is what is most characteristic of the social ethic of capitalistic culture, and is in a sense the fundamental basis of it. It is an obligation which the individual is supposed to feel and does feel towards the content of his professional activity, no matter in what it consists. . . . Of course, [we do not] . . . maintain that a conscious acceptance of these ethical maxims on the part of the individuals, entrepreneurs or labourers, in modern capitalistic enterprises, is a condition of the further existence of present-day capitalism. The capitalistic economy of the present is an immense cosmos into which the individual is born, and which presents itself to him, at least as an individual, as an unalterable order of things in which he must live. It forces the individual, in so far as he is involved in the system of market relationships, to conform to capitalistic rules of action. The manufacturer who in the long run acts counter to these norms, will just as inevitably be eliminated from the economic scene as the worker who cannot or will not adapt himself to them will be thrown into the streets without a job.

Thus the capitalism of today, which has come to dominate economic life, educates and selects the economic subjects which it needs through a process of economic survival of the fittest. But here one can easily see the limits of the concept of selection as a means of historical explanation. In order that a manner of life so well adapted to the peculiarities of capitalism could be selected at all, i.e. should come to dominate others, it had to originate somewhere, and not in isolated individuals alone, but as a way of life common to whole groups of men. This origin is what really needs explanation. (Weber 1958, 53-55)[3]

I think we can all agree that there are profound insights in Weber's analysis. All who lament one and another aspect of American society — its materialism, its acquisitiveness, and so forth — ought to take Weber's analysis with utmost seriousness. It is the habit of intellectuals to attribute socially pervasive phenomena such as materialism and acquisitiveness to the influence of certain ideas. Weber invites us to consider instead that materialism and acquisitiveness may be promoted by the character formation produced by, and required for, participation in our capitalistic economy.

But does Weber's analysis give any reason for concluding that Max de Pree was either deluded or prevaricating in stating that among the

3. Cf. Weber 1958, 72-73: "At present under our individualistic political, legal, and economic institutions, with the forms of organization and general structure which are peculiar to our economic order, this spirit of capitalism might be understandable, as has been said, purely as a result of adaptation. The capitalistic system so needs this devotion to the calling of making money, it is an attitude toward material goods which is so well suited to that system, so intimately bound up with the conditions of survival in the economic struggle for existence, that there can today no longer be any question of a necessary connection of that acquisitive manner of life with any single *Weltanschauung*. In fact, it no longer needs the support of any religious forces, and feels the attempts of religion to influence economic life, in so far as they can still be felt at all, to be as much an unjustified interference as its regulation by the State. In such circumstances men's commercial and social interests do tend to determine their opinions and attitudes. Whoever does not adapt his manner of life to the conditions of capitalistic success must go under, or at least cannot rise. But these are phenomena of a time in which modern capitalism has become dominant and has become emancipated from its old supports. But as it could at one time destroy the old forms of medieval regulation of economic life only in alliance with the growing power of the modern State, the same, we may say provisionally, may have been the case in its relations with religious forces. Whether and in what sense that was the case, it is our task to investigate. For that the conception of money-making as an end in itself to which people were bound, as a calling, was contrary to the ethical feelings of whole epochs, it is hardly necessary to prove."

goals which guided him in the operation of the Herman Miller Company were those of providing to his employees worthwhile work in a pleasing environment, and of providing to his customers products which satisfy their genuine needs and are aesthetically good in design? I fail to see that it does. Weber reminds us that unless the Herman Miller Company turns a profit and unless there are persons available who will work for the wages it offers, it will go out of existence. Of course de Pree knew that. And the Herman Miller Company was in fact making a profit; it was successful. But instead of setting profit making as the all-consuming goal of his economic endeavors, de Pree viewed profit making simply as a condition that must be satisfied if he and his company were to serve employees and customers in the way he desired.

Of course, at some point in the future he might be forced to make some difficult choices. The competition might prove such that for the company to continue to make a profit, it would have to diminish the quality of the work or of its environment, or skimp on good design, or produce items which, in de Pree's view, do not satisfy any genuine need. But that is no reason for concluding that ethical considerations *did not in fact* motivate his actions. And the case of Japan, to which Sen referred, makes clear that concern of one and another sort for the welfare of one's workers is not always, given one's competition, an affordable luxury, although sometimes it "makes good business sense."

What's also true is that the charity which came to expression in de Pree's actions was, as it were, extra-systemic in origin. Whereas to learn the role of lord was to learn one's moral rights and duties vis à vis one's serfs, it can scarcely be said that to learn the role of entrepreneur in a capitalist economy is to learn one's moral rights and duties vis à vis one's workers and customers. One has to learn those elsewhere. But of course the important point is not *where* they are learned but *whether* they are learned. Perhaps there are good reasons for supposing that the "ethos" of capitalism endangers the moral life, whereas the "ethos" of feudalism promoted it; but if so, that then is the point to make, rather than that the capitalist system snuffs out ethically motivated action.

Capitalism, says Weber, "is identical with the pursuit of profit, and forever *renewed* profit, by means of continuous, rational, capitalistic enterprise. For it must be so: in a wholly capitalistic order of society, an individual capitalistic enterprise which did not take advantage of its opportunities for profit-making would be doomed to extinction"

(Weber 1958, 17). The claim of the last sentence is correct: the enterprise in a capitalist economy that doesn't turn a profit is doomed, sooner or later, to extinction — unless it is in some way "propped up." Hence it is also true that the pursuit of profit is an essential component in the defining structure of a capitalist economy. But it doesn't follow that all entrepreneurs — not even all *successful* entrepreneurs — are motivated in their economic activity just by the prospect of profit. There is no reason to question the appearance: ethical considerations play a prominent role in the economic activities of many entrepreneurs, sometimes even at the cost of what unadulterated self-interest would call for. Lest too idealized a picture emerge, let us add that motives and emotions such as jealousy, spite, and vindictiveness also play a role, also sometimes at the cost of what unadulterated self-interest would call for. Self-interest is supplemented in the economy not just by interest in the welfare of the other but also — let us admit it — by interest in the diminishing of the other!

Is Justice Irrelevant?

Let us move on, then, to the level of appraisal of the social outcome of a given capitalist economy. Are moral categories, such as that of *justice,* irrelevant to such appraisal? More particularly, are *religiously grounded* principles making use of the category of justice — such as the one I retrieved from the Christian tradition — somehow irrelevant to such appraisal?

Here I fail to see any reason for supposing that this is the case which has even the pretense of plausibility. In each of our modern democratic polities, we the citizens do in fact appraise the social outcome of our capitalist economies; and in each of them influential groups of citizens do in fact take steps to alter, or to try to alter, that outcome so that it becomes, in their judgment, more desirable, the most obvious of these steps being the passing of laws of various sorts. Libertarians argue that the outcome would be better if we refrained from all such attempts at manipulation; but of course their argument presupposes that influential citizens do in fact manage to alter the social outcome of the economy. It's true that modern economies confront us with difficult problems of "steerage" — to say the least! But steerage does in fact occur, all the time.

Often the appraisals of outcome that motivate attempts at steerage make no use of moral categories; politicians aim just at increasing the GNP, or aim just at increasing the wealth of what they identify as their group. But that scarcely shows the irrelevance of moral appraisal and of morally guided attempts at steerage. In particular, I fail to see anything about a capitalist economy which renders irrelevant that ancient Christian principle of justice: that every human being has a natural right to genuine and fair access to adequate means of sustenance. So far as I can see, the fact that this principle is seldom embraced, and rarely used as a principle for appraisal of social outcome or as a guide for attempts at steerage, has nothing at all to do with the fact that ours is a capitalist economy. Something else has led to its demise, and to our almost-exclusive concern, when it comes to rights, with negative rights and civil liberties. Perhaps it's true that in the modern Western world Christianity is more a shaper of inward life and private relations, and less a shaper of economic life in particular and of public life in general, than was previously the case in the West. But if so, that, I suggest, is due more to the religious and convictional pluralism of modern Western society than to the fact that our economy is capitalist.

Rethinking Weber

Weber's overarching theory of modernization was that the essence of modernization is located in two related phenomena. It is located, in the first place, in the emergence of *differentiated spheres* — specifically, in the emergence of the differentiated *social spheres* of economy and state, along with household, and in the emergence of the differentiated *cultural spheres* of science, art, and law and ethics. The effect of this differentiation is that modes of thought and activity which once were subject to extraneous demands are now free to follow their own autonomous internal "logic." Previously art was intertwined with other cultural and social phenomena and in their service; now the artistic sphere has been differentiated from the other spheres of thought and action, liberated from their extraneous demands, and set free to follow its own internal dynamics so as to come into its own. Previously economic activity was intertwined with other social and cultural phenomena and in their service; now the economic sphere has been differentiated from other spheres of thought and action, liberated from their extraneous demands, and set free to follow its own internal dynamics and come into its own. So too for *Wissenschaft*, for politics, and so forth.

The essence of modernization is located, secondly, in the spread of rationalized thought and action within these spheres. Just as the fundamental dynamic of action without a modern, capitalist economy is the rationalized pursuit of profit, so the fundamental dynamic of action within our modern, bureaucratic states is rationalized administration, and the fundamental dynamic of *Wissenschaft* is rationalized pursuit of the facts. In the words of Weber's famous speech entitled "Science as Vocation," "The fate of our times is characterized by rationalization and intellectualization and, above all, by the 'disenchantment of the world.' Precisely the ultimate and most sublime values have retreated from public life either into the transcendental realm of mystic life or into the brother-liness of direct and personal human relations" (Weber 1946, 155).

We are all fated to work within the differentiated spheres of modern society and culture as if placed within a calling rather than as applying an ethic. To speak for a moment of the calling of those who labor in *Wissen-schaft*, "one cannot demonstrate scientifically what the duty of an academic teacher is. One can only demand of the teacher that he have the intellectual integrity to see that it is one thing to state facts, to determine mathematical or logical relations or the internal structure of cultural values, while it is another thing to answer questions of the *value* of culture and its individual contents and the question of how one should act in the cultural community and in political associations. These are quite hetero-geneous problems. If he asks further why he should not deal with both types of problems in the lecture-room, the answer is: because the prophet and the demagogue do not belong on the academic platform. . . . I am ready to prove from the works of our historians that whenever the man of science introduces his personal value judgment, a full understanding of the facts *ceases*" (Weber 1946, 146).[4]

---

4. "The task of the teacher is to serve the students with his knowledge and scientific experience and not to imprint upon them his personal political views. It is certainly possible that the individual teacher will not entirely succeed in eliminating his personal sympathies. He is then exposed to the sharpest criticism in the forum of his own conscience. And this deficiency does not prove anything; other errors are also possible, for instance, erroneous statements of fact, and yet they prove nothing against the duty of searching for the truth" (Weber 1946, 146).

The view that embedded within *Wissenschaft* is a relentless value-free "logic" impervious to ethical and religious values, and that all who choose the "calling" of teacher or researcher must submit to that logic or be tossed out as prophet or demagogue, today seems less and less plausible to more and more of us. I submit that we ought to be just as skeptical of those counterpart claims of Weber concerning the economy. Religious commitments and ethical concerns have not disappeared from art, nor from politics, nor from academic learning, nor from the economy. There is, admittedly, something compellingly gripping in the icy melancholy of Weber's elegant picture of differentiated sectors each relentlessly playing out its own internal autonomous meaningless logic on a disenchanted world, with religion consigned to the mystical and the privately personal. The truth is much more messy. Religious commitment and ethical concern shape economic activity under capitalism very differently from the way they shaped it under the "traditionalism" that is Weber's ever-present foil to capitalism; but they continue to shape it. It is those differences, then, that we must study — rather than assuming present-day absence and studying to see how absence emerged from once-upon-a-time presence. Possibly it is also true that religious commitment and ethical concern shape economic activity less under capitalism than they did under "traditionalism." But do we know that? Charity for workers and customers and justice for the impoverished are widely held to be virtues, but they have never been put widely into practice.

In the Cage of Vanities:
Christian Faith and the Dynamics
of Economic Progress

MIROSLAV VOLF

A Cloak and a Cage

AT THE END OF *The Protestant Ethic and the Spirit of Capitalism,* at the
point where what its author calls "purely historical discussion" edges
toward "the world of judgments of value and of faith," we read, "In
Baxter's view the care for external goods should only lie on the shoulders
of the 'saint like a light cloak, which can be thrown aside at any moment.'
But fate decreed that the cloak should become an iron cage" (Weber
1958, 181). The intriguing questions about the nature of "fate" and its
decree and about how it was carried out need not concern us here.
Important for my purposes is the double irony entailed in the transformation of the "cloak" into the "cage."

The first irony was intentional. Richard Baxter, the old Puritan
fool, thought mammon's yoke was easy and its burden light — provided

This essay was prepared for a conference entitled "Rethinking Materialism:
Sociological and Theological Perspectives," held at the Center for the Study of
American Religion, Princeton University, 11-13 June 1993. I am grateful for
the assistance I received in preparing this paper from my students Robert Cahill
and Telford Work. My friends Professor Philip Clayton, Professor Judith Gun-
dry Volf, and Professor James William McClendon Jr. read a draft of the essay
and offered valuable advice. I benefited also from the discussion during the
conference, especially from the comments by Professor Neil Smelser, Professor
Nicholas Wolterstorff, and Professor Robert Wuthnow.

one's heart was set on the things of God. But in fact the powers unleashed by transplanting asceticism "out of monastic cells into everyday life" (Weber 1958, 181) — and by a few other things, like the changes in economic organization and social structure (see Tawney 1958; Goudzwaard 1978) — have proved stronger than the heart's desire to serve the one true master. The burden of care for external goods became heavy and the worldly saints weary; the light cloak turned into an iron cage. From behind the closed doors of the cage, Christ's call to come and find rest (Matt. 11:28-30) could be heard only as a faint echo from a distant past.

The obverse of Christ's offer of rest was the warning that one cannot serve both God and mammon (Matt. 6:24). For many in the seventeenth century and after, mammon seemed an increasingly attractive lord, however. In order to pursue the creation and enjoyment of wealth with a good conscience, one needed cleanly to separate economic and religious spheres, treating them no longer "as successive stages within a larger unity, but as parallel and independent provinces, governed by different laws, judged by different standards, and amenable to different authorities" (Tawney 1926, 279). This disjunctive maneuver was calculated to render Christ's call and his command ineffectual in the economic sphere. When it succeeded, it seemed that the age of freedom had dawned. But as time went by, it became apparent that it was freedom to do what one wanted — in an iron cage. The "tremendous cosmos of the modern economic order" has come to determine "the lives of all individuals who are born into" it, "with irresistible force," wrote Weber (1958, 181). Weber exaggerated. There are people who successfully resist the force of modern economic order. Yet most succumb while cheerfully believing that they are exercising the greatest of all freedoms: the freedom of the consumer. This is the second irony in the talk about the replacement of the light cloak by an iron cage, the one Weber does not seem to have intended.

The double irony illustrates well a fundamental *aporia* at the interface of religion and economic life in the modern age: the virtual powerlessness of religious moral appeals and the slavery of "material boys and girls" — what used to be called *homo oeconomicus* — to endless desires if they refuse to heed these appeals. Have we locked the door of the cage from the inside and misplaced the key? Before proceeding with a search, it might be good to ask some deceptively simple questions:

Are we indeed in a cage? If we are, how have gotten into it? Might our "gods" be partly to blame?

The questions I propose to address betray at the outset the relatively narrow focus of this essay. Various deeply disturbing aspects of life in the cage will remain outside its scope. For instance, I will say nothing about the injustice of excluding people from the basic means of livelihood. My silence does not come from a lack of concern (see Volf 1988; Volf 1991). In any case, the futility of acquisitive materialism I intend to tackle here is no less significant a problem than injustice. The two are closely interrelated: Where there is justice, there will be abundance even amid scarcity (see Meeks 1989, 157ff.); where there is contentment, justice will flow like a mighty river.

The Cage . . .

1. In his classic *The Affluent Society* (1958), John Kenneth Galbraith compared the struggle in modern societies to satisfy their wants with "the efforts of the squirrel to keep abreast of the wheel that is propelled by his own efforts" (154). More recently, Juliet B. Schor (1992) joined him and deplored "capitalism's squirrel cage": people are entrapped in the endless "cycle of work-and-spend," whose poles mutually reinforce each other (117-65).

For Galbraith (and Schor), capitalist *production* is the culprit. Contrary to the widespread assumption that existing needs call for products to satisfy them, in modern capitalism the production "creates the wants the goods are presumed to satisfy." In other words, the production "fills a void that it has itself created" (Galbraith 1958, 155, 153). Galbraith is largely right. One must be a blind ideologue to embrace the idyllic image of producers as zealous servants, alert to any discomfort of their masters, the consumers, and ready to give a helping hand — and justly receiving generous rewards for their deft assistance. At least since Hegel, social critics have not failed to note that the spiraling wants of consumers are partly contrived by profit-seeking producers (Hegel 1976, §191; see also Hegel 1973, 593; Marx 1974, 14).

Although correct, Galbraith's diagnosis is partial. So is his proposed cure. It is futile simply to blame the producers, assuming that if their drive for profit could be tamed, then modern societies would have solved the problem of production and have freed themselves to "proceed . . . to the next task" (1958, 356). To get closer to the cure, we need to ponder why efforts at contriving wants are so easily crowned with success and why we never get around to the "next task." The answer lies not just in expert marketing but in the character of human needs. As Kant pointed out in his *Critique of Judgment* (1987), it is not human nature "to stop possessing and enjoying at some point and be satisfied" (§83; see also Hegel 1976, §190). Insatiability belongs to the basic makeup of human beings.

Ought we not be cautious, however, with talk about insatiability? Does it not impose on us as fate the unceasing quest for material goods? Moreover, is not such talk a simple-minded and arrogant projection of modern possessive individualism and of the belief in unlimited progress onto human nature in general (see Seev 1981, 43)? The alternative claim, that not all human beings have an insatiable appetite for goods and services, strikes us as plausible; many people seem content with what they have. How then can insatiability be rooted in human nature?

In a sense, however, the contentment of some people is beside the point. Just as it is true that there are content people in capitalistic societies, so it is also true that there have always been insatiable people in pre-capitalistic societies. The human race did not need to wait for capitalism to infect it with the virus of insatiability. If this metaphor is appropriate at all, then the virus was there all along. It was active in particular strata of society throughout history, until finally a general epidemic broke out with the rise of capitalism in the West. The inactive virus just needed a change in socioeconomic and cultural conditions to provide it a friendly environment. The immune system was weakened, and the insatiable appetite attacked anything it could find under the sun. The idea that the crapulousness bespoke a serious illness was suppressed.

2. As I shall argue shortly, *cultural acceptance,* even *encouragement,* of insatiability is unique to modernity. Insatiability itself is not. For proof of the latter, one has only to look at the strange world of Ecclesiastes. Insatiability is its dominant theme. Consider the following image:

> All streams run to the sea,
>   but the sea is not full;

to the place where the streams flow,
  there they continue to flow.

(1:7; see also Prov. 30:15-16)

Just as the flow of the streams never fills the sea, so humans remain forever unsatiated, all their toil notwithstanding (see Murphy 1992, 8).[1] Ecclesiastes not only registers insatiability, however. The various concrete images he employs show his clear awareness of its rootedness in human nature.

The first cause of insatiability is human animality: "All human toil is for the mouth, yet the appetite is not satisfied" (6:7). To live as an animal being is to have needs and to require their perpetual satisfaction. One might object that this is not quite what we mean by insatiability. After all, how many meals can you have in one evening? We eat, and we are satisfied. Yet the hunger invariably recurs. The only thing that can break the cycle of hunger and satiation is death. Animal beings can be satiated *fully* but never *finally*.

Human insatiability proper is not a function of animality, however, but of spirituality. Ecclesiastes writes,

. . . the eye is not satisfied with seeing,
  or the ear filled with hearing.

(1:8)

The human mouth can be satisfied — for the time being at least. But the human eye and ear are insatiable, forever eager to see and hear something new (as well as often wishing to revisit the old). One could object here, too, that a few hours spent at the Louvre and hearing Schubert's string quartet pretty much satisfy most people. Yet if we know how to appreciate art, we will want return to the Louvre and to Schubert after we have taken a rest. We might also want to see some treasures from the Hermitage and listen to Mahler. Imagination and reflection forever carry the eye and the ear beyond the point of seeing and hearing, and create a void and the need for it to be filled; indeed, they make

---

1. In the following I do not pretend to be *exegeting* select passages from Ecclesiastes. Rather, I look at the theological and philosophical insights that may lie behind Qoheleth's statements and above all at new vistas that may be opened up by them.

human beings want to see and hear "what no eye has seen, nor ear heard" (1 Cor. 2:9). We can see why the eye has come to signify desire in Ecclesiastes (see Eccles. 2:10). Its restlessness is a case in point of the self-transcendence of human beings: they are always beyond every given situation (see Scheler 1978, 36ff.; Pannenberg 1983, 40ff.). This is why the experience of insatiability glides into the experience of the *tantalous.* Human beings are never satisfied because their desire is always already beyond any given object of their desire; they are reaching for what always eludes them. And so, as Ecclesiastes writes, people find no "end to all their toil, and their eyes are never satisfied with riches" (4:8).

Since human beings are social animals, self-transcendence takes place in a social setting. The eye sees, compares, and — envies. "Then I saw that all toil and all skill in work come from one person's envy of another" (4:4). As the one envies the other, rivalry goads each to outdo the other. The effort expended increases and proficiency is sharpened (see Ogden 1987, 67). And that in turn reinforces insatiability.

Ecclesiastes' description of the dynamic of insatiability shows a striking resemblance to the dynamic of insatiability in modern societies, even if the "spirit of capitalism," which makes the pursuit of profit an end in itself, is absent from it (see Marx and Engels 1979, 22:144ff.). Might this resemblance not illustrate his claim that "there is nothing new under the sun" (1:9), a claim that strikes us as so outlandish in an age of innovation?

Whatever one might think of the presumed needs of an *infinite* being, Hegel was no doubt correct that being needful is an essential characteristic of a *finite* being (see Hegel 1963, 2:409; cf. Seev 1981, 36). Humans are finite beings, but the nature of their finitude makes their needs infinite. If we eliminated all the *contrived* wants generated by either helpful or greedy producers, the squirrel cage would no doubt turn at a much slower pace, but it would not come to a halt. Consumerism is a creation of capitalism. Insatiability is not; capitalism only capitalizes on it.

The rootedness of insatiability in human nature leads to a very simple but fundamental insight: *the economic problem cannot be solved by economic means alone,* not even in a hundred years, as Keynes suggested in his frequently quoted essay entitled "Economic Possibilities for Our Grandchildren" (1931, 366). Purely economic solutions to economic problems ignore the insatiability that keeps the squirrel wheel in motion — not only the insatiability of our hungry mouth and envious eye that seek "conveniences according to the nicety and delicacy of taste" (Smith 1896, 160), but also the insatiability of the inner vision lured by the promise of perpetual progress.

... of Vanities

1. "Among the many models of the good society no one has urged the squirrel wheel," noted Galbraith dryly (1958, 159). His sarcasm is to the point. For in fact the notion of the good society that has dominated public imagination in the West for quite some time is not so far from the squirrel wheel. It disguises itself under a different name, however. We call it progress.

In one sense, faith in progress is dead. When two centuries ago Fichte proclaimed that the true paradise was not a gift of grace that humanity enjoyed in the distant past, but a promised land to be conquered by humanity's efforts in the not-too-distant future (Fichte 1845/46, 7:342), he was not a lone voice crying in the wilderness. With many Western thinkers of the eighteenth and nineteenth centuries, he shared the belief that humanity was destined to build for itself "a paradise according to the blueprint of the one it lost" — with significant architectonic improvements, to be sure (Fichte 1845/46, 7:12; see also Volf 1988, 32-33). In the meantime, Westerners have learned through bitter lessons what they ought to have known without them: the scaffolding will never be removed from the construction site "Paradise"; even the price of pouring the foundation was much higher than anyone should have paid.

The hope of building a paradise has vanished, and with it a fixed destination for the spiral of needs. But faith in progress persists. This curiosity is easily explained when we consider that a utopian destination was never at the core of the idea of progress. As Christopher Lasch (1991) has argued, central to the modern conception of progress is not so much "the promise of a secular utopia that would bring history to a happy ending but the promise of steady improvement with no foreseeable ending at all" (47). This notion of progress takes its cue from science as a "self-perpetuating inquiry" (48). It is predicated on two sets of beliefs. The one is the positive assessment of insatiability and of the proliferation of wants (13, 45), and the other an "expectation that the expansion of the productive forces can continue indefinitely" (39).

2. The awareness is growing that what we thought to be a road of perpetual progress is in fact a dead-end street. Like many before him, Lasch has underscored the ecological limits of growth (though criticizing at the same time "a very narrow ideal of the good life" [529] that faith in progress presupposes). He writes, "[The discovery that] the earth's ecology will no longer sustain an indefinite expansion of productive forces deals the final blow to the belief in progress" (529). Others, like Fred Hirsch (1976), have drawn attention to the social limits of growth. But even if there were no ecological and social limits to growth, would the pursuit of progress predicated on insatiability make sense?

On the one hand, progress seems inextricably tied to the positive assessment of insatiability — at least an indefinite progress does. Insatiability is the fuel that keeps the engine of progress going. Were people to become content, no progress would occur. At a deeper level, however, the association of progress and insatiability is oxymoronic. The notion of progress from which a final destination has been removed cannot imply that we are asymptotically approaching the goal — as, for instance, Kant's notion of moral progress assumes the approximation toward "the highest good possible on earth" (Kant 1960, 126), or as scientific progress seems to entail an ideal explanation that is treated as true (see Clayton 1989, 178). Perfect goodness is desirable for Kant, and so is (arguably) an ideal explanation for a scientist; satiation is *undesirable* for modern believers in progress. At any moment on the time line of progress humanity is equidistant from the goal for the simple reason that progress is not conceived as a terminal enterprise. This is what insatiability does to progress. In terms of satiation, the future only *seems* better than the present; the illusion is unmasked as soon as we compare the present with the past. Today we are exactly as satiated and exactly as unsatiated as we were yesterday.

Of course, progress *does* take place. Some additional wants get both created and satisfied, and there are new and more complex means of satisfying both old and new wants. Above all, we would rarely want to go back (even if we could), partly because life has been made easier through technological inventions, but partly also because of addiction to more recent goods and services (see Scitovsky 1976, 137). *This* progress, however, never reaches below the surface. The level of satiation remains the same. As Paul L. Wachtel (1983) writes, "We keep upping the ante. Our expectations keep accommodating to what we have attained. 'Enough' is just always over the horizon, and like the horizon it recedes as we approach it" (17). We eat but remain as hungry as ever. What can the progress mean if it takes place only at the surface? Does it consist in us being better and better — *unsatiated and insatiable?* A strange kind of progress indeed! If we thrive on insatiability, we might do well to rethink the ideology of progress — unless we are so fascinated with the movement at the surface that we forget about the lack of it in the depths.

3. Ecclesiastes was not misled by surface currents. One might object that he was not sufficiently aware of them. After all, in his world there *was* nothing new under the sun (see Eccles. 1:9). Or was there? The conception that ancient societies were static is nothing more than a modern prejudice. Jacques Ellul (1990) rightly comments, "Progress did not take place then as fast as today, but it was just as basic for humanity's future" (63). Moreover, Ecclesiastes does not seem to have had a cyclical view of history; he does not "point out a cycle, an 'eternal return,' but a line of time punctuated by varying or comparable events" (66).

Important as the issue of the progress of humankind as a whole and its embeddedness in a philosophy of history is, it is not decisive for the problem we are discussing. Look at the *personal life* of Ecclesiastes:

> I made great works; I built houses and planted vineyards. . . . I made myself gardens and parks, and planted in them all kinds of fruit trees. . . . I bought male and female slaves. . . . I also had great possessions of herds and flocks. . . . I also gathered for myself silver and gold and the treasure of kings. . . . I got singers . . . and delights of the flesh, and many concubines. So I became great and surpassed all who were before me in Jerusalem. (2:4-5, 9)

This is "progress" by *our* definition. The talk about "surpassing" testifies that Ecclesiastes thought of it no differently.

What makes Ecclesiastes so different from a representative of modern Western culture is that in progress, he explained, "my wisdom remained with me" (2:9). At the very outset of the book, he posed the question our culture persistently refuses to ask: "What do people gain from all their toil at which they toil under the sun?" (1:3). He knew, of course, that hard work does bring gain, at least at the surface, and if one is lucky enough (see 9:11). The point of his question goes deeper, however. If work brings gain, *what is the gain of the gain?* This calls to mind Jesus' rhetorical question: "For what will it profit them to gain the whole world and forfeit their life?" (Mark 8:36). A person who has only superficially read Jesus might ask, "But what if they *do not* forfeit their life? Could they then strive to gain the whole world?" Ecclesiastes' question pre-empts that kind of response. He asks in effect, "What will it profit a person to gain the whole world *even apart from the destiny of her soul?*" The answer comes as the conclusion of the list of his great accomplishments: "Then I considered all that my hands had done and the toil I had spent in doing it . . . and there was nothing to be gained under the sun" (2:11). After everything was gained, there comes a realization that there was nothing to be gained!

"Vanity of vanities . . . vanity of vanities! All is vanity" (1:2) reads the programmatic statement at the beginning of Ecclesiastes' treatise. Is this the frustrated cry of an overgorged overachiever, fed up with life? Or did Ecclesiastes see something that seems veiled from most of us today? *"Nothing to be gained" is an inescapable corollary of insatiability.*

4. What about pleasure or happiness? No progress there? One would be hard-pressed to argue that a person who is permanently overcoming a lack is happier than the person who does not feel a lack, that an insatiable person is happier than a content one. It is possible, of course, that a content person is suffering from myopia: she does not see that in the future she will be happier with more and better goods and services. This perspective might be right if she is stricken with poverty. Above the life of poverty, however, better goods and services tend to contribute little to a sense of well-being. Happiness is notoriously difficult to measure, but none of the attempts to do so seem to confirm that the proliferation of wants and means to satisfy them entails progress in happiness (see Wachtel 1983, 37ff.). Adam Smith, at any rate, believed that the "greater happiness" is a delusion — useful, though, to rouse and keep "in continual motion the industry of mankind" (Smith in Ignatieff 1986, 111). Pursuit of happiness is a noble goal, but it too easily degenerates into an ideology that keeps us running in the squirrel wheel of vanities.

I am assuming that pleasure and happiness are good. And who would disagree? Ecclesiastes certainly does not. His call to enjoyment resounds like a refrain throughout the book: "There is nothing better for mortals than to eat and drink, and find enjoyment in their toil" (2:24; see also 3:12-13, 22; 5:18; 8:15; 9:7). Yet as he has dared to take a close look at the meaning of work, so also he dares to examine pleasure without shying away from disturbing questions. "I said to myself, 'Come now, I will make a test of pleasure; enjoy yourself.' But again, this also was vanity. I said of laughter, 'It is mad,' and of pleasure, 'What use is it?'" (2:1-2). As is clear from the verses that follow (2:4-8), Ecclesiastes is talking not about mindless pleasures but about the joys "understood as the good life" (Murphy 1992, 17). What is the use of *such* pleasures? The question strikes us as strange; the one who poses it seems not to know how to use the word "pleasure." But if the obvious answer to the strange question about the use of pleasure is "pleasure," the counter-answer must surely be "vanity." For pleasure is either a motif in the larger picture of a meaningful life or it is itself meaningless.

John Stuart Mill insisted that it is better to be a dissatisfied Socrates than a satisfied pig. The claim might be true; I certainly would not dispute it. But within the tradition that defines good as "what has an aptness to produce pleasure in us" and evil as "what is apt to produce pain in us" (Locke 1894, 1:340), what good reasons can be given for Mill's claim? (see MacIntyre 1984, 62ff.). Indeed, what good reasons can be given for the claim that it is better to be a *satisfied* Socrates than a satisfied pig — except that the one making the claim happens to be not a pig but a human being? Just like any decent pig, a self-satisfied modern Socrates who did not bother to learn anything from his old namesake's reflection on happiness and self-control would be enslaved in the cage of his vain pleasures.

God in the Cage

1. Taking God seriously, Richard Baxter thought, ought to have prevented the light cloak of care for external goods from turning into an iron cage. It did not. Moreover, a good argument has been made for God's complicity in the construction of the cage (see Weber 1958; Troeltsch 1986, 70ff.; for discussions, see Green 1959; Marshall 1982).[2]

2. "The cage" is not synonymous with capitalism, but stands for the self-enclosed world of *homo oeconomicus* — whether in its pre-capitalist, pure capitalist, welfare-capitalist, or communist form, or some possible post-capitalist form.

Attempts to strengthen this indictment of God have so far been unsuccessful. Max Weber, who was the first to talk of God's complicity, claimed only this much. More significant than a role God has played seems to have been the creation of an economic system in which any non-profit-making enterprise would be doomed to extinction (see Weber 1958, 91, 17). Yet God cannot be completely exonerated. God's demand for "intra-mundane asceticism" helped in the creation of the cage.

This new breed of asceticism consisted of two simple religious tenets that reinforced each other: labor must be performed with rigorous discipline since it is a calling from God, and all spontaneous enjoyment of the fruits of one's labor should be avoided. This attitude toward work and possessions, which is "irrational from the standpoint of purely eudaemonistic self-interest" (Weber 1958, 78), contributed to the formation of the modern economic order that today powerfully shapes our lives (see Troeltsch 1950, 645-46).

Initially God's complicity in the construction of the cage was unwitting; the contribution was "only an indirect and consequently involuntary one" (Troeltsch 1986, 74). During the construction, God remained partly outside. Even if the prohibition of luxury made the so-called original accumulation (see Marx and Engels 1979, 23:741ff.) possible and hence stimulated the emergence of a capitalist economic system, it still reminded people that there was a world outside the cage that ought to impinge on what was going on inside. By highlighting the instances when the world and heaven were at odds, God's command underscored that the two belonged together. Even if the effectiveness of the command was rapidly diminishing, it still served as a reminder that the religious and economic aspects of life are interdependent components of a larger unity, not "independent provinces, governed by different laws" (Tawney 1926, 279).

Over time the outside voice was silenced; God was drawn into the cage. I do not need to tell here the whole fascinating — and ultimately pathetic — story of how God was entrapped and, like some blinded Samson, made to grind at the mill in the prisonhouse of the modern Philistines. The key element in this sacrilegious conspiracy was to reconfigure the basic sentiments about morality, prosperity, and historical development (see Goldsmith 1988). In his *Enquiry Concerning the Principles of Morals* (1927), David Hume put moral alternatives well:

> Luxury, or a refinement on the pleasures and conveniences of life, had long been supposed the source of every corruption in government, and the immediate cause of faction, sedition, civil wars, and the total loss of liberty. It was, therefore, universally regarded as a vice, and was an object of declamation to all satirists, and severe moralists. Those who prove, or attempt to prove, that such refinements rather tend to the increase of industry, civility, and arts regulate anew our *moral* as well as *political* sentiments, and represent, as laudable or innocent, what had formerly been regarded as pernicious and blameable. (181)

Hume's contrast between two kinds of moral and political sentiments recalls a contrast set up by Thomas Fuller in 1648 in a sermon on contentment: "Here we have two contrary opinions set on foot together, gain is godliness, says the worldling, whose Gold is his god, looking and telling thereof his saying of his prayers. *Godliness is great gain,* says God himself, by the mouth of the Apostle" (3-4). The "worldling" and a secularized version of his creed gained the upper hand; reconfiguration of moral sentiments largely succeeded. If earlier a person of virtue was a person of few needs, now endless wants became the key not only to success of industry but also to progress in civility. Insatiability was embraced, not bemoaned. The brakes were off, and the squirrel wheel started gaining momentum.

2. The so-called secularizing effects of wealth are proverbial. It cannot suffer a god beside itself. Yet God seems to dwell quite comfortably in the cage, even making a modest contribution to the business at hand, though occasionally plagued with bouts of (well-grounded?) fear of redundancy. It is for sociologists to analyze the multiple uses to which God has been put in the cage (see Wuthnow 1993). I want to draw attention here to what I perceive to be a major shift in the function of God in economic life *as reflected in popular theological discourse*.

The God who helped build the cage demanded ascetic denial of one's desires. One was to be content in consumption and disciplined in work (which, as Hegel pointed out, can be understood as "deferred desire" [1977, 153]). This is what it meant to practice one's work as a divine calling. In the post-Protestant age, influential thinkers counsel "reappropriation of the idea of vocation" (Bellah et al. 1985, 287; Bellah et al. 1991, 106-7), though they seem less interested in discipline and contentment than in working for the common good. But strong currents in popular religion want none of the old Protestant work ethic, their solemn declarations to the contrary notwithstanding. A case in point: the neo-charismatic preachers of the "prosperity gospel" (see Copeland 1974; Copeland 1978; Avanzini 1989). One could mention also the New Age movement and its relation to the business community (see Gerschon and Straub 1989).

If one is to believe Tocqueville, it was never easy to ascertain from the discourses of American popular preachers "whether the principal object of religion is to procure eternal felicity in the other world, or prosperity in this" (Tocqueville 1945, 2:135). I am not about to decide the issue. I am rather interested in what some of today's popular preachers say about *how* religious sentiments are to be employed in procuring prosperity.

In the book entitled *The Wealth of the World* (1989), a popular neo-charismatic preacher, John Avanzini, talks about "the battle of containment," or contentment (15). But it is not a battle of the saints struggling to be content in a luring world; it is rather an unholy battle of the saints against Satan, who is seducing them through false religion into believing that they have enough (see 16). Satan needs to be resisted, however, for God wants the saints "to have exceedingly abundantly more than enough" so that they can have "all . . . needs and wants met" (125). In addition to faithful tithing and "generous offerings" (161), a sure weapon to defeat Satan is the following prayer: "No, you can't take any more of the money God intends for me. You can't keep me from the riches God intends for me to control for Him" (157).

This combative prayer tips us off as to how Christians ought to get hold of all the money God intends for them. Disciplined work is *not* the key. Rather, one needs to acquire "violent spiritual force" (21), "great quantities" of it (18): "God gives you the supernatural power to get wealth, power that goes beyond your natural abilities . . . not in some distant future life, but right now, in this life!" (114). And how does one access wealth with spiritual power? As the subtitle of the book — *The Proven Wealth Transfer System* — indicates, wealth gets *transferred* from the wicked to the saints. Avanzini writes, "God is going to literally confiscate the gold, silver, the stocks, the bonds, virtually every form of wealth that the wicked possess and *in these last days, transfer that wealth to the 'just' (dedicated, informed, committed Christians)*" (10-11). The religious purpose of the transfer is "to properly and abundantly fund the final events in His endtime plan" (10). That comes, however, only after all the needs and wants of the saints have been met.

I paused to look at Avanzini's bizarre theology of wealth not because I believe religion will deliver what he promises. Avanzini's ideology serves, rather, as an illustration of the radical change in the way Christian faith is supposed to relate to economic life. The God of the Puritans was a stern ascetic who inculcated discipline and demanded contentment — or at least it is those aspects of the personality of their God that have shaped the economic history of the West most significantly; the God of the prosperity preachers is a bon vivant who promises empowerment and abundance, along with the healing of wounds that the rough life of the market inflicts. Though not without a good deal of foot-dragging, the first God helped create the squirrel cage of vanities; with the zeal of a convert, the second God wants people to have fun in it and tries to help its smooth turning as much as God can.

3. A change in God's job description could have been foreseen. To give the merry-go-round of vanities an initial push, one needed accumulation and therefore contentment. To keep it going, one needs spending. "If you want to have more cake tomorrow, you have to eat more today" (Hobson in Reich 1992, 45). This is the magic paradox of wealth creation. Since a reluctant buyer needed to be replaced by an obsessive shopper, the God who demanded asceticism needed to give way to the God who encouraged self-indulgence. Furthermore, the God who commanded disciplined work had become expendable; the inner forces of the economic system itself were exacting discipline much more efficiently than God ever could. You can resist God with impunity — or so it seems; capitalism, however, punishes promptly and implacably.

In the meantime, however, skill and insight have become much more important than hard work or even talent. As Robert B. Reich (1992) has recently argued, in the modern economy the emphasis has shifted "from high volume to high value" (81ff.). As a consequence, "symbolic-analytic" services, which include "problem-solving, problem-identifying, and strategic-brokering activities" (177) and for which "creative use of knowledge" is central (182; see also Volf 1991, 27ff.), overshadowed in importance routine production and in-person services. And that created a new market niche for God. As George Gilder puts it in "The Necessity of Faith," the last chapter in his book entitled *Wealth and Poverty* (1981), "Our greatest and only resource is the miracle of human creativity in a relation of openness to the divine" (314). From now on, God will empower and inspire creators of high value and periodically relieve overdoses of stress. High performers will not suffer divine moralizing, but they are superstitious enough to believe that they can use a bit of theurgy and religious therapy.

4. Who are the gods I dare to talk about in such an irreverent manner? Should I not rather be talking about religious *beliefs* — false religious beliefs, for that matter? But what is the difference between a false religious belief and an idol, except that one is *in* your head and the other *outside* it? A Christian who finds himself protesting against my insolence would insist that one god or the other — depending on the camp he comes from — was none other than the God of Jesus Christ. In response I would not deny some resemblance, but would underscore that the difference is glaring. Masters of subtle religious ideological manipulation engineered a gradual metamorphosis of the God of Jesus Christ into the god of this world. They were shrewd enough not to overdo it, however. The mask of the old God was retained; appearances must be kept up, you know.

The subtlety of the metamorphic solution might be new. The project of discarding uncomfortable gods is old. Consider Deuteronomic warnings for Israel not to forget the Lord their God who brought them out of the land of Egypt: "When you have eaten your fill and have built fine houses and live in them, and when your herds and flocks have multiplied, and your silver and gold is multiplied, and all that you have is multiplied, then do not exalt yourself, forgetting the Lord your God" (Deut. 8:12-14).

If a person is religious, when he forgets the one true God, he will not simply develop a "self-made-man"-style faith with the simple credo "My power and the might of my own hand have gotten me this wealth" (Deut. 8:17); he will also "follow other gods to serve and worship them" (8:19) — gods that, like the Baal of old, promise to do marvels in stimulating infinite growth and creating boundless prosperity. If not carefully attended to, wealth develops occult powers that erase memories of the one true God and generate new gods that are more congenial to its well-being.

What is good for wealth might not be good for its owners, however.

Deuteronomy 8 ends with a threat of judgment to those who run after the gods whose only function is to bless insatiability and all the means to play up to it: ". . . so shall you perish" (v. 20). The cage will self-destruct and its gods will perish with it. For all their iron grip on the lives of people, both the cage and its gods are "like grass" and all their "glory like the flower of grass" (1 Pet. 1:24).

Unlocking the Door

1. Here is the predicament of the God *in* the cage: If God rebels, God gets discarded; if God does not rebel, God gets co-opted; other less stark options are combinations of these two. I have no scruples about siding with a discarded God; rather, I have qualms about co-opting God myself. A discarded God might have lost usefulness for some people or even whole cultures; a co-opted God has lost divine dignity. One *ought not* have any use for a God without dignity. A God *with* dignity, on the other hand, might be of some benefit even to those who know no better than to want to discard that God. God's dignity can be preserved only if God steps outside the cage. This is, of course, where the true God was all along; caught in the predicament inside the cage were the idols of this world.

The Voice from the outside said to the prophet Isaiah, "Cry out!" Perplexed, the prophet asked, "What shall I cry?" The Voice responded,

> All people are grass,
>   their constancy is like the flower of the field. . . .
> The grass withers, the flower fades;
>   but the word of our God will stand forever.
>
> (Isa. 40:6, 8)

In the previous sections I was concerned mainly with the fading of the flower. Here I want to look briefly at what the abiding word of God might have to say to our withering world. My direct interest is not to reconfigure our moral sentiments and reformulate our moral duties but to reshape our vision of the good life.

In the search for escape from the cage, I will look at some aspects of human work and consumption (in the broadest sense) and ask about their relation to religious commitments.[3] I am well aware that the cage, at least in its capitalist form, consists of much more than just attitudes and practices relating to work and consumption; it has powerful institutions and a corporate culture. The suggestions that I will make below cry out for structural underpinning. I will have to leave it to others, however, to look for possible alternatives to the present economic system (or, more precisely, for its structural improvements, for, if past experience is any guide, attempts at replacing the capitalist economic system are likely to produce worse forms of slavery). But whether we work on the institutional or the personal aspects of the problem, our task is essentially one, for the "spirit of the cage" is but one. It is totalitarian in intent too. Yet people do resist, with greater or lesser success; the cage never manages to be as nasty as it would want to be. Its inability to break down the spirit of opposition gives hope for a serene rebellion, at least on the part of a small but spirited resistance movement.

For a sufficiently disgruntled inhabitant of the cage, two simple solutions seem tempting. The first is the flight of the soul from the contingencies of the material world to the eternal and unchanging world of the Divine, to the spiritual heights of the Father in heaven. The second is the flight of the flesh-and-blood human being from the vicissitudes of the historical world to the stable cycle of nature, to the life-giving womb of "mother earth." The problem with both solutions is that one can never carry them far enough to be successful. They run counter to some stubborn features of human nature. Since we are not naked souls, our bodies in the end always triumph over any attempts at completely spurning materiality; the umbilical cord connecting us to the earth cannot be cut. But since we are not merely animal beings, our spirits always rebel against being confined to the world of pure nature; we must separate from "mother earth" and create a culture. Any viable alternative vision of the good life will have to take seriously not only God and environment but also *culture* — the world of human work and its fruits (see McClendon 1989, 93ff.).

2. At first sight it might seem that in the cage one takes work too seriously. The Puritans were called to work by God and motivated by

---

3. In the following I am drawing on more extended discussion in my two books, *Zukunft der Arbeit* (1988) and *Work in the Spirit* (1991), while at the same time developing further some aspects of that discussion.

heavenly rewards; we are forced to work and lured to it by earthly recompenses. They worked hard; we work even harder (see Schor 1992). On reflection, however, it becames clear that the problem with the cage is exactly the opposite: it *does not take work seriously enough.* Work itself is not important; what matters is that goods get produced and money put into the pocket. The less one needs to work, the better. To borrow a phrase from Horace Bushnell (1883), the cage is hard "at work to get rid of work" (22). Its view of work is purely instrumental. As Adam Smith (1937) expressed it, consumption is "the sole end and purpose of production" (625).

To free ourselves from captivity to the cage, we need to discover the *intrinsic value of work.* As the Genesis accounts of creation suggest, work is a fundamental dimension of human existence (see Volf 1991, 124-33). Work is not merely a means to life but one aspect of life. Luther and Calvin were therefore right to insist not only that human beings were originally created to work but also that God intended them to work "without inconvenience" and, "as it were, in play and with the greatest delight" (Luther 1883, 42:78; see also Calvin 1948, 125). If work is to have full human dignity, it must be important not simply as a necessary means of earning; it must be significant *as* work. The more work is its own reward, the more human dignity it will have.

But doesn't stressing the intrinsic value of work play into the hands of the cage? Won't it make the squirrel wheel spin even faster? No. It will actually slow it down. If work has intrinsic value, one will resist the pressure to produce frantically and instead take time to delight in work. In order to guard the dignity of the worker and subvert the dominance of the cage, we need to replace a production-oriented concept of work with "a *work-oriented* concept of work" (Moltmann 1984, 56; see also Johnston 1983, 136-37).

A producer in the cage is interested in production mainly because she is interested in the profit or a paycheck. As it happens, one cannot make profit without a product; consumers may be blockheads, but they cannot be persuaded to give something for nothing. Hence a producer must be indirectly interested in the product too. But a worker who cares about what she is producing only enough to ensure that consumers are willing to purchase it is not likely to enjoy her work. Henri de Man (1929) rightly spoke of the "instinct" for the finished product, which is a presupposition for enjoyment of work (39). Every good worker is something of an artist, not only enjoying what she does but also taking pride in what she has created. Paradoxical as it might sound, a work-oriented concept of work requires a *product-oriented* concept of work. If the worker does not psychologically own both the process of work and the product of work, production offends human dignity, irrespective of how high the profits or how large the paycheck may be.

3. The cage is defined today not only by fascination with efficiency in production but also by obsessive *consumption;* the two constitute a mutually reinforcing and powerful work-and-spend syndrome (see Schor 1992, 112). The cure for the syndrome cannot be found in the "light cloak" therapy of the kind Baxter suggested. For one, the therapy has never worked. Moreover, it is bad for the patient. It aggravates the existing condition, and it has serious negative side-effects. The therapy is supposed to work by combining a positive assessment of the sustained outward pursuit of wealth with the requirement of inner detachment from it. But stress on unlimited economic growth is precisely the problem with the cage. The cure can consist only in finding ways to limit growth. If the positive assessment of the pursuit of wealth takes wealth too seriously, the requirement of inner detachment from it does not take it seriously enough. The readiness at any moment to throw aside the cloak of the care for external goods assumes tacitly that the soul *can* take flight from the material world to the spheres of pure spirit. As my wife noted, only a male who merely works but does not nurture life could have come up with the idea of "the light cloak"; at *no* moment can the cloak be thrown aside without falling onto somebody else's shoulders. It has to be carried — and that is not only our fate but also our privilege. The question is, how do we keep the cloak from turning into the cage?

The answer does not lie in setting up some new version of the old distinction between necessities and luxuries that disregards the dynamic character of human needs. Rather, we should embed the valid care for external goods in the larger framework of what I have elsewhere called fundamental human needs: the need for enjoyment of God's creation, for the exercise and development of personal capacities, for cultivation of communion with our close and distant neighbors, and for the need to delight in God. All four of these closely interrelated needs coalesce in the single need for the new creation as the realm of freedom. Permit me to quote what I wrote on this need in *Work in the Spirit* (1991):

In relation to the *need for God*, the realm of freedom is a realm of perfect fellowship with God, of seeing "face to face" and of understanding as fully as one is "fully understood" (1 Cor. 13:12). In relation to the need for *solidarity with nature*, it is the realm of peace between human beings and nature liberated from corruptibility and the realm in which human beings jointly participate with nature in God's glory (Rom. 8:19ff.; Isa. 11:6f.; 65:25). In relation to the *need for fellow human beings*, it is the realm of unadulterated fellowship with one another, of pure "love, which binds everything together in perfect harmony" (Col. 3:14). In relation to the *need for personal development*, it is the realm in which life is "realized only to be opened up to as yet unrealized possibilities" (Jüngel). (154)

The realm of freedom is an eschatological vision of the good life. This vision is the broadest framework in which we ought to place the creation of wealth and the satisfaction of dynamic needs for external goods. The more our production and consumer choices are guided by this vision rather than simply by our private satisfaction, the more humane they will be (see Meeks 1989, 157ff.).

4. Although the God I am talking about might not be sufficiently interested in efficiency and productivity to be useful to the cage, this God delights in good work. From Genesis 1 and 2 we learn that work "belongs to the very purpose for which God originally made" human beings (Hengel 1986, 179). Correspondingly, the Spirit of God calls and inspires people to use their abilities in doing good work in anticipation of God's new creation. Any remnants of the notion that, apart from keeping the worker's body and soul together, the only significance of work lies in the exercise it provides for our spiritual muscles ought to be discarded.

The God who inspires good work ensures that none of it will be ultimately wasted. Without God, all human work has "the life span of a sand castle at the ocean's edge" (Haughey 1989, 99): the worker and his work will ultimately dissolve into the thin vapor of vanity; even their memory will be erased (see Eccles. 2:12-17; 3:18-21). With God, however, all good work — everything good, true, and beautiful that human beings create — will be eternally preserved (see Volf 1991, 88-102; Haughey 1989, 99-115). "God seeks out what has gone by," reads an obscure passage in Ecclesiastes (3:15b). Could the idea be that "nothing that the slippage of time drives away is lost" (Lohfink 1980, 33), that "God gathers up forgotten time, lost works, all that has taken flight"? (Ellul 1990, 68).

Life in the cage is predicated on insatiability. The cage perceives correctly that human "wants cannot be satiated" (Thurow 1980, 120), but it resists the notion that striving to satisfy them by economic means only encloses human beings into a circle of what Hegel (1976) called "false infinity" (§185). The only proper "object" of human insatiability is the mystery of the infinite God. As Karl Rahner (1966) points out, the supreme act of knowledge of God "is not the abolition or diminution of the mystery but its final assertion" (40; see also Jüngel 1978, 341). Every act of knowing God both satisfies and engenders human curiosity; every encounter with God both quenches and deepens human thirst. In the infinite being of God, the incessant movement of the human spirit begins to arrive at its final rest.

How different is the endless exploration of the mystery of God from the futility of the earthly progress predicated on insatiability? How different are the divine quenching and deepening of human thirst from the cage's satisfying and creating of wants? As different as the heavens are from the earth! But why then should we not call the encounter between the inexhaustible God and the insatiable human being a *heavenly* cage of vanities? Because human beings are made to find ultimate fulfillment in the mystery of God. The cage thrives because it capitalizes on our longings for the inexhaustible God. It could be that we project our worldly ideals onto God, as Feuerbach (1957) argued. God's infinity would then be the reverse side of human insatiability (Meeks 1989, 168). But I rather suspect that we are involved in an inverse projection by which we infuse the works of our own hands with the ability to satisfy hunger for infinity. The endless stream of new goods and services has become a cornucopia of mystery, protection, and salvation. We call it progress. But its real name is *prayer* (so Yalom 1992, 233, of love).

"What do they not know, who know him who knows all things?" asked Saint Gregory rhetorically. Thomas Aquinas (1975) used the idea to argue "that those who see the divine substance do see all things" (III/I, 196-97). If Aquinas is right, then it should be legitimate to modify Gregory's question to read, "What do they not enjoy who enjoy God, who makes all things new?" Because God does not desire to be without the created world, because God gathers all lost works, enjoyment of God cannot be a purely "spiritual," worldless enjoyment. It may seem that in turning to the mystery of God, we turn our backs to the whole created world of the good, the true, and the beautiful. In fact, when we turn to God, we find that same world in God, sanctified and glorified. In God, in whom nothing worth preserving is lost, everything worth enjoying can be enjoyed.

Deep Ecology
and Moral Community

ALBERT BERGESEN

THE REAGAN/THATCHER 1980s raised the moral status of avaricious materialism, greed, and self-interest, in response to which, in the 1990s, assertions of the importance of communitarian values are pouring forth (Bellah et al. 1985, 1991; Wuthnow 1991; Etzioni 1993). Community, collective values, and caring human institutions are poised as counters to the untrammeled freedom of materialism as the moral foundation for the good society. In this context I want to consider environmentalism as another alternative moral position to self-seeking materialism.

In its most general outline, the environmental critique of materialist ethics is well known: our culture of personal desire for more and more goods whatever the cost to the ecosystem and our placing of profits above environmental concerns represent the heart of what is thought to be responsible for a deteriorating environment. We must change our ways of living and thinking to reduce the continuing damage to the ecosystem, or any number of severe crises will ensue. There is also a consensus on this mainstream environmentalism across the political spectrum. The conservative George Bush wanted to be known as the environmental president, and the more liberal Al Gore (1992) wrote a passionate book in defense of the environment. There are disagreements

For helpful comments I would like to thank Robert Wuthnow, James Ranger-Moore, Marc Schneiberg, David Gibbs, Rebecca Salome Shaw, Max Herman, and Richard Hutchinson. This research is supported by the University of Arizona.

on whether global warming is a real problem and the extent of the hole in the ozone layer, but preserving the environment as a way of preserving humanity seems beyond disagreement.

Such mainstream environmentalism is a clear alternative to a destructive materialism. There is, however, another branch of environmental thinking that challenges not only self-seeking materialism but also the social values of anti-materialist communitarian ethics. This radical environmentalism, which is associated with the idea of "deep ecology" (Naess 1986; Devall and Sessions 1993; Fox 1990; LaChapelle 1988; Shabecoff 1993), attributes equality to all forms of life, human and nonhuman, in what is called "biocentric equality." The environment should be preserved not because of its instrumental value to humans, but because of its inherent value and the right of all life forms to develop on their own. While the specific idea of deep ecology is associated with the Norwegian philosopher Arne Naess, who coined the term, and the California environmentalists Bill Devall and George Sessions, who explicated the idea, the radical environmentalist movement includes a range of groups and beliefs: animal-rights philosophers (Singer 1977), ecofeminists (LaChapelle 1988; Plant 1989; Merchant 1993), and the ecoreligion of primitive and indigenous peoples on the sacredness of the earth (Badiner 1990; Oelschlaeger 1992).

The central idea of deep ecology has been articulated by Naess and Devall: "The well-being and flourishing of human and nonhuman Life on Earth have value in themselves (synonyms: intrinsic value, inherent value). These values are independent of the usefulness of the nonhuman world for human purposes" (quoted in List 1993, 43). The Australian philosopher Warwick Fox puts the key assumption this way: "It is the idea that we can make no firm ontological divide in the field of existence: That there is no bifurcation in reality between the human and the non-human realms. . . . To the extent that we perceive boundaries, we fall short of deep ecological consciousness" (quoted in Devall and Sessions 1993, 39).

Deep Ecology Broadens the Moral Community

What animal rights, deep ecology, and the radical environmental movement in general reflect is a growing dissolution of the moral boundary between human and nonhuman life. This moral line is not changing all at once, nor for all aspects of the natural world. The willingness to grant membership in a broadened community seems to decline with distance from humans, in what could be called a concern-distance ratio. By the late twentieth century, the idea of universal human rights extending to all people seems, in theory at least, firmly in place, and violations are reported around the globe. These rights are, of course, defended and enforced more in some areas than others, and much work remains to be done to have them extended around the world. The barrier to extending this moral community to nonhumans has been broken through with growing prohibitions against using animals in laboratory experiments, where they might be injured in the testing of cosmetics or explicitly killed for nonessential products such as fur coats. Where the experimentation involves medical research tied to human betterment, animal rights are more controversial and less forcefully fought for.

When we move beyond animals, the moral concern thins quickly. If we jump in a broad categorical way from animals to plants of all sorts, the deep ecological idea of intrinsic unalienable rights and moral worth gives way to the position of preservation for usefulness to humans. It is argued that we need to preserve wilderness areas for human needs — for example, that we need to preserve the Brazilian rain forest because of its effect on the atmosphere, or because of the medicines that can be extracted from it. When we move all the way out to the category of things called "inanimate," like the land, there is the least moral sympathy and little of a moral defense that isn't tied to human betterment. The progress in extending the moral community, then, is slow, but it is occurring, and in theory it poses a clear challenge to the human-centeredness of traditional religious and social moralisms. How the moral community is broadening, and what challenges this poses to the moral foundations of traditional communitarian ethics, are the issues I want to examine here. In the late twentieth century, we are rethinking not only materialism but also the social ethics of anti-materialism.

The challenge of deep ecology to communitarian social ethics is to broaden the operative moral base from that of humans to the ecosystem as a whole. If there is no fundamental divide in the realm of existence between human and nonhuman life forms, then "humanism" implicitly becomes an eco-tribalism, a moral primacy of one species over others. No matter how radical or "humanitarian," moralism about human betterment (at minimum) or secular or religious salvation (at maximum) — socialism or heaven — is now, by definition, a redemption of only some members of the ecosystem. The past goal of a perfected, free, human community is now simply too narrow. This is the moral challenge of environmentalism. Schemes that do not include nonhuman life forms in their plans for ultimate redemption are, by definition, less than total, and hence are based on a less than ultimate morality. The secular morality of human betterment has been based on sentient, feeling, conscious beings — us, humanity. The body of moral human thinking since the Renaissance has been based on the idea that everyone was included in the liberation project. Equal rights for all, freedom for all, democracy for all, unalienated labor for all — and, with these things, emancipation for all. But now, assuming the deep-ecology value of biocentric equality, the "all" of the human liberation project is reduced to "some," one species over others.

Environmentalism is usually thought of in terms of the more physical issues of waste products, ozone layers, animal extinction, rain forests, and so on. There is an ongoing debate over these issues in the scientific community. But the idea of preserving or caring for the ecosystem has also begun to raise philosophical issues about the value and rights of nature — instrumental versus intrinsic value, the rights of trees (Stone 1974), and so forth. These debates have occurred primarily among environmental philosophers, ethicists, and legal scholars. But these issues also raise a direct challenge to the sociologist's bounding of community and the human centricity that has been the bedrock of morality since the Renaissance. While the morality issue is key, it is clearly interconnected with the sociological issue of where the line of membership in the moral order should be drawn. Deep ecology suggests that moral community may be broader than sociology, Marxism, or liberalism ever conceived. The ecological sense of community includes all living things, which broadens and alters not only ideas of membership rights but also ideas about the classic social issues of who exploits and who dominates whom. Previously the question of hierarchy and domination was contained within the human community, and what was to be overcome was, accordingly, intrahuman exploitation and oppression.

For Marx, for example, the domination of nature was a goal, something to be done willfully to further the liberation project of humankind. That this is wrong, or a kind of oppression, creates confusion over exactly who is to be liberated from what. If nature is no longer an inanimate object to be owned, used, exploited, and conquered, but a primal subjectivity of equivalent moral status to humankind, then how is it to be included in the revolutionary project? What role does nature play? Does it act for itself? And if not, what are the moral responsibilities of nature's ecosystemic brothers and sisters in facilitating nature's emancipation? Obviously, no one knows the answers to these questions. They are just coming to the edge of progressive consciousness. Ironically, those most committed to various programs for radical social change find themselves threatened by nature's claim for equal moral status. Those who are most imaginatively progressive are often the most resistant to a progressive agenda for nature. Progressives, leftists, and humanists have long been cynical about environmentalists and the rights of animals, let alone the rights of trees and rocks. There are hopeful signs, however, that this is changing, with the left becoming more concerned with issues of "green justice" and "environmental racism" (Bullard 1993).

Social moralists have been aware of and have sought to correct the exploitation of poor by rich, of women by men, of people of color by white Europeans and their descendants. But these moral struggles against classism, sexism, and racism are only attempts to heal the wounds of a single species. These social movements and theories of liberation and emancipation do not, per se — and this is the important point — heal the wounds between humans and nature. These attempts to heal the schisms of humanity and, with such a fundamental reunification, to attain a kind of secular salvation and human redemption, do not include nature.

Put most boldly: all theories of liberation, emancipation, salvation, and redemption that are centered only on humans, even if successful, will have redeemed only a portion of the living sentient universe, and as a consequence, any claims to a very profound and deep — hence religious — redemption are limited in scope. Environmentalism, then, undercuts and cripples the certainty of the redemptive claim to moral healing that was humanism. Some could argue that each life form is responsible for its own salvation project, and that human responsibility ends where animals begin. But when the fates of humans and animals — and the rest of nature — are interconnected, then "going it alone" is practically impossible and morally indefensible.

From this point of view, we are at the end of the era of social morality as the morality of human totality. Whether heaven or socialism — if only humankind qualifies, that is not enough. If the full range of life forms do not also have the possibility for heaven (some kind of religious redemption) or socialism/liberalism (some kind of economic/political emancipation), then Heaven isn't heaven and Socialism isn't socialism. As long as other species and, in principle, the earth as a living entity (Lovelock 1979) are left out of prescriptive theologies and social philosophies, they become more limited in scope, less potent in moral claim, and more irrelevant to what will be the moral issues of the twenty-first century.

From the Social to the Ecological Revolution

This coming change of which I speak can be better understood by considering it in the context of the human-centered moral revolution that environmentalism is now replacing. Starting with the Renaissance or, more clearly, the Enlightenment, the sacred and the moral were secularized in a way that separated "modernity" from earlier times. Sacredness was moved from the heavens to humankind, and it was explicated in the specification of human rights thought unalienable. From the age of faith in the Middle Ages to the age of humanism, we felt that through our moral principles, economics, and politics, we were the masters of our destiny. We believed that we wrested our fate from the heavens and gave it to ourselves. We made society, laws, and politics, and in a growing body of moral political philosophy, we defined ourselves as creatures with unalienable rights to freedom, dignity, and independence, rights derived from nothing more than our humanness. This unalienable status gave human rights their moral and religious significance. Accordingly, anything that would block the realization of these rights and freedoms would be opposed in moral theory.

Governed neither by the laws of nature nor by those of heaven, humankind, having carved out a middle zone of existence between the heavens and the animal kingdom, was its own master (Wolfe 1993). As such, we could make our world fit pictures of future societies that our moral imagination could construct. And construct we did. Through the ideals of secular humanism, the documents of the American and French Revolutions, the ideas of socialism in the nineteenth century, and the concepts of human rights in the twentieth, we have constructed a body of moral theory about who we are, what rights are ours, and what we want out of life. The key assumption is that all humans have an intrinsic worth regardless of their hierarchic division by class, ethnicity, race, gender, nationality, or sexual preference. That is, divisions within the human community are illegitimate and immoral to the extent that they block and deny the realization of fundamental rights. The prescriptive component is that humans should work against these divisions, by reform or revolution, so that at some future time a better, more egalitarian, and freer world of human relations will come into being.

The moral breach is not so much between God and humankind as between classes, genders, people with different sexual preferences, races, and ethnic groups. We are separated not from the divine but from each other and from ourselves. From attitudinal bigotry to patriarchal hierarchy to class division, we are divided and alienated by political and economic systems that do not allow the mastery of our own political fate, physical bodies, and labor power. Healing this breach in the human community by creating a new wholeness that would reunify was the essence of the modern path of moral salvation and redemption. This moral impulse to align the human world with idealized blueprints of human association includes all political persuasions. Conservatives wish to protect freedoms that already exist, liberals work for change within the system, and radicals work to overthrow the system.

Since the Renaissance, division after division has been opposed. In the sixteenth and seventeenth centuries, it was religion. The religious barrier was removed with the idea that everyone was, in principle, entitled to his or her own religious beliefs as a fundamental right. By the eighteenth century, the targets were unrepresentative political forms, the aristocracy, the monarchy, and the absolutist state. Rights to free assembly, to free speech, and to direct access to political decisions were fought for, won, and embodied in the moral documents of the American and French Revolutions. By the nineteenth century, the hierarchical division of humankind by wealth through capitalism came under attack, and in the twentieth century, the ideals of universal human rights fill out the packet of secular morality that makes up the humanist project of moral redemption. Each of these surges toward religious, political, and economic equality built upon what went before, so that liberal democratic theory included religious freedom, and the socialist utopia included both democracy and religious freedom (in theory at least).

This brings us to the end of the twentieth century and to the next stage in the expansion of egalitarian moral community. The jump this time is much greater and will involve a much deeper rethinking of morality. As the idea of moral community is broadened to include all life forms, there is an implicit decentering of humankind and its morality. This does not mean a degradation of humans, although in the fervor to elevate the rights of the environment, that sometimes appears to be the case. The goals of humanism are not to be discarded but subsumed within a larger and more fully encompassing moral theory in which redemption is granted not only to humans but to other life forms as well. This means a new conception of moral community and the means for its redemption or reunification. The claim that we are entering a period of post-socialist, post-Marxist, or post-Enlightenment moral projects has been raised before, but the post-modernist pluralistic celebration of the distinctions of gender, race, ethnicity, and sexual preference, while a new particularism different from the hegemonic universalism of traditional social, economic, and political theory, represents only a further advancement of the rights of members of the human community. This furthering of human emancipation is not new. It just involves new people. Post-modernism and multiculturalism do not include animals or nature per se. They involve more rights for more humans — different humans, exploited humans, yes, but still humans.

The depth of the new moral claim and the breadth of the included community go together. The broader the community that a theoretical perspective encompasses, the more inclusive — and hence the deeper — its moral claim. To the utilitarian ethicists of unfettered individualism, the socialists and contemporary social communitarians have posed the rights and obligations of a larger institutional and societal community. But now, the deep ecologists define this human community as but another form of unfettered individualism, humanity as but one "individual species." Just as social philosophy of a moral and redemptive nature (from Marxism to today's new communitarianism) critiqued self-seeking individualism, now it is a self-seeking human "species-ism" that is critiqued from the perspective of a still larger community — the ecosphere.

One way to understand the changes is to see what we have been through as something that could be called waves of moral widening: first the social over the individual, and now the ecological over the social. Each claims a broader and deeper morality, and each indicts the other for narrow self-centeredness. For so long the social communitarian perspective seemed the "broadest of the broad," embracing as it did all of humankind — and as such the most profoundly selfless, caring, and moral stance. So what a shock it is to have the humanist moral high ground attacked as but an amoral, destructive force within the new wider biocommunity. From the fifteenth to the twentieth century, humanism broadened the bounds of moral community to include, in principle, all humans. But now, as we move into the twenty-first century, the holism of the past six hundred years appears as a self-centered partialism. In effect, the critique of the social moralists — that individual materialism is self-seeking and indifferent to the broader community — is now leveled at them by the deep ecologists. Again, the key is the broadening of the moral community, which has the effect of transforming the previous holism of humanism into a partialism from the viewpoint of deep ecology. The sacred is also moving from humanity to the ecosystem, and those philosophies, theologies, and prescriptive ethics that aim toward the reunification and redemption of this widened ecocommunity will soon supplant those of the earlier socialism, humanism, and communitarianism.

The Counterattack of Social Morality

Because of this development, social ethicists are on the defensive, lashing out against the green challenge to their moral hegemony. Charged with putting human rights before animal rights and with promoting an elite use of national parks over the masses' enjoyment of unspoiled nature, the counterattack of social ethicists has been strong. From what we know about the sociology of boundary maintenance and defensiveness, it would make sense that those most committed to the humanistic ideal would be the most threatened by a challenge to their status. Therefore, it is not surprising that those most committed to ideals of human progress, human rights, and a caring social community are the most defensive about sharing their hard-won rights to the moral life with the new claimants from nature. For them, the extension of rights to other species seems a loss for humans and a downgrading of human achievement: "Human affairs become not especially noteworthy, their patterns and activities a by-product of majestic ecological laws, in comparison to which our own fears, desires, and needs seem puny" (Wolfe 1993, 83). Gains for animals are seen as losses for humans: "To live by the tenets of animal rights is to bring about equality between the human and other animal species not by elevating the latter but by lowering the former" (Wolfe 1993, 91).

One response to the green challenge is to reassert the values of the threatened humanist position. For example, consider how Alan Wolfe justifies "some cruelty" to animals: "Hunting is no doubt cruel. But here, too, animal rights advocates lack appreciation for the symbolic meaning of human practices such as hunting. . . . Is it preferable to live life without religion, sport, and creativity and at the same time not be cruel or to accept at least some cruelty for the sake of a greater richness of meaning?" (Wolfe 1993, 89, 90). Wolfe argues for cruelty to animals from the position of the highest of human values, and if maintaining those values requires "at least some cruelty" — well then, so be it.

But this picture looks very different from the deep ecological view. What was once so high and noble is now a self-centered individualism that creates pain and cruelty for others. To see the difference, just substitute "human" for "animal" in the above quotation and see how Wolfe's position reads. Is "at least some cruelty" shown to human beings morally tolerable for the sake of sport or religion? Of course not, which illustrates the importance of the location of the boundary of moral community. In his now classic essay entitled "The Land Ethic" (1987), the environmentalist Aldo Leopold argues, "The land ethic simply enlarges the boundaries of the community to include soils, waters, plants, and animals, or collectively: the land" (204). If moral boundaries were to be so enlarged, cruelty to animals would be as immoral as cruelty to humans.

Social Ecology

Wolfe represents arguments for the continued supremacy of human interests above those of other life forms, but there are also representatives of halfway positions — half social project and half ecology project. But note that the human and social half comes first, because for many, as Murray Bookchin (1990) explains, "all ecological problems are social problems" (24). The moral imperative of Bookchin and other social ecologists is to heal the breach within the human community before attempting to heal the breach between humans and the environment. An outspoken opponent of deep ecology, Bookchin argues that to speak of the whole of humanity vis-à-vis the environment is to diminish the moral importance of relations within humanity, such as those of class, oppression, and gender. "Of course," Bookchin says, "we are not any less animals than other mammals, but we are more than herds that browse on the African plains. The way in which we are more — namely, the *kinds* of societies that we form and how we are divided against each other into hierarchies and classes — profoundly affects our behavior and our efforts on the natural world" (23). For Bookchin, humans and their society still come first, and only by altering the materialism of capitalism will it be possible to deal with nature on better terms. As long as the human community is dominated by the capitalist mode of production that places profits before nature, it will be impossible to change our relationship to the ecosystem.

Eco-Marxism

With the growing pressure of environmental concerns, some traditional theories of change, like Marxism, are building a distinctly ecological component into their social logic. But in this adaptation, as in the adaptation by social ecologists, the human and the social still come first: change capitalism, and that will change relations with the environment. The alternative of deep ecology would be: change relations with nature, and that will change capitalism. The ecological Marxists are merely extending the logic of the old social model of relations within the human community (class relations under capitalism) to the environment, such that the crisis of capitalism now manifests itself in a crisis of the environment.

One example of eco-Marxist thinking can be found in an essay by James O'Connor (1992), who argues that neither labor power nor external nature are produced capitalistically, although both are bought and sold capitalistically. Thus he speaks of a capitalization of nature. Now the crisis-ridden nature of capitalism means that it destroys external nature and thereby destroys the conditions of its own existence. According to O'Connor, "Examples of capitalist accumulation impairing or destroying capital's own conditions, hence threatening its own profits and capacity to reproduce and accumulate more capital, are well known. The warming of the atmosphere will inevitably destroy people, places and profits. . . . Acid rain destroys forests and lakes and buildings and profit. . . . Salinization of water tables, toxic wastes, soil erosion, etc. impair nature and profitability. The pesticide treadmill destroys profits as well as nature" (189). Therefore, external nature can be part of the internality of capitalist production because external nature is commodified and capitalized.

Ecofeminism

Another example of the social/environmental mix is ecofeminism. Ecofeminists, like the social ecologists and eco-Marxists, argue that social relations will have to change if our relations with nature are to change. Carolyn Merchant (1993) states the problem succinctly: "For socialist ecofeminism, environmental problems are rooted in the rise of capitalist patriarchy and the ideology that the Earth and nature can be exploited for human progress through technology" (51). According to Merchant, "Radical ecofeminism analyzes environmental problems from within its critique of patriarchy and offers alternatives that could liberate both women and nature" (49). Ynestra King (1993) offers this sobering comment: "The special message of ecofeminism is that, when women suffer through both social domination and the domination of nature, most of life on this planet suffers and is threatened" (76).

While there are a great variety of ecofeminist positions (for a review, see Merchant 1992, 183-210), the central thrust of them is that the domination of nature grows out of the domination of women by men. Since society is patriarchal, societal domination of nature is domination by men; accordingly, the end of patriarchy will result in the end of nature's domination. Here again we see the anthropocentrism of assuming the central place of humankind: changing gender relations will change the relations between humankind and nature.

The Eco-Paradigm Revolution

Each of these three groups sees nature from its own perspective. Social ecologists and eco-Marxists see environmental problems as capitalist problems, and ecofeminists see them as patriarchal problems. If these problems can be solved, they say, then the problems with nature can be solved. This causal logic can be contrasted with that of the position of deep ecology. These alternative causal models for environmental change are diagrammed below:

Social Model

Change Capitalism   →   Change Human Relations to Nature
Change Patriarchy   →   Change Human Relations to Nature

Deep Ecology Model

Change Human Relations to Nature   →   Change Capitalism
Change Human Relations to Nature   →   Change Patriarchy

The social model and the deep ecology model represent two fundamentally different approaches that have different implications for strategies of change (Bergesen 1980, 1990). The first employs something more like micro logic, working from the parts to whole, and the second employs something more like macro logic, working from the whole to the parts. Historically, microanalysis is associated with utilitarianism and neoclassical economics, in which it is assumed that people have pre-social wants, needs, and desires, the free pursuit of which results in the institutional fabric of collective economic and social life. This logic undergirds the self-seeking materialism that the new communitarian ethics seeks to replace with a more caring, companionate web of human institutional relations. Macroanalysis is associated with the rise of sociology, in which it is theorized that social structure exists prior to individual behavior, and thereby exercises a constraint upon it. "Micro" causal logic reasons upward from the individual parts to the social whole. "Macro" causal logic reasons downward from the structural relations of the larger community to the behavior of individuals. Today these differences are seen in micro rational-choice theory (Coleman 1990) versus macro sociological structuralism.

It is important to realize, however, that "macro" and "micro" are relative terms. In the theory of utilitarians, the larger social structure, whether it be capitalism or patriarchy, constitutes a "macro" extra-individual environment. But when the definition of "macro" is broadened, as it was broadened here in the discussion about including the ecosystem in the moral community, then capitalism and patriarchy are transformed into micro objects. From the ecosystem perspective, the human species is a self-seeking "individual maximizer," a sort of collective utilitarian entity, that is wreaking destruction on the ecocommunity of earth. When the macroanalysis is based on the structural relations of the ecosystem, focusing on capitalism and patriarchy is a kind of microanalysis that does not take into account the larger structures in which capitalism and patriarchy are embedded. Macro eco-relations are now mystified, creating a new Robinson Crusoe myth, except that instead of free-willed individuals devoid of society, we now have social orders devoid of the ecosystem.

The radical analyses of social ecology, eco-Marxism, and ecofeminism are "radical" only when the human species is the totality of analysis. Then these economic and gender relations are the brackets that shape, control, and constrain the individual behaviors within their parameters. However, they are not so radical in an ecosystem analysis, because then they are no longer the external brackets but an internal component, now bracketed and framed by a still broader and higher level of analysis. The societal frame is itself being framed: gender and economic relations are structured by the relations of the larger human/environmental system.

The emerging crisis for social theory, from Marxism to feminism to liberalism, is that the level of analysis is being ratcheted up a notch, making yesterday's macroanalysis today's microanalysis. The key to the macro position was the insight that to focus only upon individual actors was to miss the larger web of relations in which they were embedded. If we apply that macro position from the perspective of deep ecology, we see that to ascribe the environmental crisis to human gender or economic relations is to blindly focus upon a part of the ecosystem without seeing the larger set of ecostructural relations within which capitalist and gender relations are embedded.

This is the same error that pre-sociological economic thinkers made in arguing that individuals who buy and sell make capitalism, rather than realizing that it is capitalism which makes people buy and sell. On an environmental scale, the argument would be that it is not an individual species acting capitalistically and patriarchally that makes for a malfunctioning ecosystem, but a malfunctioning ecosystem that makes a species act in a capitalistic and partriarchal way. Humans are still the most powerful and hierarchically privileged within the ecosystem, just as the upper class is the most privileged class within the capitalist social system. But the human species, like the upper class, is still governed by the laws of the larger system in which it is embedded.

In the nineteenth century, sociology constituted a revolution in the human sciences because it inverted the parts-to-whole logic of the utilitarian classical economists. In the twenty-first century, the revolution in thought will involve a similar paradigm shift. Societal analysis (whether of capitalism, patriarchy, racism, world systems) is based on the mistaken notion that the behavior of an individual species is eco-structurally free and therefore creates the resulting ecosystem. By this I do not mean to say that greedy human behavior isn't tied to the environmental crisis, any more than the behavior of greedy capitalists isn't tied to the problems of the working class. But capitalists are not intrinsically or naturally greedy and "self-maximizing." That was Adam Smith's error: assuming that humans had a natural propensity to barter, when such behavior was a necessity forced and prescribed by a particular historical mode of production. Max Weber noted the error and attributed the rational calculating of the capitalist to the religious ethic of Protestantism, while Marx argued that the capitalist mode of production made necessary such self-maximizing buying and selling. The same point holds for men dominating women. It isn't an intrinsic or natural propensity so much as it is a product of the larger system of patriarchy.

Revolutionize patriarchy and change the behavior of men; revolutionize the capitalist mode of production and change the behavior of capitalists; and, following the same logic, revolutionize the ecological system of human/nature relations and change the behavior of the human economy (capitalism) and gender relations (patriarchy). That is the truly radical implication of deep ecology. Humans dominate nature not because of their intrinsic nature, any more than capitalists dominate labor or men dominate women because of something intrinsic about capitalists or men. They occupy positions within an order, a system of relations, or a mode of production, and it is at that level, at the systemic level, that revolutionary action must be targeted for any real change to occur. Otherwise, the change will be piecemeal and ameliorative and will not get at the root causes of the environmental problem.

What is required, then, is a new set of scientific principles that deal with the human species in structural relation to the rest of the ecosystem, the same way that sociology and other social theories dealt with the structural relations between groups of humans, whether by class, race, ethnic group, or gender group. What we now need is a theory of species to species, of human to earth, of species to ecosphere relations. Any such ecological theory will have to present a further deepening of human emancipation above and beyond that specified in the human-centered proposals for liberation over the past six hundred years. Turning things over to the animals, to the "laws of nature," at the expense of human well-being, will not be a successful strategy. In the redemptive social philosophy of the past, everyone gained: there was liberty for all, democracy for all, equality for all, economic justice for all — in short, salvation and redemption for all. The emerging ecological theory will also have to have promises for "all," except now the "all" is more than just humans — it is all living things. Marxism versus liberalism, capitalism versus socialism, patriarchy versus feminism, or the developed versus the underdeveloped countries — these are simply debates within the human community. This discourse has its place and is important. But it can no longer have the hegemony — in scientific theory or moral discourse — that it has had over the past six hundred years. The era of human-only discourse is at an end. The era of eco-human discourse is just beginning.

Is Deep Ecology Enough?

Is deep ecology as it is presently formulated ready to be the successor to the social model of change not only for intra-human relations (e.g., issues of class, gender, race, and ethnicity) but also for human-to-nature relations? The answer is both yes and no. Yes, in terms of the previously discussed effort to broaden the moral community. From what I have seen, arguments against such a moral broadening are principally defensive. I would include here the foot-dragging of the social ecologists, the eco-Marxists, and the ecofeminists, who are willing to go along with the environmental agenda as long as their social project is given primacy. But I would say that deep ecology is not ready to replace any other model of change in a substantive way because there is little in deep ecology theory other than utopian ideas of altering consciousness as a strategy for revolutionizing human/environmental relations.

While deep ecology's strategies for change seem radical to most, including many within the environmental movement, they are actually more idealist and utopian than materialist and radical. Consider for a moment an analogy with the development of another radical theory of change — socialism. If we compare deep ecology theory with the theory of socialism, deep ecology is very similar to the stage known as "utopian socialism," during which the program to bring about a changed world involved changing personal beliefs and ideas, along with withdrawing into local, communal, small-scale living arrangements. This pre-1848 "utopian socialism" is associated with the ideas of Saint-Simon, Charles Fourier, and Robert Owen, and can be contrasted with the "historical materialist socialism" associated with the writings of Marx and Engels. Here change was linked to the laws of the new field of economics and to the material specifics of the historical process, including the objective conditions of the working class. By contrast, the nineteenth-century utopians focused their strategies upon changing existing religious, moral, and political ideologies, which is very similar to the present strategy of deep ecology, which involves urging people to develop as deep and broadened an "ecological self" or "earth consciousness" as possible. Arne Naess speaks of the importance of developing as "expansive a self as possible," meaning a self that identifies with nature and the larger cosmic totality rather than one that is narrowly defined by itself. This is a primary emphasis found in the work of many writers on deep ecology:

> When we use the word "Deep Ecology" here, we are referring to the philosophical approach described by George Sessions, Bill Devall, Arne Naess, and others. . . . Using Naess's terminology, we can say that the follower of the Deep Ecology Way practices extended self-identification . . . [which] involves an extension of one's concerns, commitments, and political actions. (Drengson quoted in Fox 1990, 235)

I shall only offer one single sentence resembling a definition of the ecological self. The ecological self of a person is that with which this person identifies. This key sentence (rather than definition) about the self shifts the burden of clarification from the term "self" to that of "identification," or rather "process of identification." . . . [This] outlook is developed through an identification so deep that one's *own* self is no longer adequately delimited by the personal ego or the organism. One experiences oneself to be a genuine part of all life. (Naess quoted in Fox 1990, 230)

Ecological consciousness is the result of a *psychological* expansion of the narrowly encapsulated sense of self as isolated ego, through identifications with all humans (species chauvinism), to finally an awareness of identification and interpenetration of self with ecosystem and biosphere. (Sessions quoted in Fox 1990, 234)

The key point here is that the deep ecological means for revolutionizing relations between humans and the environment is a mystical process of self-willed personal identification with nature: See yourself as one with nature, and good things will follow:

As the implications of evolution and ecology are internalized and replace the outmoded anthropocentric structures in your mind, there is an identification with all life. . . . [Thus] "I am protecting the rain forest" develops to "I am part of the rain forest protecting myself. I am that part of the rain forest recently emerged into thinking." (Seed quoted in Fox 1990, 239)

If one can identify with nature, then benevolent behavior toward the environment outflows, naturally, organically — hence the environmental revolution. But, as I argued before, trying to change only beliefs and attitudes and consciousness without altering the larger matrix of human/environmental material relations will not produce the desired change. Like utopian socialism, what could be called *utopian ecology* is a theoretical perspective devoid of a deep sense of transformative dynamics or of a process linked to the evolutionary dynamics of our present malfunctioning ecostructural system. The "utopian" element of deep ecology is that it is an ideal blueprint for a transformed set of relations between humans and the environment that is attainable solely through imaginative efforts, the goal being to see oneself as part of, or as one with, the larger universe.

To see this more clearly, imagine a theory of social change that would tell feudal serfs, Roman slaves, or industrial factory workers that to change their condition, all they would have to do was think of themselves differently. But if there is only a change in self-identity but no change in the real, material, structural relations of the people with these changed identities, it is naive and utopian to expect real change. Without changing the lord-serf relations of feudalism, the patrician-slave relations of slavery, or the capital-labor relations of capitalism, serfs, slaves, and workers could imagine themselves any way they wanted to; nothing of significance would happen. The notion of "false consciousness" arose to describe this very phenomenon, in which the class position that class actors perceived themselves as occupying was different from the position they actually occupied.

Seen in this light, isn't Naess's broadened "ecological self" a similar kind of false consciousness? When John Seed says, "I am part of the rain forest," and when Robert Aitken says, "Deep ecology . . . requires openness to the black bear, becoming truly intimate with the black bear, so that honey dribbles down your fur as you catch the bus to work" (quoted in Fox 1990, 239), in what sense are these anything but psychological sleights of hand that, while possibly making the environmental activist feel better, are only delusions at best, and, at worst, mystifications of our malfunctioning ecosystem's objective human/environmental relations?

The reality of human domination of nature continues in objective fact, perpetuated and reproduced in the ecostructural relations of our present malfunctioning ecosystem. Seeing oneself as one with the bear or the rain forest is not the same as *being* one with the bear and the rain forest. They are subjective actors oppressed in our malfunctioning ecosystem, and revolutionizing the existent ecosystemic relations is the path to their liberation, not merely developing the expansive-as-possible ecological self, which amounts to only a kind of sympathy vote.

In the development of the theory of socialism, the designation "utopian" was attached by the later historical materialists, who felt that a theory of transformation which was not rooted in the dynamics of the materialist historical process was utopian. The new socialist world was to be an outcome of objective historical development, not correct thinking, cooperative consciousness, or efforts at withdrawing from society into microworlds of harmony and cooperation. In the nineteenth century, Robert Owen went to America and established the New Harmony community, and Saint-Simonians founded a short-lived Saint-Simonian church and community in Menilmontant in 1832 (Bottomore et al. 1983, 506). In the twentieth century, there are proposals for "bioregionalism," a kind of localized close living with nature (Sale 1991). Here is Doge's definition of bioregionalism: "a decentralized, self-determined mode of social organization; a culture predicated upon biological integrities and acting in respectful accord; a society which honors and abets the spiritual development of its members" (quoted in List 1993, 114). That definition could have been written by a nineteenth-century utopian socialist. While social ecologists like Bookchin disagree with the deep ecologists, both share a similar belief in small-scale living arrangements as the best way to alter relations with the environment. But the notion that living close to the earth allows the logic of an organic ecosystem to seep into the logic of a human social system is very mystical, and a weak foundation on which to build a program for altering our relations with the environment. Tying our rhythms to nature's rhythms and letting the logic of the natural and organic take precedent over the logic of the urban, industrial, capitalistic, socialistic, or patriarchal seems not only mystical but forced and naive.

It is interesting that the scientific part of ecology seems to flee when it comes to the strategical part of deep ecological analysis. The moralism is there — broaden the community — but the praxis of concrete steps to be taken seems as utopian as the visions of the early utopian socialists. My guess is that just as the theory of socialism evolved into one that tied change to the laws of economics and the specifics of the historical process, environmental theory will also evolve to a point where change will no longer be something thought to arise from correct thinking and communal living, but will be seen as part of the larger evolutionary dynamics of the eco-social formation itself.

The next stage required of deep ecology theory, then, is the transition from a *utopian ecology* predicated upon changing beliefs to an *ecostructural materialist ecology* predicated upon the laws of the human-to-nature ecosystem. Bookchin and the social ecologists have also noted the spiritual emphasis of deep ecology, but they have responded by moving backward in thought to the earlier social model and emphasizing the importance of transforming human relations first. Their emphasis upon structural relations is correct — but what need to be transformed are not the social structures among humans, but rather the relations between humans and nature. That is where the truly "macro" and truly radical analysis is located. Bioequality, the goal of deep ecology, is correct, but the means of reaching that goal need to be shifted from revolutionizing consciousness to revolutionizing ecostructural relations. If only a self-willed change in consciousness is promoted, deep ecology will remain lodged at the utopian stage of theory development. It needs to move on to become a more materialist-based theory in which change is tied to specific human-to-nature structural relations, not just human consciousness.

Such an *ecostructural materialist deep ecology* will represent a truly radical environmental program because it will not reduce environmental problems to the social logic of capitalism (the goal of social ecologists and eco-Marxists) or to patriarchy (the goal of ecofeminists), or reduce their solution to prescribing new thoughts (the present goal of deep ecologists). The path to revolutionizing ecostructural relations simply won't be changed by imagining a oneness with the bear, the mountain, and the river. These are simply imaginative exercises and have nothing to do with the reality of ecostructural relations between humans and nature. Deep ecologists champion the "expansive self," but if human-to-nature structural relations remain unchanged, then our ecological realities will remain unchanged.

Materialism and Morality:
The Role of Social Science

ALAN WOLFE

Introduction

THERE ARE NO SIMPLE WAYS to explain a society's commitment or lack of commitment to materialism. Both rich and poor countries will be concerned with materialistic values, even if for different reasons. Anthropologists are unlikely to discover that societies with relatively underdeveloped economies are somehow more spiritual, and less concerned with material things, than those that provide high standards of living to their people; it is far more likely that their materialism will merely take a different form (Turnbull 1972). Communism, we now know, was as much concerned with the accumulation of material things as capitalism; it was only the performance that was different (Havel 1985). Clearly there is no exclusive correlation between materialism and ethnicity or religion, as demonstrated by the preponderance of entrepreneurs in London or Los Angeles who are neither white nor Christian (Light and Bonacich 1988).

In spite of these constants, however, materialism is surely also a variable. Not only will there be differences between different countries

---

This essay was prepared for a conference entitled "Rethinking Materialism: Sociological and Theological Perspectives," held in June 1993 at the Center for the Study of American Religion, Princeton University. I would like to thank the participants at the conference for their suggestions, especially Neil Smelser, Robert Wuthnow, and Patrick Allitt.

with respect to their appreciation of non-materialist values, but there will always be differences within one country at different periods of time. In the United States, the 1980s were perceived as a particularly materialistic decade, especially in contrast to the 1960s. This was a period symbolized by junk bonds, jet setters, and Yuppies, while decreasing economic growth and a reluctance to tax contributed to a decline in the standard of living for the poor and lower middle class. In the 1990s, by contrast, there is once again talk of more altruistic values, symbolized by a focus on national service and a renegotiated welfare state. No modern society will ever be anti-materialistic, but the degree to which materialist considerations trump all others can and will change.

If materalism varies over time and between places, one needs a method of measuring it. No method will ever be perfect, for the ways we might measure the strength or weakness of a commitment to materialistic values — church attendance, the frequency of what Wuthnow (1991) calls "acts of compassion," the proportion of the GNP spent on consumer goods — will always measure both more and less than the materialism of any particular society. Everyone has a stake in the issue of materialism, but those who have a professional interest as well are sociologists, for, since the time of Durkheim, sociology has been trying to make sense of and measure the degree of materialism — or altruism — in society. As I will try to show in this essay, this aspect of sociology has not declined in recent years; if anything, it is more alive than it has been in some time.

Besides assessing participation in voluntary associations, church attendance, blood donations, and other measures of altruism, one additional way to shed light on the materialism or non-materialism of a society is to look at the social sciences as indicators of larger processes. I argued in a previous work (Wolfe 1989) that the social sciences, despite their claims to the contrary, are inevitably linked with questions of moral obligation. If so, then the degree to which different social sciences rise and fall in popularity — as well as the subjects and methods each uses — may tell us something about the overall material preoccupations of the society. Because its subject is the market and its unit of analysis the individual, economics tends to predominate when society is becoming more materialistic. Because its subject is society at large, and its focus is on the often irrational ways by which individuals take group needs into account, the rise of sociology would indicate that a society is becoming less materialistic.

There is little doubt that during the Reagan years, when Americans seemed far more concerned with material goods, economics grew rapidly in popularity and sophistication of technique. It also expanded into new areas of inquiry that had direct relevance for public policy, such as the field of law and economics (Epstein 1992). These were also years in which sociology declined: not only did the number of college sociology majors and the number of members of the American Sociological Association decrease, but the field also seemed to lose its focus and its sense of self-importance (D'Antonio 1992; Turner and Turner 1990, 128). Contrariwise, sociology experienced its golden years as a result of the 1960s, a decade during which it was popular to speak of the triumph of "post-materialist" values among the citizens of advanced industrial societies (Inglehart 1977; Inglehart 1990). It may, in short, be possible to measure at least some aspects of the materialism of a society simply by counting the relative number of sociologists and economists.

But there is obviously more to the problem than this, for both economics and sociology can be taught and practiced in different ways. Although economics remains primarily an exercise in model building, there have been traditions in the history of economics that have focused on larger social questions, questions in which other countries have retained an interest, and we have seen the rise of "socioeconomics" primarily among economists who do not make their living in economics departments (Coughlin 1991; Bürgenmeier 1992). Similarly, not all sociologists are directly concerned with altruistic behavior or non-materialist values; rational-choice theory — which proposes to explain all social interaction by concentrating on the rationality of the decisions made by individuals — has become an important strain in sociology, and there are efforts to replace the economic imperialism of one discipline with the sociological imperialism of the other. (On the relationship between these disciplines, see the autobiographical essays in Swedberg 1990.) It is not only how many individuals practice a particular social science that measures materialism, but how they practice it as well.

In this essay I will take for granted that sociology is beginning to attract more students and practitioners. The more important development that indicates a turning away from materialist values, I will argue, lies in the way sociologists are doing their work. Sociologists have, since the very origins of the discipline, been torn between a desire to be scientific and a concern with moral order. While these two things are not necessarily contradictory, sociologists sometimes lean in the direction of one pole and sometimes in the direction of the other. I will argue here that at the very same time that economistic models are becoming popular in sociology, we are also witnessing a re-engagement with the moral questions that brought the field into being in the first place.

It is possible to cite many examples of the continued relevance of the grand tradition of sociology, especially Tocqueville, Durkheim, and Weber. Robert Bellah and his collaborators' *Habits of the Heart* (1985; see also 1991), Amitai Etzioni's *The Moral Dimension* (1988), Robert Wuthnow's *Acts of Compassion* (1991), Philip Selznick's *The Moral Commonwealth* (1992), and my own *Whose Keeper?* (1989) are just some of the books that put moral considerations at their heart.[1] To this list should surely be added one recent book by a political scientist: James Q. Wilson's *The Moral Sense* (1993). Moreover, these works may be the tip of the iceberg. Seventy-nine dissertations were listed in *Dissertation Abstracts* between 1985 and 1987 under the classification "morality and the social sciences," and each year saw an increase over the previous one (twenty-three in 1985, twenty-four in 1986, and thirty-two in 1987).[2] *Sociological Abstracts* conveys much the same sense: in the mid-1970s, between eight and sixteen entries could be found under the heading "morality," whereas in the mid-1980s, as few as fifteen and as many as thirty-four were listed.[3] As far as the social sciences are concerned, morality is a subject whose time has once again come.

This blossoming of moral discourse in sociology could hardly have been predicted. One would expect its inspiration to come from the sociology of religion, a specialty of the discipline that rises and falls with religion itself. The secularization hypothesis — which predicted that as societies became more modern, they would also become more secular — did not prove to be true (Bruce 1992; Martin 1978). As people

---

1. In addition, I am editing a book series on morality and society for the University of Chicago Press.

2. Information is also available for 1982, 1983, 1984, and 1988, but it is too scanty to be reliable.

3. There are some exceptions to this pattern. There were sixty entries under "morality" in 1978, the largest number for any year since 1973.

recognized that religion was still a compelling force in the world — in some parts of the world, *the* compelling force — religious sociology did not die out but experienced something of a revival, although it remains a minor current within sociology. (For examples, see Burns 1992; Casanova 1994; and Wuthnow 1988a.) Yet not all the interest in moral sociology comes from the study of religion per se. Four of the authors responsible for books in the field — Selznick, Wilson, Etzioni, and Wolfe — worked previously in the general areas of organizational and political sociology, fields far removed from religion. Indeed, Selznick begins his book with a recounting of his years as a Trotskyite, while my own work grew out of earlier experiences with the radical politics of the 1960s. And, as if to drive the point home that the rekindling of an interest in morality in the social sciences is not driven by any particular political point of view, James Q. Wilson, a political scientist usually characterized as conservative, has also been part of this development. In short, the revival of moral discourse in sociology is part of, but also goes beyond, the revival of interest in religion.

Although morality has once again taken its place among the human sciences, the return of moral discourse has been accompanied by little agreement on what morality is. As if representing the fact that American society is experiencing both the fascination and the confusion that come after a decade or two of focusing on more materialistic values, the revival of moral discourse in sociology has resulted in a proliferation of different ways to think about the conditions that make morality possible. No one, of course, can know whether the moral tradition in sociology will continue to flourish, or whether there will be another stage in the cycle that will emphasize more the value neutrality and scientific objectives of the sociological enterprise. But whatever happens, we might be able to gain greater insight into questions of morality and materialism by trying to provide some conceptual clarification to guide this interest in moral questions. Economists, in one way or another, spend a considerable amount of time bringing conceptual clarification to materialistic behaviors and institutions. Sociologists ought to do the same for questions involving morality.

Multiple Meanings

Social scientists use the term *moral* to refer to a number of different phenomena. The concept of moral obligation has given rise to one important branch of philosophy, while the notion of moral development has become a subfield. Important as these usages are, in what follows I will concentrate on the major ways in which the term *moral* is used by sociologists. Among the most important of these uses are the following seven:

1. Moral Order

In sociology, the most common usage of the term *moral* involves the concept of order. Sociologists want to know what it is that holds things together. Born in an intellectual milieu distrustful of marginal utility analysis, utilitarianism, and other efforts to reduce the whole to the actions of its parts, sociologists typically believe that the moral order can be sustained only when there is some imperative that channels and directs individual self-interest to some kind of common good. In the absence of mechanisms of socialization or institutions, people will be self-interested rather than disinterested. "Morality," Durkheim wrote, "begins with disinterest, with attachment to something other than ourselves" (1973, 151). For Durkheim, the moral and the social were, for all intents and purposes, synonymous. When *morality* is used in this sense, the opposite of the moral is not the immoral but the individual; morality stands in contrast to instinct or drive, which is understood to be what people act upon in the absence of moral constraints.

Understanding morality as synonymous with the social order makes sociology the moral science par excellence. That may be the way Durkheim wanted it, but making too close an identification between the social and the moral has its disadvantages. First, the dominant intellectual trend in the social sciences at the present time is individualistic, and while there is much to criticize in the rush toward rational-choice models, they also possess the important grain of truth that individuals and their acts do matter. Second, strict adherence to the Durkheimian formulation solves the tension between the macro and the micro by absorbing the one into the other, but it may be preferable to play off the tension between them. If the social and the moral are the same, the moral order can be sustained by immoral individuals — which, I take it, is one of the messages Erving Goffman wanted to leave for us (something I will discuss presently).

Third, locating the moral in the realm of the social means that all too little attention is paid to the profane; one of sociology's major intellectual contributions has been to come down from the Durkheimian peaks to look at real people in the conditions of real life. Fourth, it is questionable whether the proper response to economic imperialism is to substitute sociological imperialism, as if any one field or way of looking at the world possessed a moral monopoly. Finally, it is quite possible that individual choices can in themselves be moral, even if they are motivated by self-interest. Indeed, rational-choice theory does not ignore the problem of order so much as it represents an effort to generate principles of order from assumptions rooted in individual action.

In short, there is a good deal of truth in the fundamental sociological insight that society requires something more than self-interest. But whether *everything* that stands outside the individual and guides his or her choices to harmonious ends ought to be called moral is questionable. The term *moral* ought to be reserved for *some* constraints on individual action. Or, to put the matter another way, it is proper to speak of a moral order, but it does not make sense to use the terms *moral* and *order* as synonymous. Legal order is different from moral order; it matters when people are willing to consider the point of view of society as a whole for reasons other than the fear of punishment that would follow from not doing so (Ellickson 1991). Nor would it make sense to use the term *moral* to apply to those forms of order that are unthinkingly generated in spontaneous fashion from the dynamics of any complex system (Luhmann 1990; Hayles 1991); order can be produced by the invisible hands of independent economic actions, or even by autopoietic self-organization, but because such forms of order lack human intentionality, little is gained by thinking of them as moral accomplishments. Finally, we ought to recognize that the achievement of moral order, while always an accomplishment, is not necessarily always associated with the rich symbolic tapestry celebrated by Durkheim; a moral order can also be minimal, in the sense that it holds people together without demanding strong pledges of allegiance (Baumgartner 1988). The complete identification of the moral with the social tells us both too much and too little about the moral order — that is, about the reasons why societies reproduce themselves over time.

2. Moral Rules

Avoiding some kind of Hobbesian civil war and maintaining moral order requires *rules*. Rules can take many forms, ranging from informal norms to highly codified laws. In the strong version of disinterest associated with Durkheim, adherence to such moral rules is hard work, often requiring the sacrifice of what may be immediately pleasurable. But there are also weaker understandings of what the moral order demands, such as Erving Goffman's. Although suspicious of even the idea of a common or collective good, Goffman by no means dismisses the notion of morality. Because the binding acts and rituals that hold society together "occur infrequently or take a long time for their consummation," Goffman (1967) would have us look at the rules encoded in everyday interactions rather than those written as social commandments (90). To be sure, in Goffman's world the person is a construct, but that "construct" is created by "moral rules that are impressed upon him from without," rules that "determine the evaluation he will make of himself and of his fellow-participants" (45). Although Goffman is often viewed as sympathetic to individualism, his world, like Durkheim's, contains little allowance for free individuals engaged in free acts. "Approved attributes and their relation to face make of every man his own jailer," Goffman says; "this is a fundamental social constraint even though each man may like his own cell" (10).

Moral rules are obviously central to the organization of society, so central that every society has them: "All human societies acknowledge moral rules, rules that are right, imperative, and unchangeable," claims Robert Edgerton (1985, 41). It is even the case that while the specific content of moral rules varies depending on the cultural values of any particular society, some specific prohibitions achieve a kind of universality. Shweder, Mahapatra, and Miller (1990), for example, found that Americans, Indian Brahmins, and Indian Untouchables all agreed that some actions — for example, asking a stranger how much his watch costs and whether he would part with it; discriminating against disfigured persons in hotels — were immoral (193). At the same time, it is also widely agreed that exceptions to rules are also universal; as Sally Falk Moore (1978) has pointed out, manipulation of rules is as common as adherence to them. By emphasizing the unchangeability of moral rules as distinct from other kinds of rules, Edgerton suggests that the moral is the sphere of the timeless. But this conflicts with one of the most important recent developments in sociology: the idea that people are active participants in shaping their own lives, including the rules by which they live. If that insight is to be taken into account, as it should be, the distinction between moral rules and other kinds of rules must lie somewhere else than in the realm of permanence.

Moral rules ought to be understood as those rules that make moral order possible. And since, following Durkheim, a moral order exists when there are constraints on individual self-interest, moral rules are those rules that define how one ought to treat others (Gewirth 1978, 1). "Follow your self-interest" can therefore be an example of a moral rule if a society believes that the net effect of an individual's following his or her own self-interest will be to enhance the interests of everyone else. What defines a moral rule, in this sense, is not its content; it would be a mistake for sociologists to classify as moral rules only those prohibitions with which they were in sympathy. We look to moral rules to understand how people expect others to be treated, not just as ways to tell people how to treat others.

Although most moral rules exist in negative form, specifying what people ought not to do, there are also examples of positive injunctions that could be classified as moral rules. Indeed, to some degree the debate in America over morality has become so passionate because Americans are being asked not just to say no to some things but also to say yes to others. Debates over speech codes, elementary school curricula, and the right of homosexuals to serve in the military raise the question of whether it is sufficient that majorities *not* trespass on the rights of minorities; increasingly, majorities are being asked to show minorities positive respect and appreciation, rather than negative tolerance and acceptance. Because as a society we have not reached — and perhaps will never reach — consensus on these issues, we will be confronting the nature and dynamics of moral rules for some time to come.

3. Moral Sense

Even if moral rules exist, why would anyone obey them? It is an established tradition in Western social thought that human beings are predisposed by their very natures to feel a sense of sympathy with or concern toward others. Before the rule comes an instinct or a drive, one that makes it possible for human beings, unlike other animal species, to organize their lives on some basis other than constant aggression. (Depending on how it is understood, this point of view stands in contrast to Durkheim's idea that morality is cultivated by society to curb animal instincts.) The same thinkers who brought to modern society an appreciation of self-interest — Francis Hutcheson, David Hume, Adam Smith — also brought an appreciation of sympathy. Interests, after all, are not passions (Hirschman 1977); the moral sense tames what is wild in order to make what is civilized possible.

The concept of moral sense — lying, as it does, close to biological theories about human nature — went into abeyance in the social sciences as culture, rather than nature, became the key explanation of human development (Degler 1991). Contemporary social science, believing that most things are the products of how human beings construct social meanings out of the materials of everyday life, seems reluctant to accept that anything, even something so apparently "natural" as a mother's love, can have a biological basis (Scheper-Hughes 1992; Eyer 1992). It is in this atmosphere of suspicion toward biological explanations that James Q. Wilson, in his recent book entitled *The Moral Sense* (1993), suggests the following: "We have a moral sense, most people instinctively rely on it even if intellectuals deny it, but it is not always and in every aspect of life strong enough to withstand a pervasive and sustained attack" (12).

But even if Wilson is correct that there is an innate moral sense, this does not, by his own formulation, answer the question of why people obey moral rules. For if the moral sense is weak, unable to defend itself against concerted attack, the question of how it survives becomes essentially a cultural and sociological one. Whether biology gives human beings an innate moral sense makes for interesting speculation, but the question is in some ways irrelevant. We tend to be interested in the question of moral sense when we notice that some people seem to lack moral sense. The concern of social scientists is not with the moral sense in itself but with the conditions under which the moral sense flourishes. And those conditions are inevitably the product of our social institutions, not our human nature.

An appreciation of moral sense, in short, need not be an argument in favor of biological or genetic determinism. To be sure, biologists such as Gunther Stent (1978) are correct when they argue that only human beings have the capacity to take a Kantian position of disinterested morality. But the question of whether human biological givens are more conducive to morality than the biological givens of other species is the wrong question. Human beings add to their biological inheritance the capacities not only of culture but also of mind. (For more on this point, see Wolfe 1993.) The capacity to be moral, in particular, is likely one of those capacities that is dependent not only on history, culture, and tradition, but also on the ability of human beings to think for themselves when confronted with new conditions. The possession of moral sense, as its name implies, "sensitizes" the person toward a moral response, but such a response does not mean much until the classical questions of sociological inquiry are introduced, questions involving institutions, norms, culture, socialization, responsibility, and leadership.

4. Moral Duty

For many writers, especially those rooted in religious traditions, morality means doing what is right, especially from the point of view of God. But religion is not the only source of this emphasis on doing one's duty. Lawrence Kohlberg's concept of moral development, inspired by Kant, also emphasizes duties that call from beyond the world of daily life (Kohlberg 1980). Both traditions tend to stress the out-of-the-ordinary nature of moral action. Because the world is filled with sinners, not everyone will act in accordance with God's will. And because this century — characterized by world war and genocide — has been particularly immoral, only the actions of those few inspired by what Kohlberg calls "post-conventional" moral reasoning can point the way for others.

Kohlbergian conceptions of morality that emphasize duty tend to be individualistic, and they therefore stand in sharp contrast to the equation of the moral and the sociological just discussed. The image conveyed by writers in this tradition is that of the heroic inner strength of the moral person, driven, like Martin Luther, by an inner certainty of what must be done. For this reason there is a certain tension between Kohlbergian notions of moral duty and the requirements of social order, for the latter often demand that we take the viewpoint of others as our own, while the concept of moral duty looks not to obedience and conformity but to psychological strength and autonomy. To use a once-popular language, the moral order hangs on outer-directed people, while moral duty requires a substantial amount of inner-directedness.

It is therefore understandable that morality-as-duty would be associated more with a psychologist such as Kohlberg than with the sociological tradition. For what is often a matter of individual duty can be, in Parsonian terms, "dysfunctional" for the smooth reproduction of society. In many ways, moral people are poor constituents for a moral order; the existence of a moral order often requires less heroic moral actors. Duty demands saints; society requires subjects. It is important, obviously, to have both moral individuals and moral societies, but the one usually has to be sacrificed to obtain the other.

The tension between individualistic and social conceptions of morality comes out most strongly when we try to attach moral labels to specific behavioral imperatives. It is part of the higher stages of Kolhbergian morality not to discriminate against people on the basis of their race. There thus arises the inevitable tendency to characterize individuals who want to preserve the all-white character of their neighborhoods as immoral. But to the residents of many racially exclusive neighborhoods — one thinks of those who live in Jonathan Rieder's Canarsie — the highest moral imperative is a Durkheimian stress on collective values and traditions. Indeed, many of Rieder's informants, far from believing that their racially exclusionary attitudes make them immoral, believe that most of the blacks with whom they come into contact are themselves immoral, because, in their opinion, they take drugs, refuse to work, and engage in crime (Rieder 1985, esp. 57-94). What makes an example like this a rich one for sociologists is that at stake are two very different conceptions of what morality is. To discuss the issue in Kohlbergian terms too narrowly constrains what morality means, the same result that is produced by too Durkheimian an emphasis. Duty is an essential concept in any effort to understand society, for if we are to call "moral" those actions taken in the interests of others that are not coerced by states or enforced by laws, the sense of obligation that comes with a duty will be crucial to understanding how society functions. Moreover, it is probably the case — although data on this topic is notoriously weak — that a sense of duty has been in decline in modern societies, which causes significant problems for the maintenance of moral order. (For some evidence to the contrary, see Wuthnow 1991.) But duty cannot be fully equated with morality, just as society cannot be, for there are moral acts which are not dutiful, such as those that come about through an individual's desire to please others or those that are the product of routine and ritual. Furthermore, the concept of a duty, particularly a higher duty, can never be specified in full detail, for moral acts are often ambiguous and contradictory. Kohlberg's conception of moral duty can never be neglected, but the controversies surrounding the term itself indicate why it always needs to be supplemented.

One way to link an individualistic notion of duty together with society's need for continuity and obedience is to make a distinction between critical and conventional morality, as Selznick does (1992, 392-427). Sociologists must develop an appreciation for the less than heroic forms of conventional morality that Kohlberg tends to slight. Everyday life is made possible and moral order is secured when individuals do not retreat, like Antigone, to some inner sanctum in order to do what is right. At the same time, critical morality, which is based, in Selznick's words, "on reason and principle rather than passion and historicity," enables society to change and respond to new challenges (392). A moral order that does not permit individuals under certain conditions to challenge convention in the name of some higher good is also one that will not survive, because it will become frozen in its own traditions and patterns of obedience. One of the fundamental tasks of a moral sociology is to find the ways in which critical and conventional morality can, despite the tension between them, work together.

5. Morality and Ethics

Although Durkheim is the clear inspiration for the moral revival currently underway in the social sciences, there were at least two Durkheims, and each one deals with the relationship between morality and ethics in a different way. Durkheim the functionalist is associated with a "thin" treatment of ethical concepts. As Derek Phillips (1986) has pointed out, Durkheim at his most functionalist tends to find justified the institutions of any particular society so long as they contribute to the maintenance of that society (21-23). Missing from functionalism, in other words, is any independent criteria for determining the ethical goodness of society. Here again, Goffman and Durkheim are quite similar, for Goffman refuses on principle to stand in judgment of the content of social interaction; indeed, his reputation as a cynic stems from the evenhandedness with which he moves from discussions of the trivial to discussions of the serious — at least as those terms are used in the conventional wisdom.

If any society is as good as any other so long as each finds ways to express its collective sense — or if all social practices are equally interesting from a sociological point of view — then ethics, as we usually understand the matter, is something distinct from the possession of a moral point of view. It is thus important to note that some writers make a distinction between the moral and the ethical in which a concern with the good society would belong to the latter category, not the former. Goffman (1971), for example, uses Simmel's distinction between ethics — which involves the practices of particular subgroups within the society — and morality, which involves the rules that govern society as a whole (97). If we were to build on this distinction, we would reserve discussions of ethics for issues involving professions, clans, and other groups that speak for particular group interests, and reserve discussions of morality for issues of concern to the entire group in question.

This whole matter looks quite different, however, if one treats Durkheim more as an explicit moral theorist than as a functionalist. Robert N. Bellah — who perhaps more than any other contemporary practitioner of the art deserves to be described as a "moral sociologist" — was one of the first who attempted to rescue Durkheim as a moral thinker from the then prevailing interpretation of him as a functionalist (Bellah 1973). In *Habits of the Heart* (1985), and more recently in *The Good Society* (1991), Bellah and his colleagues lay claim to — and are often criticized for — adopting a moral point of view. In particular, *The Good Society* seeks to identify sociology to some degree directly with ethics: good societies are those that cultivate beneficial ethical imperatives; bad societies are those that do not. It is precisely this ethical imperative that marks the major difference between the functionalist and the moralist inheritances which contemporary sociology has received from Durkheim. For any effort to provide substantive content to the adjective "good" as it modifies the noun "society" runs counter to a functionalist understanding of reproduction as an end in itself.

Should we, then, make a distinction between ethics and morality, the former associated with the practices of groups such as professional associations, the latter referring to the rules that make it possible for societies to function? One thing is clear: the contemporary moral revival in sociology pays attention both to organizations that express the interests of particular groups and to society as a whole. Bellah and his colleagues certainly do so. Indeed, in *The Good Society* (1991), they focus more on institutions ("Moral ecology," they write, "is only another way of speaking of healthy institutions") than on society as a whole (6). In like manner, Selznick, in his inquiry into the conditions that make a moral community possible (1992), spends considerable time on the institutions that constitute modern society. To "live through institutions" — the phrase belongs to Bellah et al. (1991, 3-18) — is to be as concerned with the ethical dilemmas of and demands on such institutions as with the overall moral order as Durkheim understood it. Institutions have, in fact, become so crucial to the functioning of modern society that the interests they serve can barely be described as particularistic. For this reason, the Simmelian way of distinguishing between ethics and morals may not make sense, at least under modern conditions. The study of morality cannot restrict itself to universalistic institutions speaking for the entire society without overlooking the dramatic importance of corporations, unions, professional associations, and other such institutions that inevitably assume a moral character.

Although I will turn to a discussion of some of the methodological issues involved in the study of morality later in this essay, it is worthwhile anticipating one of those points now. One place in which it does make sense to make a distinction between morals and ethics involves not what sociologists study but how they study it. To develop an ethics, an author must have a strong sense of what is proper and what is improper and be prepared to defend the one and condemn the other. The tools of ethical analysis range from the logical to the rhetorical; one's aim is to convince, to win others to one's point of view. By contrast, a strong ethical sense is *not* a necessary prerequisite to developing a moral sociology and can, under some circumstances, be counterproductive. The task of the sociologist of morality is to understand how people themselves understand their moral rules; animal-rights activists are probably not going to understand the moral rules involved in animal sacrifice. When Durkheim called sociology a moral science, he meant it; there was no contradiction between morality as a subject of inquiry and a commitment to value neutrality and scientific rigor as a method of inquiry.

The revival of interest in ethical conceptions of the good society is a healthy development for the social sciences. That development will be even healthier, however, if a way is found to maintain a scientific interest in the ways in which societies work, which is different from an ethical concern with how they ought to work. Both tasks can be pursued, and often by the same person in the same text. But they are different tasks, and the different implications of each should always be kept in mind.

6. Moral Boundaries

While the concept of a moral order is generally understood to involve society as an organic entity, it is also true, as Robert Wuthnow points out, that "order consists mainly of being able to make distinctions — of having symbolic demarcations — so that we know the place of things and how they relate to one another" (Wuthnow 1987, 69; for an account of how moral boundaries are constructed, see Lamont 1992). If it is primarily boundaries that give meaning to the moral order, then the Simmelian distinction between ethics and morals needs to be turned on its head. From this point of view, it makes perfect sense to examine institutions — or any other subdivision of society, such as ethnic groups, communities, and particular identities — for it is within these least abstract and more identity-filled boundaries that individuals are more likely to feel a sense of obligation to others.

Boundaries not only reinforce moral obligations within, but also tend to loosen moral obligations without. Sociologists are naturally interested in boundaries, for without them there would not be found the identities, ties, networks, bonds, and all the other grist for the sociologists' mill. (For recent expressions of this interest, see Lamont and Fournier 1992 and Zerubavel 1991.) But most sociologists are also liberal democrats, and there is a liberal democratic impulse to universalize moral obligation, to believe, as Kohlberg does, that the more universal and generalizable the obligation, the more egalitarian, just, and therefore presumably moral the society. (I explore this point at greater length in Wolfe 1992.) Hence the distinction between a moral boundary and a more organic moral unity overlaps and crisscrosses with all the diverse ways in which *morality* is used in the social sciences. If our focus is on the particulars, such as the way in which men and women (or whites and blacks, or Catholics, Protestants, and Jews) develop their sense of moral duty, we will tend to appreciate moral boundaries as justified and worth keeping. (For example, see Gilligan 1982.) But if our focus is on our more abstract obligations to others — let alone on even more abstract concepts such as future generations, the biosphere, and potential life on other planets — then moral boundaries will strike us as limiting and parochial. (This dilemma is explored in Benhabib 1982.) Richard Rorty's suggestion that we need both Habermas and Foucault — the one to remind us of our universality, the other of our threatened particularity — may be the only sensible way out of the dilemma (Rorty 1989, 61-69).

Perhaps the single most important distinction relevant to sociologists is the distinction between the private and the public (Weinstein and Kumar forthcoming). There is a tendency in contemporary social theory to equate the moral with the public, a tendency best represented in the thought of Jürgen Habermas. (This is particularly true of Habermas's early work, less true of his later work; see Habermas 1991.) This is a sensible approach, for modern individuals have received the benefits of a private realm into which public morality ought not necessarily intrude. Yet a host of complicated issues — AIDS, abortion, date rape, discriminatory harassment — raise awkward questions about what is private and what is public. In other words, the moral boundary that creates moral boundaries is itself ambiguous, which suggests that morality ought to operate on both sides of the public/private distinction, if in different ways. Habermas, with his preference for the public over the private, needs always to be read in the context of Goffman, with his preference for the private over the public.

7. Morality and Altruism

Once again because of Durkheim, altruism and its related spin-offs —
the gift relationship, reciprocity, the generalized other — have been a
central concern of the sociological tradition. Altruism is a stronger
expression of the Durkheimian concern with disinterest; to be disinterested, we merely have to tie ourselves to the mast and resist the siren
call to self-interest. But to be altruistic, we have to take positive steps,
willingly giving to others as a way of acknowledging the interdependence we share with them.

During the post–World War II economic boom, driven by Keynesian economic techniques and increasing reliance on the public sector,
altruistic concerns tended to be embodied in states, particularly welfare
states. The welfare state made the affairs of everyone the affairs of
everyone else. No other single feature of modern life became more
charged with moral significance than the tax code, for without sufficient
money, the ability of the state to serve as the collective conscience of
the society could not survive. The central, overriding reason for welfare,
according to Robert E. Goodin (1988) is to prevent exploitation; that is
what gives the welfare state its moral character (22). When the state
becomes responsible for altruism, sociology is replaced by political
science. For the question of what we owe to strangers is answered by
developing the correct bureaucratic or administrative apparatus designed to carry out those obligations most efficiently. To take the most
conspicuous example, there can be little doubt that the poorest individuals in a society like the United States are better off under welfare than
they would be if they were at the mercy of private charity. But at the
same time they also become wards of the state, dependent on the
willingness of taxpayers to continue to assess themselves so that the
welfare system can continue to function.

In recent years, the limits of the Western welfare state have clearly
been reached. Whether this means "the end of equality" is another
matter entirely (Kaus 1992), but it is clear that states are looking more
toward the world of civil society — families, communities, churches —
to play a greater role in promoting individual and collective welfare.
This will mean a greater role for sociology in the sense that focus is
placed on those social institutions that have been at the heart of the
sociological enterprise since its founding. There is a certain logic in this

development, for the questions that are being asked as the welfare state reaches its limits — questions about how many children one should have and under what conditions, not to mention questions about paternal responsibility, work, child care, and reciprocal obligations between society and the individual — all possess a strong moral dimension. In short, during the peak of the welfare state, questions involving the relationship between morality and altruism went into decline, since altruism was routinized and automated. But since that is no longer the case, altruism is a key concept in any continued revival of the moral tradition in the social sciences.

There are also other ways in which the term *morality* is used in the contemporary social sciences that I have not discussed. There is, for example, the question of whether the moral behavior of individuals — whether members of the "underclass" or corporate executives — ought or ought not to be considered in the making of public policy, a topic I have not chosen to address in this essay. (On the moral behavior of corporate executives, see Jackall 1988; see the essays in Katz 1993 for arguments that the urban poor are the victims of economic transformations, not moral failures.)

Moreover, subjects that are closely linked to the question of morality — such as trust, responsibility, and loyalty — have themselves been increasingly studied. (On trust, see Gambetta 1990 and Luhmann 1979; on responsibility, see Heimer [unpublished]; and on loyalty, see Fletcher 1993.) Even economists and others associated with individualistic understandings of human behavior have been examining such concepts. (On trust, see Oliver Williamson n.d.; for a rational choice approach to morality, see Gauthier 1986.) It is becoming increasingly obvious that seemingly "hard" issues — such as the way prices are established by a supply-and-demand auction or the dynamics of labor markets — are themselves the products of complex social processes that contain important dimensions (Smith 1989; Granovetter 1973). Those who strive for highly systematic accounts of the way humans behave cannot ignore the fact that one of the ways in which they behave is morally. (Two recent efforts to approach moral questions from a sophisticated theoretical basis are Coleman 1990 and Elster 1992.)

As all these developments make clear, a moral revival within the field of sociology is most definitely taking place. There is hardly an approach or a method that has not been affected. If the rise and fall of different approaches in the social sciences measures in any degree the way in which the larger society thinks about materialism, this revival indicates that American society is increasingly looking beyond economics to a concern with moral obligation.

Conclusion

Interest in the sociology of morality rises at a time when such contentious moral issues as abortion, AIDS, and homosexuality divide American society. A political system that is already asked to achieve peace and stabilize the economy — two tasks that in themselves can defy the best efforts of public officials — is also asked to decide when life begins, who should live, how they should live, and where the line between individual rights and collective obligations ought to be drawn. This is by no means the first time that American society has been riven by moral conflicts, nor are these the most serious. (Slavery, which produced a civil war, was a moral conflict.) But it is also true that American society, like the social sciences, goes through phases of materialism and morality, and that we are currently in a phase in which (morality) has assumed a particular importance.

The moral controversies that swirl around American politics suggest that the developments in the sociology of morality discussed in this essay are likely to be with us for some time. We are constantly reminded of the moral order, even as we debate whether people have a moral sense and can (or should) follow moral rules. Duty, ethics, and altruism are anything but abstractions of interest only to the social scientist; the daily newspaper provides examples of each of them in action in the lives of ordinary people. It is surely more than coincidental that the revival of a concern with morality in the social sciences has been matched in the larger society by a movement toward communitarianism and other ways of thinking about people's obligations to one another. Indeed, some individuals, such as Amitai Etzioni, are responsible for both (Etzioni 1993).

To a considerable degree, the questions with which America is preoccupied as it enters the latest version of its post-materialistic phase are questions that can be approached with the benefit of a sociological concern with moral obligation. In at least some of its versions, liberal political theory emphasizes the importance of individual rights in dealing with important political controversies, while a sociological approach emphasizes the importance of group obligations. Both are essential if liberal democracy is to remain strong, but in a primarily individualistic culture, the sociological aspect is usually downplayed. Should abortion be understood as involving primarily a woman's right to choose or as symbolizing society's commitment to the sanctity of life? Ought we be more concerned about behavior that spreads AIDS or protecting the privacy of those who are at risk from it? Does a community's religious belief that homosexuality is a sin override a school system's desire to teach respect for all individual lifestyles? Is the moral behavior of individuals who receive public assistance a proper concern of those whose taxes pay for public assistance? Should we regulate private speech in order to uphold group dignity? Are solutions to the racial discrimination practiced against groups in the past morally justified if one of their effects may be to harm individuals in the majority group in the present? These kinds of questions usually do not have right and wrong answers. They pose instead the issue of how we can use the best analytic methods we have, from very different disciplines, to shed light on the complexities that surround these questions.

The moral revival taking place in the social sciences should therefore be a welcome affair. In the wake of a turning away from the materialism of the Reagan years, American society is clearly re-evaluating itself. As Americans confront a world in which manufacturing jobs are declining, the middle class is shrinking, and government can no longer do everything, they are wondering more about their moral values and the role such values can play in their public and private lives. What is taking place in sociology is a piece, however small, of that re-evaluation. Americans will be looking to a number of sources — religion, tradition, community values — to receive insight on the question of how to act in the face of the new realities around them. Although social scientists may not realize it, their ideas also become part of the mix that offers people moral guidelines. The moral revival will take place whether or not the social sciences actively participate, but this revival is likely to be more thoughtful if they participate as actively as they can.

POSTSCRIPT

Materialism and Spirituality in American Religion

MARTIN E. MARTY

"The Old Tag of American Materialism" disturbed French philosopher and American visitor Jacques Maritain. In a seminar in Chicago in 1956 and in a book published in 1958, during the peak years of "the affluent society," he built upon an observation he had made in New York en route to Rome in 1945, as World War II ended. The American people, he argued, "are the least materialist among the modern peoples which have attained the industrial stage." He found "sickening" the stock remarks, the "fable," of many Europeans — who, he said, were "themselves far from despising the earthly goods of this world" — about the "so-called materialism" of America.

The philosopher found this fable issuing from "an old prejudice, confusing spirituality with an aristocratic contempt for any improvement in material life (especially the material life of others)." As a social critic, Maritain faulted Hollywood for its projection of unmixed materialist images. He knew that America was also

> infected by the miasmata that emanate from the structures and ritual
> of our modern civilization; the noise made by a crowd of vulgar
> assertions, which measure everything either in terms of statistics and
> facts and figures or in terms of success, fun, and practical power, hold
> "ideas" to be only something to be "sold" to a possible consumer,
> silent partner, or sucker, and see human conduct as a by-product
> either of hormones or of economic factors.

Maritain was also aware of "the process of materialist contagion" in personal lives, of egotism and greed, of open devotion to money; but to invoke all this as proof of so-called American materialism was "to talk nonsense." American materialism compared to what? he kept asking. The vices and afflictions were "in no way specifically American." Europe especially displayed them in comparable ways. And there were opposing trends.

Over against the charges of so-called materialism, Maritain credited Americans with "generosity, good will, [and] the sense of human fellowship." Americans liked to give, through foundations, institutions, private groups, and personal initiatives, a fact that he set out to document. He pointed to the readiness for change and the fluidity of American life, "the concern of the American people for moral and religious values, their attitude toward moral conscience." The philosopher in him linked their love of free discussion, their support of the humanities and liberal arts, an eagerness for knowledge, and a spiritual dimension in the literature of Melville and Hawthorne, Wolfe and Faulkner, Poe and Dickinson, Crane and Tate and Eliot, whose writing "has been preoccupied with the beyond and the nameless which haunt our blood."

Specifically, Maritain set out to surprise Europeans and self-denigrating Americans by pointing to

> the thirst for spiritual life which is deep in the American soul, and the signs of which are more and more manifest, especially among young people. In a number of people it is more or less unconscious, more or less repressed by the conditions of existence and the tyranny of unceasing activity. For all that it is real and alive, and exercises continual pressure on souls. . . . There [are] in America great reserves and possibilities for contemplation; the activism which is to the fore appears . . . in many cases as a remedy against despair, and masks a hidden aspiration to contemplation.

As final documentation, Maritain pointed to the best-seller status of modern classical works on spiritual life by Thomas Merton and the growth of contemplative orders beyond the Trappists of Gethsemani.

A Thesis against "Pure Forms"

Jacques Maritain cannot be asked or permitted to do our work for us. He was by no means the "unbiased" Frenchman he advertised himself to be; he brought his own perceptions and agenda. His observation came from the world of 1956, during the putative "American century," before the voices of women and men who carried the debates over materialism and spirituality beyond the orbit of European and American high culture had become a part of generally recognized public discourse. He appears here in part to set up the received polarities, to provide a template for discussions of comparative generalizations about nations, to suggest some complicating factors, to show how proverbial the inherited "old tags" had become, and for one more reason: he helps frame what will become the thesis of this paper. As Maritain summarized it, "There is no end to the enumeration of the various features peculiar, quite peculiar indeed, to so-called *American materialism*" (Maritain 1958, 29-42).

Among the "peculiar, quite peculiar" distinctives in American materialism and spirituality has been a widespread endeavor to overcome pure versions of the materialism/spirituality poles. Thesis: In the American experience, citizens and believers have been figuratively at war with sharp dictionary definitions that pose *pure form materialism* against *pure form spirituality*. To make this point, I shall cite the *Oxford English Dictionary*. It is not the only dictionary, just as Maritain is not the only commentator. But its definitions "on historical principles" encapsulate what I have called the sharp posing of two alternatives. They point to the mutually exclusive character of materialism and spirituality as this had been hardened through centuries of usage in the linguistic traditions that shape discourse today.

We should be very clear about which "materialism" is being scrutinized: not the philosophical or theological view that nothing exists or matters except matter. The "matter" in question here refers to possessions, goods, property, and money to which there is attachment. In the *OED*, this attachment is defined in [2.c]: "Devotion to material needs or desires, *to the neglect of spiritual matters;* a way of life, opinion, or tendency based entirely upon material interests." In radical opposition is the *OED* definition of our other term, *spirituality:* "[3.] The quality or condition of being spiritual; attachment to or regard for things of the spirit *as opposed to material or worldly interests.*" (In both cases, the italics are mine.)

"Historical principles" and usages gave Europeans other than Maritain good reason to tag America for materialism. They did observe plenty of "material needs or desires [and] interests" in a nation in which material goods were indeed abundant. And they did not always discern much "attachment to or regard for things of the spirit" as divorced from material or worldly interests. They were not prepared to understand some of the ways in which significant numbers of Americans worked to transcend these poles in human experience elsewhere, poles that were sharpened by the words "to the neglect of" and "as opposed to." This is not to make a case for American uniqueness or simple exceptionalism: the United States draws upon experiences from many times and places, and does some exporting as well. But in the American unfoldings, there were reasons for citizens and believers to develop "peculiar, quite peculiar" fresh understandings.

On Pervasiveness and Persistence

Compare this situation, for example, to Seymour Martin Lipset's discussion of America as "The First New Nation." It was such, among other things, because the United States freshly related two poles that had previously and elsewhere been seen in simple opposition: "all-pervasiveness" of religion with "secularity" as "a persistent trait of American religion." Hitherto (at least in the Western historical experience that provided the contrast for Lipset, as it did for Maritain), to find religion to be "all-pervasive" would have meant that there was no room for the secular to be invasive. To find "persistent secularity," on the other hand, would have meant that there was no time for religion. Yet both were present. I have often spoken of the American resolution as "religiosecular," just as in the present case one might have to patent — and then quickly tuck away and hide — linguistic barbarisms such as materiospiritual or spiritomaterial to do some justice to the emergence (Lipset 1963, 140-58).

Both Maritain and Lipset wrote during a time when many people spoke with more confidence than they do now about "*The* American Pilgrimage," which was Maritain's choice, or "*The* American Character," which was Lipset's. Today Americans in their subgroups are perceived as living in proverbially distinct universes of discourse that follow lines of gender, class, ethnicity, race, and religion. This fact leads me here to speak at times about "significant numbers of Americans" more readily than about "*The* Americans." But I am ready to contend that in these separate universes there are also some common features, especially with respect to the present topic.

For example, white males of European descent have long been in positions of power and wealth that have brought them more consistently into the orbit where materialisms find expression. Yet newcomers from other subcultures who have come into similar positions have displayed similar ranges of response; the evidence for that is massive. At the risk of distracting us from the main thesis but in order to suggest that we are talking about widespread inventions in America, let me provisionally, and with readiness to do some circumscribing on other issues, agree with an observation by Louis Menand (1992) in a day of "multicultural" awarenesses:

> In so far as ["multiculturalism"] refers to functionally autonomous subcultures within a dominant culture, or to conflicting tastes and values specifically associated with ethnicity, gender and sexual preference — the United States is becoming not more multicultural, but less. For when the whole culture is self-consciously "diverse," real diversity has disappeared. Real diversity is what the United States *used* to have — when women and men, black and white Americans, Christians and Jews, gays and straights, and the various ethnic communities of recent immigrant groups led, culturally, largely segregated lives. . . . People in the United States still want, as people in the United States always have, to be "American." It is just that being American is now understood to mean wearing your ethnicity, religion, gender and sexual history — your "differences" — on your sleeve. You would be naked, in fact, without them. . . . If you didn't advertise your differences, then you really would be different. . . . The United States is a country in which people, permitted to say whatever they like, all somehow end up saying the same thing. (3-4)

That last sentence is hyperbolic, but only slightly overstates what I believe to be documentable on the present point: that Americans across a wide subcultural spectrum have been "all-pervasively" and "persistently" struggling to display a new combination of "religious" and "secular," as well as — the present topic — to violate the simplicity of distinction between "materialist" and "spiritual."

On "-isms" versus -"ities"

The terms "material*ist*" and "spiritual*ity*" bias the linguistic and conceptual cases. Words ending in "-ism" denote ideology, system, the integral, the closed, the propositional; that which attracts and demands attack and defense. Words ending in "-ity" suggest instead experience, what is processive, unfinished, open, to-be-conversed-about; that which attracts and demands the guidance of questions more than of argument, debate, or examination.

Note that in the present case, in inherited American usage, the situation cannot be evened up by transferring endings now and then. "Spiritual*ism*" has nothing in common with spirituality; it refers to a specific religious movement devoted to spirits and seances. And "material*ity*" in turn has little except "matter" in common with materialism. Therefore, we are alerted that when materialism is posed against spirituality, the temptations to bring ideology into the designation of the "-ism" itself are strong and are usually acted upon.

Defenders of "materialism" to the neglect of the spiritual have been rare. One of the few qualifiers for this defense has been Ayn Rand, with her school of "Objectivism." She and her followers were militantly anti-spiritual. They would not merely neglect the spiritual; they would oppose it. Thus, if altruism is a virtue with spiritual groundings and overtones, Randites would see that as a vice. If selfishness looks like pure materialism, the Objectivists would celebrate that as a virtue. Today this would be called "in-your-face materialism." Many others on libertarian and free-market fronts, where ideology commends them to admit and enjoin "devotion to material needs or desires," choose to or must make it a point to show that this attachment is not "to the neglect of spiritual matters." Thus in *Wealth and Poverty* George Gilder defends the heritage of Adam Smith against charges of materialism, using a kind of theological argument. Far from being selfish and materialist, he argues, this heritage was based on ultimate trust and on the very altruism that Rand despised (Rand 1961; Gilder 1981).[1]

Murray N. Rothbard, considered by Walter Block to be "the second most influential person after Ayn Rand within the libertarian community," stresses the importance of the impulse to spiritualize and render religious the movement so often seen as atheist:

> The libertarian movement . . . will get nowhere in America — or throughout the world — so long as it is perceived, as it generally is, as a movement dedicated to atheism. . . . Many libertarians have habitually and wrongly acted as if religious people in general and Christians in particular are pariahs and equivalent to statists. This pernicious attitude, combined with aggressive luftmenschship, has managed to turn off a huge number of middle-class Americans. (Rothbard 1988)

What matters here is not the argument within the libertarian movement but the reading by Rothbard of the "huge number" of middle-class Americans who are turned off by deliberately materialist "as opposed to" spiritual advocacies.

This is not the place to develop the historical or social-scientific case, including the citation of surveys and polls; a reading of business history in America would produce plenty of evidence. Critics might call the apologias the hypocrisies of robber barons or the self-justifications of a self-delusive bourgeoisie. Rather than attempt to engage in a hermeneutics of suspicion or an examination of the hearts of others, I think it is important now only to make the case that those who had reason to be inclined to "so-called materialism" on the inherited model kept telling themselves, their diaries, their families and friends, and the recipients of their philanthropies that they saw wealth and property not as materialist ends but as part of an also spiritual means.

---

1. For further elaboration of the theme, see Nash (1986) and Schall (1989).

Pure Spiritualism

Conversely, from what might be called the economic, political, and theological left, there has been little resort to frank materialisms in support of addressing the physical needs of the poor, the material necessities of the oppressed, or the institutional revisions necessary for social welfare programs. From the time of colonial-era appeals to doctrines of stewardship for the common good, through the Protestant Social Gospel with its approach to "the Kingdom of God," through the Catholic Bishops' Program and its reference to Pope Leo XIII's explicit theological rationales, through the more recent range of liberation theologies from the whole "pentagon of peoples" (African-, Asian-, Native-, Hispanic-, and Euro-Americans), to the voices of feminist and gender-based interest groups with their cries that God shows "a preferential option for the poor," the oppressed, and the victimized, there has been a consistent claim that it is the right, the free-market advocates, who are materialist, while "we" are spiritual. On this point, Menand is right: groups "all somehow end up saying the same thing" out of their diverse backgrounds.

This means that on the left in general and, by definition, the religious left in particular, there has been little undialectical *or* dialectical materialism. The anti-spirituality and anti-religion of Karl Marx have been overlooked. There has been a "great evasion," says historian William Appleman Williams (1964, 12-13).[2] Thus Marx's attacks on religion as the opium of the people were heard as European but were seldom domesticated in America. Of course, some in radical movements like the I.W.W. (Industrial Workers of the World) imported the charge that to be religious or spiritual meant to be distracted by the promise of heaven, of recompense and reversals of fortune in the life to come, to be preoccupied with the time-wasting delusion of the practice of prayer and worship. But the votes were simply not there in large numbers for those who made such charges.

Harder-line ideologues and softer-line right-wing analysts of the left and left-wing analysts of the right were not and will not easily now be convinced of the spiritual preoccupations and interpretations of their

2. For a book-length defense of the spiritual side of the economic left in American religion, see Craig (1992).

opponents. But whoever listens to what anthropologists call "agents' descriptions" will find that both "sides" pervasively and persistently have refused to "neglect" or "oppose" the spiritual dimensions of existence. And there have always been explicitly Christian voices, from the nineteenth-century Protestant political economists like Francis Wayland to the twentieth-century activists like Walter Rauschenbusch, Martin Luther King, and Dorothy Day, who infused the social-welfare movements with biblical, religious, and broadly spiritual motifs and impulses.

It is not possible or necessary here to give equal time to materialism and spirituality. Let it be said, however, that American spirituality — from Anne Hutchinson and Roger Williams, through Mary Dyer, William Penn, and John Woolman, and then still further through Frances Willard, Walter Rauschenbusch, and Reinhold Niebuhr, down to Martin Luther King, Thomas Merton, Dorothy Day, Abraham Joshua Heschel, and some of our contemporaries — has always been "activist," to use Maritain's designation. Its partisans have made efforts to make a difference in the material world.

To put it provocatively but, I think, defensibly: If one were to assemble anthological material into two books, *Classics of American Activism* and *Classics of American Spirituality*, in the vast majority of cases the same authors would be in both. There would not be one book on practical, productive, pragmatic, and programmatic sorts who care about the material world and another on mystical, passive, meditative, and contemplative types. These exemplars can hardly be accused of being "opposed to material or worldly interests." Indeed, the Christians among them in their lives seemed to be writing footnotes to the contention of the late Anglican Archbishop William Temple that "Christianity is the most materialistic of all great religions." Temple was arguing against spiritualistic and gnostic translations of Christianity in the Anglican and English world, but some American believers may have needed his reminder as well. If so, he was giving good conscience and theological clarity to people who in effect said or showed that they knew all along what Temple was declaring.

The accent, then, falls on the religious and spiritual side of the fused material and spiritual dimensions. Sometimes the social theologians had a good deal of interpreting to do as they transacted with those who were considered to be pure materialists, people who were charged with gathering money through questionable means "to the neglect of spiritual matters." My favorite tale of the transactors has to do with Graham Taylor, a major advocate of the Social Gospel at the (Congregationalist) Chicago Theological Seminary. The seminary needed funds to propagate, among other things, Taylor's advocacy of addressing the material needs of the urban poor. Its leaders looked with some envy on the decade-old, Baptist-founded University of Chicago to the seminary's south. It was having success drawing millions from Baptist John D. Rockefeller.

The most noted Congregationalist congregational minister of the time, Washington Gladden of Columbus, Ohio, preached a sermon entitled "Malefactors of Great Wealth." Rockefeller's fortune, Gladden preached, "is laid in the most relentless rapacity known to modern commercial history. He has organized a system of plunder and a system of brigandage." When, in 1905, the American Board of Commissioners for Foreign Missions accepted an unsolicited gift of $100,000 from the pious Rockefeller, Gladden protested the "dishonorable alliance. . . . Benevolences cannot atone for wrongs." But Taylor, though he was a friend of Gladden, disagreed. What counted in a penny, he said, was "not its pedigree but its destiny" (McGiffert 1965, 137-38).

Taken at their own word, the Rockefellers and other "relentlessly rapacious" plunderers and brigands saw things quite differently. With few exceptions, they left behind legacies of spoken and written words showing that they did not want to be devoted to material needs or desires "to the neglect of spiritual matters." Their failures may have been gross, depending upon the standards that one uses to judge them. But their efforts are part of a continuum that complicates — some would say compromises — the life of prophets in a for-profit society. From the libertarian, free-market, and material-celebrating right, for instance, has come a countering set of observations about and charges against this kind. The religious social-welfare advocates, it was regularly claimed, spoke more out of the security of academic tenure than in the trenches of congregational life, where there was no insulation from the laity; the professors, journalists, and prestigious pastors were no less devoted to material concerns like pensions and financial security than were those who defended material acquisitiveness. Now more than then it gets pointed out that those who are seen as critics of the social order often produce best-sellers. Those who decry the materialism of the advertising and promotional worlds welcome it when their publishers advertise their books and promote their personas.

I am pointing to something structural, hard to escape, and almost impossible to transcend in a culture where material affluence has been accessible across a wide range of classes, professions, and interests. Some Americans have been egregiously materialist "to the neglect of spiritual matters." Not everyone in their concerns has been obsessively attached to things of the spirit "as opposed to material or worldly interests." But the American situation has allowed for few pure separations of the two sets of impulses. Such separation may have been possible during the periods of the rise of pure market or pure collective economic advocacies in Protestant and secular Europe. It may have been possible in the long memory of Catholic Europe, where "contemplatives" were radically distanced by space and calling from "activists," "secular" priests, and the laity. But the American mix has not permitted much of such pure defining. People have had to improvise interpretations, legitimations, and ways of life that transect or transcend the old distinctions. How they have done this makes up much of the plot of American religious history.

Two Sources of the American Ethos

Ordinarily, two main sources are seen as the historic feeders into the American ethos, and they will have to be considered when the longer history of "rethought materialism" and "spirituality" is written. One of these can be coded by the word *Enlightenment;* Sidney E. Mead calls it "the religion of the republic." He likes to quote historian Crane Brinton: "[In] the late seventeenth century . . . there arose in our society what seems to clearly be a new religion. . . . I call this religion simply Enlightenment, with a capital E" (Brinton 1964, 315). This "religion of the republic," comments Mead, "provides, or legitimates, the premises of the Declaration of Independence, the Constitution, and a long line of Supreme Court decisions" (Mead 1975, 118).

Mead traces only the *civil* consequences of the Enlightenment religion of virtually all of the founders, the Franklins and Washingtons, the Jeffersons and Adamses and Madisons. In their own time and since, they were also seen as promoting *material* ("propertied") outlooks.

Theirs was a God of Reason and Nature who called them to responsibility in the things of this world, a call apart from the mystical and metaphysical calls that accompanied often otherworldly scriptural religion. Many founders were people of property, of wealth, preoccupied with gaining more — even to the extent of their employing systems of human slavery. But being "antimetaphysical," as Jefferson would have it, never meant working "to the neglect of spiritual matters." Whoever traces their economic thought will find that, in Franklin's spirit, they promoted frugality and opposed luxury, a sign of awareness that "devotion to material . . . interests" could be corrupting, debilitating, and anti-spiritual. Sidney Mead is not alone in complaining at book length in *The Nation with the Soul of a Church* that critics using the "prophetic" tradition associated with Judaism and Christianity have scored their points against the Enlightenment and its successor, the "American Way of Life" religion, by measuring them at their realized worst against the standards of a Jewish and Christian idealized best. Critics of church and synagogue who used vantages of the Enlightenment heritage have done the same thing.

It should be clear from this that comment on the spiritual strivings of Americans — from Enlightenment foreparents, through ordinary practical people and the industrial and corporate magnates, to modern apologists for attachment to free-market and libertarian economies — cannot be a normative or definitive statement on the *quality* of their expressions. To attempt to make such a statement raises the issue of the measurement of values — it is notoriously difficult to assess just *how* materialist or spiritual anyone is! — and, even more, the question of where one gets the agreed-upon norms for judgment. What needs stating here is an observation that looks to me to be well-based on the historical record and the empirical data: that significant representatives among those prone to and accused of being pure materialists have, in ways that qualify as being pervasive and persistent, *not* devoted themselves to the material "to the neglect of spiritual matters" — any more than many a preoccupied priest or guru might have done.

I have just referred to the other source on which the majority — over 80 percent in any poll — of Americans claim to draw for their thinking about material and spiritual interests: the prophetic, biblical, Jewish, and Christian traditions. These traditions show concern for both the material and the spiritual *and* make demands upon adherents to be stewards of one and devotees of the other — at the same time! That almost goes without saying, but is said anyhow by most biblical scholars and historians of theology. The drastic separation of spheres in our language has derived in part from the prophetic notice of the idolatrous lures of the material: "You cannot serve God and mammon!" is quoted from Jesus. Christians more than Jews have been warned not to "love the world, nor the things that are in the world." Ascetic, world-denying, otherworldly, and purely spiritual impulses have been encouraged a few times in New Testament scriptures and often in monastic and other ascetic traditions. These influences naturally fed into the norm-setting perceptions of those Europeans who applied the "old tag" of materialism to Americans, and into the perceptions of Americans who, Maritain knew from conversation, often accepted it. The countertexts about loving the created order, tending the earthly garden, seeking the welfare of the human city, being stewards, and enjoying material goods occur just as frequently. These always suggest that the material world is the scene of spiritual striving. Texts like Isaiah 58 and scores more reveal prophetic and Yahwist disdain for the spiritualizers who devoted themselves to fasting and prayer at the expense of attention to material needs and interests.

The biblical tradition in Protestantism arrived in America during an unfolding that saw lay and clerical leadership alike devoted to the material realm. The fabled Calvinist "work" ethic mitigated or compromised the compulsive material quest through doctrines of vocation, stewardship, and mission. The move "from Puritan to Yankee," to use the title of the book by Richard Bushman, and comparable moves in other variations of the tradition have meant some secularization of the spiritual impulse. But in American economic moves, the pervasively and persistently religious claims have been sufficiently consistent that they could help a Maritain counter the charges of American materialism.

Culture-Specific Instances: South and North America

That adaptation by citizens and believers to the needs and desires for the material and the attachment to or regard for things of the spirit is culture-specific. It varies somewhat, depending upon which peoples are doing adapting in which environments with which resources and ide-ologies; this is made clear by comparisons between historic North Amer-ican and traditional South American developments. In an ingenious and often overlooked book entitled *The Public Man: An Interpretation of Latin American and Other Catholic Countries* (1977), Glen Caudill Dealy contrasts the two. His generalizations are too broad, but his insights are sharp. He refers to the Protestant ethos à la Max Weber as the favoring of capitalism as "a whole pattern of civilization" and not simply a mode of economic exchange. Dealy argues that this ethos "does not hold a unique place within the Western world as a culture integrator," but "reflects the particular stance of bourgeois man: the economists and social scientists that capitalistic society has fostered." The system "is not a unique and inexorable life style toward which all societies are moving," even if, I would add, subcultures in the United States in some ways are.

Dealy believes that the Latin American Catholic-based ethos, which he calls a *caudillaje* (rooted in *caudillo*, meaning "leader" or "chief"), is an alternative ideal-type value system. The stereotypical North American Protestant accumulates possessions and material wealth for security. The stereotypical South American Catholic, who is a "public" person, accumulates friends of and relations to the *caudillo* (whether politician, priest, or person of means) for similar security. The Catholic pursues public power the way the Protestant strives for private wealth. The theological rootages differ in the two contexts, as do the modes of rationalization and the expressions of piety. It is not that one is materialistic and the other is not so, or that one is spiritual and the other is not so. They are material and spiritual in different fusions and interactions (Dealy 1977, 1-12, and passim).

It would be foolish to make too much of these ideal types. The Protestant type has recently come to stamp Latin American cultures, thanks to conversions to evangelicalism and the spread of free-market economic patterns. Catholic liberation theology meanwhile and all along has drawn on some European Protestant and secular impulses. It is also important to note that the United States is and has long been one-fourth Catholic. Both continents belong to an international economic *oikoumene* whose fusing energies only increase in an age of rapid transportation and world-shrinking mass media. But Dealy is suggestive in reminding us that different cultural contexts give people different repertoires for relating to material and spiritual worlds alike.

The Fusion Illustrated:
A Nineteenth-Century Instance

In the United States the fusion of Enlightenment and biblical (often specifically Protestant) modes was far along in the nineteenth century. One of the ways to gain an understanding of its pervasiveness and persistence is to read Ruth Miller Elson's canvass of all the public-school textbooks of the century. They were popularizations of the Enlightenment ethos and the biblical expression. I'll let her summarize:

> Throughout the century the virtues most frequently praised in the individual are economic ones, industry and frugality, and these are given the sanction of religion. Idleness is not only economically unproductive, but "It is a great sin to be idle." Ideal economic behavior rests on the combined precepts of Calvin and Benjamin Franklin; both the Bible and Franklin are liberally quoted. Nature itself is always busy by the ordinance of God; the bees, ants and beavers are the usual illustrations. The most popular selection on this subject is, of course, Isaac Watts' "How doth the little busy bee. . . ." The Calvinistic doctrine of the stewardship of wealth is applied to life itself: "Existence is a sacred trust; and he who misemploys and squanders it away is treacherous to its author." . . . The all-pervading religious emphasis in schoolbooks, then, sanctions virtues likely to lead to materialism rather than otherworldliness. . . . Throughout the century religion sanctions the process of making money; by the bestowal or withdrawal of material goods God rewards or punishes men immediately in the temporal realm.

The level of spirituality may not have been very high in these translations of the Enlightenment and the Bible. It is hard to read Elson's well-documented summaries without finding in the texts great potential contributors to cruel economic practices and psychological adaptations. But the main point gets reinforced: even children in this culture were not to be obsessed with "devotion to material needs or desires, to the neglect of spiritual matters." And Elson does adduce scores of textbook citations that do suggest direct attention to more nearly "pure" but never antimaterial spirituality. The critics of religious calls for asceticism or otherworldliness would find little documentation in such texts (Elson 1964, 245-61, esp. 252-53; also 41-64).

The Situation Today;
Prospects for Tomorrow

We do not live in the world of the *caudillo*, though it may be closer and better represented here than before. We do not congenially live in the worlds of John Calvin and Adam Smith or Benjamin Franklin; of nineteenth-century public-school textbooks; of the Social Gospel or George Gilder. America is more diverse and multicultural in ways that Louis Menand's observation did not exhaust. Ideal types are ever harder to discern or create, and exceptions to rules about American identity and character increase exponentially. It is too soon to learn what the presence of "public woman" in wealth and power — as well as in the forefront of spiritual expression, as is increasingly the case — will do to the improvisations about the materialism that does not neglect spiritual matters, or the spirituality that is not opposed to the material. Given the record and much of what is observable today, however, there are good reasons to believe that both will be pervasive and persistent.

Looking ahead, as I am not called to do, however, I would look in certain directions that Maritain, back in 1945 and 1956, already indicated were evidences of a fresh emergence. More has to be made now of the voluntary and independent sectors, of philanthropy and charity and volunteering — in directions to which Robert Wuthnow and others in the Princeton and Lilly orbits have for some time been pointing. Wuthnow's *Acts of Compassion: Caring for Others and Helping Ourselves* (1991) is but one of many settings forth of examples. The Americans he describes are devoted to the material but not neglectful of the spiritual by any measure — and on a scale probably unmatched by the Europeans who looked over Maritain's shoulder, or by many in the undeveloped nations who have good reason to experience firsthand the purer materialism of much American enterprise.

Meanwhile, the accent on spirituality has increased in recent years. In 1967 I found no less a theologian and devotee of the Spirit than Paul Tillich despairing of the concept and of attempts to resuscitate the adjective *spiritual*: it was, he said, "lost beyond hope" (Tillich 1963; Marty 1967, 99-115). There are reasons to make the qualitative judgment that much of the new spiritual obsession is superficial, "commodified," banalized in consumer culture, that it is an evasion of deeper, more established aspects of faith and religion and community. But one cannot help but notice the energy and enterprise that even the more affluent people in the culture are putting into the spiritual quest. Certainly it has to be reckoned with in a world post-Maritain.

A Key: The Modes of Experience

In all this, as often elsewhere, I am drawing upon a theory of personality and history that refuses to see life in hardened spatial terms (as in spheres of "the material" and "the spiritual") but that looks at alternatives.

Benjamin Mariante calls these differing "foci of consciousness"; Alfred Schutz, "universes of discourse" and "provinces of meaning"; William James, subjects of "attentiveness" and attention; and Michael Oakeshott, "modes of experience." Maritain's European critics of American materialism (and Marx's critics of non-material, otherworldly spirituality) thought that Americans, surrounded as they were by material resources, and welcoming as they did philosophies that legitimated material quests, had to be given over to the material at the neglect of all else, *or* to the spiritual in opposition to all else.

Not at all, or not simply. They could have a "focus of consciousness" on accumulation and at the same time focus consciousness on giving. They could inhabit a competitive free-market "universe of discourse" and at the same time contribute to a cooperative ethos and fabric. They could live in a "province of meaning" apparently unbounded by judgment and move with ease to the zone where texts and preachments effectively did judge them and move their spirits. They were "attentive" to compulsive material ventures and often able to retreat and find spiritual refuge. They lived with many "modes of experience," not without occasions of bad faith, weak faith, and unfaith. But at least they showed signs of endeavor which — and Maritain was right on this point — had often been overlooked, misperceived, or wrongly interpreted. Whatever "new tag" visitors from abroad or critics from within apply, the "old tag" of "so-called materialism" cannot survive without reservation.

References

Alcorn, Randy. 1989. *Money, Possessions, and Eternity.* Wheaton, Ill.: Tyndale Press.

Appadurai, Arjun, ed. 1986. *The Social Life of Things: Commodities in Cultural Perspective.* Cambridge: Cambridge University Press.

Aquinas, Thomas. 1975. *Summa Contra Gentiles.* Translated by Vernon J. Bourke. Notre Dame: University of Notre Dame Press.

Arrow, Kenneth. 1984. "The Economics of Information." In vol. 4 of *Collected Papers.* Oxford: Blackwell.

Avanzini, John. 1989. *The Wealth of the World: The Proven Wealth Transfer System.* Tulsa: Harrison House.

Avila, Charles. 1983. *Ownership: Early Christian Teaching.* Maryknoll, N.Y.: Orbis Books.

Badiner, Allan Hunt, ed. 1990. *Dharma Gaia: A Harvest of Essays in Buddhism and Ecology.* Berkeley: Parallax Press.

Bailyn, Bernard. 1967. *The Ideological Origins of the American Revolution.* Cambridge: Harvard University Press.

Baldwin, Stanley. 1988. *Take This Job and Love It.* Downers Grove, Ill.: Inter-Varsity Press.

Barton, Michael. 1989. "The Victorian Jeremiad: Critics of Accumulation and Display." Pp. 55-72 in *Consuming Visions: Accumulation and Display of Goods in America, 1880-1920,* edited by Simon J. Bronner. New York: W. W. Norton.

Baumgartner, M. P. 1988. *The Moral Order of a Suburb.* New York: Oxford University Press.

Becker, Gary S. 1981. *A Treatise on the Family.* Cambridge: Harvard University Press.

Belk, Russell W., Melanie Wallendorf, and John F. Sherry Jr. 1989. "The Sacred and the Profane in Consumer Behavior: Theodicy on the Odyssey." *Journal of Consumer Research* 16 (June): 1-38.

Bellah, Robert N. 1967. "Civil Religion in America." *Daedalus* 96 (Winter): 1-21.

————. 1970. *Beyond Belief: Essays on Religion in a Post-Traditional World.* New York: Harper & Row.

————. 1973. *Emile Durkheim on Morality and Society.* Chicago: University of Chicago Press.

Bellah, Robert N., and Phillip E. Hammond. 1980. *Varieties of Civil Religion.* New York: Harper & Row.

Bellah, Robert N., et al. 1985. *Habits of the Heart: Individualism and Commitment in American Life.* Berkeley and Los Angeles: University of California Press.

Bellah, Robert N., et al. 1991. *The Good Society.* New York: Knopf.

Bendix, Reinhard. 1964. *Nation-Building and Citizenship.* New York: John Wiley.

Benhabib, Seyla. 1982. "The Generalized and Concrete Other." Pp. 154-77 in *Women and Moral Theory,* edited by Eva Kittay and Diane Meyers. Totowa, N.J.: Rowman & Littlefield.

Berger, Peter L. 1986. *The Capitalist Revolution: Fifty Propositions about Prosperity, Equality, and Liberty.* New York: Basic Books.

Berger, Peter L., ed. 1990. *The Capitalist Spirit: Toward a Religious Ethic of Wealth Creation.* San Francisco: Institute for Contemporary Studies Press.

Bergesen, Albert. 1980. "From Utilitarianism to Globology: The Shift from the Individual to the World as a Whole as the Primordial Unit of Analysis." Pp. 1-12 in *Studies of the Modern World-System,* edited by Albert Bergesen. New York: Academic Press.

————. 1990. "Turning World-System Theory on Its Head." *Theory, Culture, and Society* 7: 67-81.

Berman, Morris. 1984. *The Reenchantment of the World.* Toronto: Bantam Books.

Biggart, Nicole Woolsey. 1989. *Charismatic Capitalism: Direct Selling Organizations in America.* Chicago: University of Chicago Press.

Blaug, Mark. 1992. *The Methodology of Economics: Or How Economists Explain.* 2d ed. Cambridge: Cambridge University Press.

Block, Walter, Geoffrey Brennan, and Kenneth Elzinga, eds. 1982. *Morality of the Market: Religious and Economic Perspectives.* Vancouver: The Fraser Institute.

Bloom, Allan. 1987. *The Closing of the American Mind: How Higher Education*

Has Failed Democracy and Impoverished the Souls of Today's Students. New York: Simon & Schuster.

Blumin, Stuart. 1985. "The Hypothesis of Middle-Class Formation in Nineteenth-Century America: A Critique and Some Proposals." *American Historical Review* 90 (April): 299-338.

Boli, John. 1981. "Marxism as World Religion." *Social Problems* 28 (June): 510-13.

————. 1989. *New Citizens for a New Society: The Institutional Origins of Mass Schooling in Sweden*. Oxford: Pergamon Press.

Bookchin, Murray. 1990. *Remaking Society: Pathways to a Green Future*. Boston: South End Press.

Boorstin, Daniel J. 1973. *The Americans: The Democratic Experience*. New York: Random House.

Bottomore, Tom, et al., eds. 1983. *A Dictionary of Marxist Thought*. Cambridge: Harvard University Press.

Bourdieu, Pierre. 1984. *Distinction: A Social Critique of the Judgment of Taste*. Translated by Richard Nice. Cambridge: Harvard University Press.

Brinton, Crane. 1964. "Many Mansions." In *American Historical Review* 49 (January).

Bronner, Simon J., ed. 1989. *Consuming Visions: Accumulation and Display of Goods in America, 1880-1920*. New York: W. W. Norton.

Bruce, Steve, ed. 1992. *Religion and Modernization: Sociologists and Historians Debate the Secularization Thesis*. New York: Oxford University Press.

Bullard, Robert D. 1993. *Confronting Environmental Racism*. Boston: South End Press.

Bürgenmeier, Beat. 1992. *Socioeconomics: An Interdisciplinary Approach*. Translated by Kevin Cook. Boston: Kluwer Academic Publications.

Burkett, Larry. 1990. *Business by the Book*. Nashville, Tenn.: Thomas Nelson Publishers.

Burns, Gene. 1992. *The Frontiers of Catholicism*. Berkeley and Los Angeles: University of California Press.

Bushnell, Horace. 1883. *Work and Play*. New York: Charles Scribner's Sons.

Calvin, John. 1948. *Commentaries on the First Book of Moses Called Genesis*. Translated by John King. Grand Rapids: William B. Eerdmans.

Campbell, Colin. 1987. *The Romantic Ethic and the Spirit of Modern Consumerism*. London: Basil Blackwell.

Casanova, José. 1994. *Public Religions in the Modern World*. Chicago: University of Chicago Press.

Caywood, George. 1989. *Escaping Materialism: Living a Life That's Rich toward God*. Sisters, Ore.: Questar Publications.

Chase-Dunn, Christopher. 1989. *Global Formation: Structures of the World-Economy.* Cambridge: Basil Blackwell.

Christon, Lawrence. 1991. "She Doesn't Make It Easy: Diane Ford's Sly, Earthy Humor," *Los Angeles Times,* 27 January, p. 8.

Chrysostom, St. John. 1984. *On Wealth and Poverty.* Translated by Catherine P. Roth. Crestwood, N.Y.: St. Vladimir's Seminary Press.

Clayton, Philip. 1989. *Explanation from Physics to Theology: An Essay in Rationality and Religion.* New Haven: Yale University Press.

Coleman, James S. 1990. *Foundations of Social Theory.* Cambridge: Harvard University Press–Belknap Press.

Collins, Randall. 1980. "Weber's Last Theory of Capitalism: A Systematization." *American Sociological Review* 45 (December): 925-42.

———. 1986. "A Theory of Technology." Ch. 4 in *Weberian Sociological Theory* by Randall Collins. Cambridge: Cambridge University Press.

———. 1988. "The Micro Contribution to Macro Sociology." *Sociological Theory* 6 (Fall): 242-53.

Colson, Charles, and Jack Eckerd. 1991. *Why America Doesn't Work.* Dallas: Word Publishing.

Copeland, Gloria. 1978. *God's Will Is Prosperity.* Tulsa: Harrison House.

Copeland, Kenneth. 1974. *The Laws of Prosperity.* Forth Worth, Tex.: Kenneth Copeland Publications.

Coughlin, Richard, ed. 1991. *Morality, Rationality, and Efficiency: New Perspectives in Socio-Economics.* Armonk, N.Y.: M. E. Sharpe.

Craig, Robert H. 1992. *Religion and Radical Politics: An Alternative Christian Tradition in the United States.* Philadelphia: Temple University Press.

Crowley, J. E. 1974. *This Sheba, Self: The Conceptualization of Economic Life in Eighteenth-Century America.* Baltimore: Johns Hopkins University Press.

D'Antonio, William V. 1992. "Recruiting Sociologists in a Time of Changing Opportunities." Pp. 99-136 in *Sociology and Its Publics: The Forms and Fates of Disciplinary Organization,* edited by Terence C. Halliday and Morris Janowitz. Chicago: University of Chicago Press.

Daun, Åke. 1983. "The Materialistic Life-Style: Some Socio-Psychological Aspects." Pp. 6-16 in *Consumer Behavior and Environmental Quality,* edited by Lisa Uusitalo. Helsinki: Gower.

Davis, Kingsley. 1949. *Human Society.* New York: Macmillan.

Dayton, Edward. 1992. *How to Succeed in Business without Losing Your Faith.* Grand Rapids: Baker Book House.

Dealy, Glen Caudill. 1977. *The Public Man: An Interpretation of Latin American and Other Catholic Countries.* Amherst: University of Massachusetts Press.

Deetz, Stanley. 1991. *Democracy in an Age of Corporate Colonization.* Albany, N.Y.: SUNY Press.

Degler, Carl. 1991. *In Search of Human Nature: The Decline and Revival of Darwinism in American Social Thought.* New York: Oxford University Press.

De Man, Henri. 1929. *Joy in Work.* London: George Allen & Unwin.

Demerath, N. J. III, and Rhys Williams. 1992. *A Bridging of Faiths: Religion and Politics in a New England City.* Princeton: Princeton University Press.

Devall, Bill, and George Sessions. 1993. "Deep Ecology." Pp. 39-46 in *Radical Environmentalism: Philosophy and Tactics,* edited by Peter C. List. Belmont, Calif.: Wadsworth.

Douglas, Mary. 1966. *Purity and Danger: An Analysis of Concepts of Pollution and Taboo.* London: Routledge & Kegan Paul.

Douglas, Mary, and Baron Isherwood. 1979. *The World of Goods: Towards an Anthropology of Consumption.* New York: Basic Books.

Dumont, Louis. 1977. *From Mandeville to Marx: The Genesis and Triumph of Economic Ideology.* Chicago: University of Chicago Press.

Durkheim, Emile. 1933 [1893]. *The Division of Labor in Society.* Translated by George Simpson. New York: Free Press.

———. 1951 [1915]. *The Elementary Forms of the Religious Life.* Translated by Joseph Ward Swain. Glencoe, Ill.: Free Press.

———. 1973. "The Dualism of Human Nature and Its Social Conditions." Pp. 149-63 in *Emile Durkheim on Morality and Society* by Robert N. Bellah. Chicago: University of Chicago Press.

———. 1992 [1937]. *Professional Ethics and Civic Morals.* Translated by Cornelia Brookfield. London: Routledge.

Edgerton, Robert B. 1985. *Rules, Exceptions, and Social Order.* Berkeley and Los Angeles: University of California Press.

Elkins, Stanley. 1959. *Slavery: A Problem in American Institutional and Intellectual Life.* Chicago: University of Chicago Press.

Ellickson, Robert C. 1991. *Order without Law: How Neighbors Settle Disputes.* Cambridge: Harvard University Press.

Ellul, Jacques. 1971. *Autopsy of Revolution.* Translated by Patricia Wolf. New York: Alfred A. Knopf.

———. 1973. *Les nouveaux possédés.* Paris: Arthème Fayard. Translated by C. Edward Hopkin as *The New Demons.* New York: Seabury Press, 1975.

———. 1984 [1954]. *Money and Power.* Translated by LaVonne Neff. Downers Grove, Ill.: InterVarsity Press.

———. 1990. *Reason for Being: A Meditation on Ecclesiastes.* Translated by Joyce Main Hanks. Grand Rapids: William B. Eerdmans.

Elson, Ruth Miller. 1964. *Guardians of Tradition: American Schoolbooks of the Nineteenth Century.* Lincoln: University of Nebraska Press.

Elster, Jon. 1992. *Local Justice: How Institutions Allocate Scarce Goods and Necessary Burdens.* New York: Russell Sage Foundation.

Epstein, Richard A. 1992. *Forbidden Grounds: The Case against Employment Discrimination Laws.* Cambridge: Harvard University Press.

Etzioni, Amitai. 1988. *The Moral Dimension: Toward a New Economics.* New York: Free Press.

————. 1993. *The Spirit of Community: Rights, Responsibilities, and the Communitarian Agenda.* New York: Crown Publishing.

Evans, Peter, Dietrich Rueschemeyer, and Theda Skocpol, eds. 1985. *Bringing the State Back In.* Cambridge: Cambridge University Press.

Eyer, Diane. 1992. *Mother-Infant Bonding: A Scientific Fiction.* New Haven: Yale University Press.

Farney, Dennis. 1992. "Literary History." *Wall Street Journal,* 16 September, p. A1.

Feuerbach, Ludwig. 1957 [1841]. *The Essence of Christianity.* Translated by G. Eliot. New York: Harper & Row.

Fichte, Johann Gottlieb. 1845/46. *Sämmtliche Werke,* edited by I. H. Fichte. Berlin: Veit und Comp.

Fletcher, George. 1993. *Loyalty: An Essay on the Morality of Relationships.* New York: Oxford University Press.

Foster, Richard. 1985. *Money, Sex, and Power: The Challenge of the Disciplined Life.* New York: Harper & Row.

Fox, Warwick. 1990. *Toward a Transpersonal Ecology: Developing New Foundations for Environmentalism.* Boston: Shambhala Publications.

Fredrickson, George. 1965. *The Inner Civil War: Northern Intellectuals and the Crisis of the Union.* New York: Harper & Row.

Frey, Bruno S., Werner W. Pommerehne, Friedrich Schneider, and Guy Gilbert. 1984. "Consensus and Dissensus among Economists: An Empirical Inquiry." *American Economic Review* 74:986-95.

Frohock, Fred. 1992. *Healing Powers: Alternative Medicine, Spiritual Communities, and the State.* Chicago: University of Chicago Press.

Fuller, Thomas. 1648. *A Sermon of Contentment.* London.

Galbraith, Kenneth John. 1958. *The Affluent Society.* Boston: Houghton Mifflin.

Gambetta, Diego. 1990. *Trust: Making and Breaking Cooperative Relations.* Oxford: Basil Blackwell.

Gauthier, David P. 1986. *Morals by Agreement.* Oxford: Clarendon Press.

Gay, Craig. 1991. *With Liberty and Justice for Whom? The Recent Evangelical Debate over Capitalism.* Grand Rapids: William B. Eerdmans.

Geertz, Clifford. 1973. *The Interpretation of Cultures.* New York: Basic Books.

Gerschon, David, and Gail Straub. 1989. *Empowerment: The Art of Creating Your Life as You Want It.* New York: Dell.

Gewirth, Allan. 1978. *Reason and Morality.* Chicago: University of Chicago Press.

Gilder, George. 1981. *Wealth and Poverty.* New York: Bentham Books.

Gilligan, Carol. 1982. *In a Different Voice: Psychological Theory and Women's Development.* Cambridge: Harvard University Press.

Gilmore, Michael T. 1985. *American Romanticism and the Marketplace.* Chicago: University of Chicago Press.

Glendon, Mary Ann. 1991. *Rights Talk: The Impoverishment of Political Discourse.* New York: Basic Books.

Goffman, Erving. 1956. "The Nature of Deference and Demeanor." *American Anthropologist* 58 (June): 473-502.

———. 1967. *Interaction Ritual: Essays on Face-to-Face Behavior.* New York: Pantheon Books.

———. 1971. *Relations in Public: Microstudies of the Public Order.* New York: Harper.

Goldmann, Lucien. 1973. *The Philosophy of the Enlightenment: The Christian Burgess and the Enlightenment.* Translated by Henry Maas. Cambridge: MIT Press.

Goldsmith, M. M. 1988. "Regulating Anew the Moral and Political Sentiments of Mankind: Bernard Mandeville and the Scottish Enlightenment." *Journal of the History of Ideas* 49:587-606.

Goodin, Robert E. 1988. *Reasons for Welfare: The Political Theory of the Welfare State.* Princeton: Princeton University Press.

Goodwin, Craufurd D. 1988. "The Heterogeneity of the Economists' Discourse: Philosopher, Priest, and Hired Gun." Pp. 207-20 in *The Consequences of Economic Rhetoric,* edited by Arjo Klamer, Donald N. McCloskey, and Robert M. Solow. Cambridge: Cambridge University Press.

Gore, Al. 1992. *Earth in the Balance: Ecology and the Human Spirit.* New York: Houghton Mifflin.

Goudzwaard, Bob. 1978. *Capitalism and Progress: A Diagnosis of Western Society.* Translated by J. Van Nuis Zylstra. Grand Rapids: William B. Eerdmans.

Granovetter, Mark S. 1973. "The Strength of Weak Ties." *American Journal of Sociology* 78 (May): 1360-80.

Green, Robert W., ed. 1959. *Protestantism and Capitalism: The Weber Thesis and Its Critics.* Problems in European Civilization series. Boston: D. C. Heath.

Greene, Jack P. 1988. *Pursuits of Happiness: The Social Development of Early Modern British Colonies and the Formation of American Culture.* Chapel Hill: University of North Carolina Press.

Gregory, C. A. 1982. *Gifts and Commodities.* London: Academic Press.

Habermas, Jürgen. 1962. *Strukturwandel der Öffentlichkeit. Untersuchungen zu einer Kategorie der bürgerlichen Gesellschaft.* Koblenz: Neuwied.

———. 1987. *The Theory of Communicative Action.* 2 vols. Translated by Thomas McCarthy. Boston: Beacon Press.

————. 1991. *The Structural Transformation of the Public Sphere.* Translated by Thomas Burger. Cambridge: MIT Press.

Hacker, Andrew. 1967. "A Defense (or at Least an Explanation) of American Materialism." *Sales Management,* March, pp. 31-33.

Hadden, Jeffrey K., and Anson Shupe. 1988. *Televangelism: Power and Politics on God's Frontier.* New York: Henry Holt.

Halevy, Elie. 1928. *The Growth of Philosophical Radicalism.* Translated by Mary Morris. London: Faber & Faber.

Harris, Janis Long. 1992. *Secrets of People Who Love Their Work.* Downers Grove, Ill.: InterVarsity Press.

Hartley, Keith. 1992. "Exogenous Factors in Neo-Classical Microeconomics." Pp. 50-73 in *Interfaces in Economic and Social Analysis,* edited by Ulf Himmelstrand. London: Routledge.

Hauerwas, Stanley, and William H. Willimon. 1989. *Resident Aliens: Life in the Christian Colony.* Nashville: Abingdon.

Haughey, John C. 1989. *Converting Nine to Five: A Spirituality of Daily Work.* New York: Crossroad.

Havel, Vaclav, ed. 1985. *The Power of the Powerless: Citizens against the State in Central and Eastern Europe.* Armonk, N.Y.: M. E. Sharpe.

Hayles, N. Katherine, ed. 1991. *Chaos and Order: Complex Dynamics in Literature and Science.* Chicago: University of Chicago Press.

Hegel, Georg Wilhelm Friedrich. 1963 [1813]. *Wissenschaft der Logik.* 2 vols. Hamburg: Verlag von Felix Meiner.

————. 1973 [1818-31]. *Vorlesungen über Rechtsphilosophie.* Edited by K. H. Itling. Stuttgart-Bad Canstatt: Frommann-Holzboog.

————. 1976 [1821]. *Grundlinien der Philosophie des Rechts oder Naturrecht und Staatswissenschaft im Grundrisse.* Frankfurt am Main: Suhrkamp.

————. 1977 [1807]. *Phänomenologie des Geistes.* Frankfurt am Main: Suhrkamp.

Heimer, Carole. 1985. *Reactive Risk and Rational Action: Managing Moral Hazard in Insurance Contracts.* Berkeley and Los Angeles: University of California Press.

————. Unpublished. "Doing Your Job *and* Helping Your Friends: Universalistic Norms about Obligations to Particular Others in Networks."

————. Unpublished. "Producing Responsible People in Order to Produce Oil: Bringing Obligations, Rights, Incentives, and Resources Together in the Norwegian State Oil Company."

Hengel, Martin. 1986. "Arbeit im frühen Christentum." *Theologische Beiträge* 17:174-212.

Henry, Patrick. 1981. " 'And I Don't Care What It Is': The Tradition-History of a Civil Religion Proof-Text." *Journal of the American Academy of Religion* 49.

Herberg, Will. 1955. *Protestant — Catholic — Jew: An Essay in American Religious Sociology.* Garden City, N.Y.: Doubleday.

Hicks, John R. 1938. *Value and Capital.* Oxford: Oxford University Press.

Hinsley, F. H. 1986. *Sovereignty.* 2d ed. Cambridge: Cambridge University Press.

Hirsch, Fred. 1976. *The Social Limits to Growth.* Cambridge: Harvard University Press.

Hirschman, Albert. 1977. *The Passions and the Interests: Political Arguments for Capitalism Before Its Triumph.* Princeton: Princeton University Press.

Hochschild, Arlie. 1983. *The Managed Heart: The Commercialization of Human Feeling.* Berkeley and Los Angeles: University of California Press.

Hollinger, David. 1985. *In the American Province: Studies in the History and Historiography of Ideas.* Baltimore: Johns Hopkins University Press.

Hughey, Michael W. 1990. "Internal Contradictions of Televangelism: Ethical Quandaries of That Old Time Religion in a Brave New World." *International Journal of Politics, Culture, and Society* 4 (1): 31-47.

Hume, David. 1927 [1777]. *Enquiries Concerning Human Understanding and Concerning the Principles of Morals.* Edited by L. A. Selby-Bigge. Oxford: Clarendon Press.

Hummon, David M. 1988. "Tourist Worlds: Tourist Advertising, Ritual, and American Culture." *Sociological Quarterly* 29, no. 2:179-202.

Hunter, James D. 1983. *American Evangelicalism: Conservative Religion and the Quandary of Modernity.* New Brunswick, N.J.: Rutgers University Press.

———. 1987. *Evangelicalism: The Coming Generation.* Chicago: University of Chicago Press.

Hybels, Bill. 1982. *Christians in the Marketplace.* Wheaton, Ill.: Victor Books.

Iannaccone, Lawrence. 1992. "The Economic Orientation of American Protestant Fundamentalism." Pp. 342-66 in *Fundamentalisms and the State,* edited by M. Marty and R. S. Appleby. Chicago: University of Chicago Press.

Ignatieff, Michael. 1986. *The Needs of Strangers: An Essay on Privacy, Solidarity, and the Politics of Being Human.* New York: Penguin Books.

Inglehart, Ronald. 1977. *The Silent Revolution: Changing Values in Politcs and Styles among Western Publics.* Princeton: Princeton University Press.

———. 1990. *Culture Shift in Advanced Industrial Society.* Princeton: Princeton University Press.

Jackall, Robert. 1988. *Moral Mazes: The World of Corporate Managers.* New York: Oxford University Press.

Jardin, André. 1988. *Tocqueville: A Biography.* Translated by Lydia Davis with Robert Hemenway. New York: Farrar, Straus & Giroux.

Jeppersen, Ronald L., and John W. Meyer. 1991. "The Public Order and the Construction of Formal Organizations." Ch. 9 in *The New Institutionalism in Organizational Analysis*, ed. Walter W. Powell and Paul J. DiMaggio. Chicago: University of Chicago Press.

Johnson, Paul. 1978. *A Shopkeeper's Millennium: Society and Revivals in Rochester, New York, 1815-1837.* New York: Hill & Wang.

Johnston, Robert K. 1983. *The Christian at Play.* Grand Rapids: William B. Eerdmans.

Johnstone, Ronald L. 1975. *Religion and Society in Interaction: The Sociology of Religion.* Englewood Cliffs, N.J.: Prentice-Hall.

Jüngel, Eberhard. 1978. *Gott als Geheimnis der Welt. Zur Begründung der Theologie des Gekreuzigten im Streit zwischen Theismus und Atheismus.* Tübingen: J. C. B. Mohr (Paul Siebeck).

Kahneman, Daniel, and Tversky, Amos. 1986. "Choices, Values, and Frames." In *Behavioral and Social Science: Fifty Years of Discovery*, ed. Neil J. Smelser and Dean R. Gerstein. Washington, D.C.: National Academy Press.

Kaiser, Susan B., Richard H. Nagasawa, and Sandra S. Hutton. 1991. "Fashion, Postmodernity and Personal Appearance: A Symbolic Interactionist Formulation." *Symbolic Interaction* 14, no. 2:165-85.

Kant, Immanuel. 1960 [1794]. *Religion within the Limits of Reason Alone.* Translated by T. M. Greene and H. H. Hudson. New York: Harper & Row.

———. 1987 [1790]. *Critique of Judgment.* Translated by W. S. Pulhar. Indianapolis: Hackett Publishing Co.

Katz, Michael. 1993. *The "Underclass" Debate: Views from History.* Princeton: Princeton University Press.

Kaus, Mickey. 1992. *The End of Equality.* New York: New Republic Books.

Kertzer, David I. 1988. *Ritual, Politics, and Power.* New Haven: Yale University Press.

Keynes, John Maynard. 1931. "Economic Possibilities for Our Grandchildren." Pp. 358-73 in *Essays and Persuasions* by John Maynard Keynes. London: Macmillan.

———. 1936. *General Theory of Employment, Interest, and Money.* New York: Harcourt Brace.

King, Ynestra. 1993. "Toward an Ecological Feminism and a Feminist Ecology." Pp. 70-80 in *Radical Environmentalism*, edited by Peter C. List. Belmont, Calif.: Wadsworth.

Klamer, Arjo, Donald N. McCloskey, and Robert M. Solow, eds. 1988. *The Consequences of Economic Rhetoric.* Cambridge: Cambridge University Press.

Knight, Frank H. 1921. *Risk, Uncertainty, and Profit.* Boston: Houghton Mifflin.

Koenenn, Connie. 1990. "Tree Wizards." *Los Angeles Times*, 16 September, p. E1.

Kohlberg, Lawrence. 1980. "The Future of Liberalism as the Dominant Ideology of the West." Pp. 55-68 in *Moral Development and Politics*, edited by Richard W. Wilson and Gordon J. Schochet. New York: Praeger, 1980.

LaChapelle, Dolores. 1988. *Sacred Land, Sacred Sex, Rapture of the Deep: Concerning Deep Ecology and Celebrating Life*. Durango: Kivaki Press.

Lamberton, Don. 1992. "Information Economics: 'Threatened Wreckage' or New Paradigm?" Pp. 113-23 in *Interfaces in Economic and Social Analysis*, edited by Ulf Himmelstrand. London: Routledge.

Lamont, Michele. 1992. *Money, Morals, and Manners*. Chicago: University of Chicago Press.

Lamont, Michele, and Marcel Fournier, eds. 1992. *Where Culture Talks: Exclusion and the Making of Society*. Chicago: University of Chicago Press.

Lane, Christel. 1981. *The Rites of Rulers*. Cambridge: Cambridge University Press.

Lane, Robert E. 1991. *The Market Experience*. Cambridge: Cambridge University Press.

Lasch, Christopher. 1979. *The Culture of Narcissism: American Life in an Age of Diminishing Expectations*. New York: Warner Books.

———. 1991. *The True and Only Heaven: Progress and Its Critics*. New York: W. W. Norton.

Lash, Scott. 1990. *Sociology of Postmodernism*. London: Routledge.

Lears, T. J. Jackson. 1983. "From Salvation to Self-Realization: Advertising and the Therapeutic Roots of the Consumer Culture, 1880-1930." Pp. 1-38 in *The Culture of Consumption: Critical Essays in American History, 1880-1980*, edited by Richard Wrightman Fox and T. J. Jackson Lears. New York: Pantheon Books.

———. 1989. "Beyond Veblen: Rethinking Consumer Culture in America." Pp. 73-98 in *Consuming Visions; Accumulation and Display of Goods in America, 1880-1920*, edited by Simon J. Bronner. New York: W. W. Norton.

Leinberger, Paul, and Bruce Tucker. 1991. *The New Individualists: The Generation after the Organization Man*. New York: Harper & Row.

Leopold, Aldo. 1987 [1947]. *A Sound County Almanac and Sketches Here and There*. New York: Oxford University Press.

Levine, Donald L., ed. 1971. *Georg Simmel on Individuality and Social Forms*. Chicago: University of Chicago Press.

Light, Ivan, and Edna Bonacich. 1988. *Immigrant Entrepreneurs: Koreans in Los Angeles, 1965-1982*. Berkeley and Los Angeles: University of California Press.

Lipset, Seymour Martin. 1963. *The First New Nation: The New United States in Historical and Comparative Perspective*. New York: Basic Books.

List, Peter C., ed. 1993. *Radical Environmentalism: Philosophy and Tactics*. Belmont, Calif.: Wadsworth.

Locke, John. 1894 [1690]. *An Essay Concerning Human Understanding.* 2 vols. Edited by A. C. Fraser. Oxford: Clarendon Press.

Lohfink, Norbert. 1980. *Koheleth.* Berlin: Echter Verlag.

Lovelock, J. E. 1979. *Gaia: A New Look at Life on Earth.* Oxford: Oxford University Press.

Luhmann, Niklas. 1979. *Trust and Power.* New York: John Wiley & Sons.

————. 1982. "The Self-Thematization of Society." Ch. 14 in *The Differentiation of Society* by Niklas Luhmann. New York: Columbia University Press.

————. 1990. *Essays on Self-Reference.* New York: Columbia University Press.

Luther, Martin. 1883. *D. Martin Luthers Werke. Kritische Gesamtausgabe.* Weimar: Böhlau.

MacIntyre, Alasdair. 1981. *After Virtue: A Study in Moral Theory.* Notre Dame: University of Notre Dame Press.

————. 1984. *After Virtue: A Study in Moral Theory.* 2d ed. Notre Dame: University of Notre Dame Press.

Malinowski, Bronislaw. 1955. *Magic, Science, and Religion and Other Essays.* Garden City, N.Y.: Doubleday.

Maritain, Jacques. 1958. *Reflections on America.* New York: Charles Scribner's Sons.

Marsden, George. 1980. *Fundamentalism and American Culture: The Shaping of Twentieth-Century Evangelicalism.* New York: Oxford University Press.

Marshall, Alfred. 1880. *Principles of Economics.* London: Macmillan.

Marshall, Gordon. 1982. *In Search of the Spirit of Capitalism: An Essay on Max Weber's Protestant Ethic Thesis.* New York: Columbia University Press.

Martel-Van Doorne, Martine. 1977. "Approche historique de l'évolution de la marque." *Revue de l'Institut de Sociologie (Solvay),* 1:73-88.

Martin, David. 1978. *A General Theory of Secularization.* New York: Harper & Row.

Marty, Martin E. 1967. "The Spirit's Holy Errand: The Search for a Spiritual Style in Secular America." *Daedalus* 96 (Winter): 99-115.

Marx, Karl. 1974 [1857/58]. *Grundrisse der Kritik der Politischen Ökonomie. Rohentwurf.* Berlin: Dietz Verlag.

Marx, Karl, and Friedrich Engels. 1947 [1846]. *The German Ideology.* New York: International Publishers.

Marx, Karl, and Friedrich Engels. 1979. *Werke.* Berlin: Dietz Verlag.

Mauss, Marcel. 1976. *The Gift: Forms and Functions of Exchange in Archaic Societies.* New York: W. W. Norton.

McClay, Wilfred M. 1993. "The Strange Career of *The Lonely Crowd:* Or, The Antinomies of Autonomy." In *The Culture of the Market: Historical Essays,* edited by Thomas L. Haskell and Richard F. Teichgraeber. New York: Cambridge University Press.

McClendon, James W. Jr. 1989 [1986]. *Ethics: Systematic Theology.* Nashville: Abingdon Press.

McCloskey, Donald N. 1985. *The Rhetoric of Economics.* Madison: University of Wisconsin Press.

———. 1990. *If You're So Smart: The Narrative of Economic Expertise.* Chicago: University of Chicago Press.

McGerr, Michael. 1993. "The Persistence of Individualism." *Chronicle of Higher Education,* 10 February, p. A48.

McGiffert, Arthur Cushman Jr. 1965. *No Ivory Tower: The Story of Chicago Theological Seminary.* Chicago: Chicago Theological Seminary.

Mead, Sidney E. 1975. *The Nation with the Soul of a Church.* New York: Harper & Row.

Meeks, M. Douglas. 1989. *God the Economist: The Doctrine of God and Political Economy.* Minneapolis: Fortress Press.

Menand, Louis. 1992. *Times Literary Supplement,* 30 October.

Merchant, Carolyn. 1992. *Radical Ecology: The Search for a Livable World.* New York: Routledge.

———. 1993. "Ecofeminism and Feminist Theory." Pp. 49-55 in *Radical Environmentalism: Philosophy and Tactics,* edited by Peter C. List. Belmont, Calif.: Wadsworth.

Meyer, John W., John Boli, and George M. Thomas. 1987. "Ontology and Rationalization in the Western Cultural Account." Ch. 1 in *Institutional Structure: Constituting State, Society, and the Individual,* edited by George M. Thomas et al. Newbury Park, Calif.: Sage Publications.

Mill, John Stuart. 1965-73. *Collected Works of J. S. Mill,* edited by V. W. Bladen. Toronto: University of Toronto Press.

Miller, Daniel. 1987. *Material Culture and Mass Consumption.* New York: Basil Blackwell.

Minirth, Frank, Don Hawkins, Paul Meier, and Richard Flournoy. 1986. *How to Beat Burnout.* Chicago: Moody Press.

Moltmann, Jürgen. 1984. "The Right to Meaningful Work." Pp. 37-58 in *On Human Dignity: Political Theology and Ethics* by Jürgen Moltmann. Translated by M. Douglas Meeks. Philadelphia: Fortress Press.

Moore, Sally Falk. 1978. *Law as Process: An Anthropological Approach.* London: Routledge.

Mulkay, Michael. 1985. *The Word and the World: Explorations in the Form of Sociological Analysis.* London: George Allen & Unwin.

Mumby, Dennis, and Linda Putnam. 1992. "The Politics of Emotion." *Academy of Management Review* 17:465-86.

Murphy, Roland Edmund. 1992. *Ecclesiastes.* WBC 23A. Waco, Tex.: Word.

Naess, Arne. 1986. "The Deep Ecological Movement: Some Philosophical Aspects." *Philosophical Inquiry* 8:10-31.

Nash, Ronald H. 1986. *Poverty and Wealth: The Christian Debate over Capitalism.* Westchester, Ill.: Crossway Books.

Needleman, Jacob. 1991. *Money and the Meaning of Life.* New York: Doubleday.

Nisbet, Robert. 1980. *History of the Idea of Progress.* New York: Basic Books.

Nohria, Nitin, Ranjay Gulati, and Robert G. Eccles. 1994. "Firms and Their Environments." In *Handbook of Economic Sociology,* edited by Neil J. Smelser and Richard Swedberg. Princeton: Princeton University Press and the Russell Sage Foundation.

O'Connor, James. 1992. "Capitalism, Nature, Socialism: An Introduction." *Society and Nature* 2 (September-December): 174-202.

O'Connor, Karen. 1992. *When Spending Takes the Place of Feeling.* Nashville: Thomas Nelson Publishers.

Oelschlaeger, Max, ed. 1992. *The Wilderness Condition: Essays on Environment and Civilization.* San Francisco: Sierra Club Books.

Ogden, Graham. 1987. *Qoheleth.* Sheffield: JSOT Press.

Otto, Rudolf. 1936 [1926]. *The Idea of the Holy.* Translated by John W. Harvey. London: Oxford University Press.

Owensby, Walter L. 1988. *Economics for Prophets: A Primer on Concepts, Realities, and Values in Our Economic System.* Grand Rapids: William B. Eerdmans.

Pannenberg, Wolfhart. 1983. *Anthropologie in theologischer Perspektive.* Göttingen: Vandenhoeck & Ruprecht.

Parry, Jonathan, and Maurice Bloch, eds. 1989. *Money and the Morality of Exchange.* Cambridge: Cambridge University Press.

Parsons, Talcott. 1935. "Sociological Elements in Economic Thought." *Quarterly Journal of Economics* 49:414-53, 646-67.

———. 1971. *The System of Modern Societies.* Englewood Cliffs, N.J.: Prentice-Hall.

———. 1979. "Religious and Economic Symbolism in the Western World." *Sociological Inquiry* 49, nos. 2-3:1-48.

Pemberton, Prentiss, and Daniel Rush Finn. 1985. *Toward a Christian Economic Ethic: Stewardship and Social Power.* Minneapolis: Winston Press.

Phillips, Derek. 1986. *Toward a Just Social Order.* Princeton: Princeton University Press.

Plant, Judith. 1989. *Healing the Wounds: The Promise of Ecofeminism.* Philadelphia: New Society Publishers.

Pocock, J. G. A. 1975. *The Machiavellian Moment: Florentine Political Thought and the Atlantic Republican Tradition.* Princeton: Princeton University Press.

Radcliffe-Brown, A. R. 1952. *Structure and Function in Primitive Societies.*
Glencoe, Ill.: Free Press.

Rafaeli, A., and R. Sutton. 1989. "The Expression of Emotion in Organizational
Life." Pp. 1-42 in *Research in Organizational Behavior,* vol. 11. Edited by
L. Cummings and B. Staw. Greenwich, Conn.: JAI Press.

Rahner, Karl. 1966. "The Concept of Mystery in Catholic Theology." Pp. 36-73
in *Theological Investigations,* vol. 5. Translated by K. Smyth. Baltimore:
Helicon Press.

Raines, Howell. 1980. "Man in the News." *New York Times,* 6 November, p. A1.

Rainwater, Lee. 1974. *What Money Buys: Inequality and the Social Meaning of
Income.* New York: Basic Books.

Rand, Ayn. 1961. *For the New Intellectual: The Philosophy of Ayn Rand.* New
York: Random House.

Reich, Robert B. 1992 [1991]. *The Work of Nations: Preparing Ourselves for
Twenty-First-Century Capitalism.* New York: Alfred A. Knopf.

Rieder, Jonathan. 1985. *Canarsie: The Jews and Italians of Brooklyn against
Liberalism.* Cambridge: Harvard University Press.

Riesman, David. 1990. "Innocence of *The Lonely Crowd.*" *Society* 27 (January-
February).

Riesman, David, with Nathan Glazer and Reuel Denney. 1950; rpt. 1969. *The
Lonely Crowd: A Study of the Changing American Character.* New Haven:
Yale University Press.

Robbins, Lionel. 1952 [1932]. *An Essay on the Nature and Significance of
Economic Science.* London: Macmillan.

Rodgers, Daniel T. 1978. *The Work Ethic in Industrial America, 1850-1920.*
Chicago: University of Chicago Press.

Rorty, Richard. 1989. *Contingency, Irony, and Solidarity.* Cambridge: Cambridge
University Press.

Rothbard, Murray N. 1988. "Freedom Is for Everyone." *Liberty* 1 (March):4.

Rozman, Gilbert, ed. 1993. *The Dismantling of Communism.* Princeton: Princeton University Press.

Sahlins, Marshall. 1976. *Culture and Practical Reason.* Chicago: University of
Chicago Press.

Sale, Kirkpatrick. 1991. *Dwellers in the Land: The Bioregional Vision.* Santa Cruz,
Calif.: New Society Publishers.

Sandel, Michael. 1984. "The Procedural Republic and the Unencumbered Self."
Political Theory 12:81-96.

———. 1989. "The Political Theory of the Procedural Republic." Pp. 19-32 in
Reinhold Niebuhr Today, edited by Richard John Neuhaus. Grand Rapids:
William B. Eerdmans.

Schall, James V., S.J. 1989. *Religion, Wealth, and Poverty.* Vancouver, B.C.: Fraser Institute.

Scheler, Max. 1978 [1928]. *Die Stellung des Menschen im Kosmos.* Berlin: Vranke Verlag.

Scheper-Hughes, Nancy. 1992. *Death without Weeping: The Violence of Everyday Life in Brazil.* Berkeley and Los Angeles: University of California Press.

Schlesinger, Arthur M. Jr. 1992. *The Disuniting of America: Reflections on a Multicultural Society.* New York: W. W. Norton.

Schor, Juliet B. 1992. *The Overworked American: The Unexpected Decline of Leisure.* New York: Basic Books.

Scitovsky, Tibor. 1976. *The Joyless Economy: An Inquiry into Human Satisfaction and Consumer Dissatisfaction.* New York: Oxford University Press.

Seev, Gasiet. 1981. *Menschliche Bedürfnisse: Eine theoretische Synthese.* Frankfurt am Main: Campus Verlag.

Selznick, Philip. 1992. *The Moral Commonwealth: Social Theory and the Promise of Community.* Berkeley and Los Angeles: University of California Press.

Sen, Amartya. 1987. *On Ethics and Economics.* Oxford: Basil Blackwell.

Shabecoff, Philip. 1993. *A Fierce Green Fire: The American Environmental Movement.* New York: Hill & Wang.

Shackle, G. L. S. 1957. "The Nature of the Bargaining Process." In *The Theory of Wage Determination,* edited by John Dunlop. Cambridge: Cambridge University Press.

Shalhope, Robert. 1972. "Toward a Republican Synthesis." *William and Mary Quarterly* 29:49-80.

————. 1982. "Republicanism and Early American Historiography." *William and Mary Quarterly* 39:334-56.

Shelley, Bruce, and Marshall Shelley. 1992. *Consumer Church: Can Evangelicals Win the World without Losing Their Souls?* Downers Grove, Ill.: InterVarsity Press.

Sherman, Doug. 1991. *Keeping Your Head Up When Your Job's Got You Down.* Brentwood, Tenn.: Wolgemuth and Hyatt Publishers.

Sherman, Doug, and William Hendricks. 1987. *Your Work Matters to God.* Colorado Springs: Navpress.

Shweder, Richard A., Manamohan Mahapatra, and Joan C. Miller. 1990. "Culture and Moral Development." Pp. 130-204 in *Cultural Psychology: Essays on Comparative Human Development,* edited by James W. Stigler, Richard A. Shweder, and Gilbert Herdt. Cambridge: Harvard University Press.

Sider, Ronald J. 1984. *Rich Christians in an Age of Hunger.* Rev. ed. Downers Grove, Ill.: InterVarsity Press.

Silverman, Kenneth. 1985. *The Life and Times of Cotton Mather.* New York: Columbia University Press.

Simmel, Georg. 1906. "A Contribution to the Sociology of Religion." *American Journal of Sociology* 11:359-76.

———. 1971a [posthumous]. "Freedom and the Individual." Pp. 217-26 in *Georg Simmel on Individuality and Social Forms,* edited by Donald L. Levine. Chicago: University of Chicago Press.

———. 1971b [1904]. "Fashion." Pp. 294-323 in *Georg Simmel on Individuality and Social Forms,* edited by Donald L. Levine. Chicago: University of Chicago Press.

———. 1978 [1907]. *The Philosophy of Money.* London: Routledge & Kegan Paul.

Simon, Herbert. 1982. *Models of Bounded Rationality.* 2 vols. Cambridge: MIT Press.

Singer, Peter. 1977. *Animal Liberation.* New York: Avon Books.

Smelser, Neil J. 1987. Introduction. Pp. xvii-xxiv in *Contemporary Classics in the Social and Behavioral Sciences,* compiled by Neil J. Smelser. Philadelphia: ISI Press.

———. 1992. "The Rational Choice Perspective: A Theoretical Perspective." *Rationality and Society* 4:381-410.

Smith, Adam. 1896. *Lectures on Justice, Police, Revenues, and Arms.* Edited by E. Cannan. Oxford: Clarendon.

———. 1937 [1776]. *An Inquiry into the Nature and Causes of the Wealth of Nations.* New York: Random House.

Smith, Charles. 1989. *Auctions: The Social Construction of Value.* New York: Free Press.

Stark, W. 1944. *The History of Economics in Relation to Social Development.* London: Kegan Paul, Trench, Trubner & Co.

Stent, Gunther S. 1978. *Morality as a Biological Phenomenon.* Berkeley and Los Angeles: University of California Press.

Stigler, George J. 1982. *The Economist as Preacher.* Oxford: Basic Blackwell.

Stone, Christopher. 1974. *Should Trees Have Standing?* Los Altos, Calif.: William Kaufmann.

Strayer, Joseph. 1970. *On the Medieval Origins of the Modern State.* Princeton: Princeton University Press.

Swedberg, Richard. 1990. *Economists and Sociologists: Redefining the Boundaries.* Princeton: Princeton University Press.

Tawney, Richard Henry. 1926. *Religion and the Rise of Capitalism: A Historical Study.* New York: Harcourt, Brace & Company.

———. 1958 [1930]. Foreword. Pp. 1-11 in *The Protestant Ethic and the Spirit of Capitalism* by Max Weber. Translated by Talcott Parsons. New York: Charles Scribner's Sons.

Thaler, Richard H. 1991. *Quasi-Rational Economics.* New York: Russell Sage Foundation.

Thomas, George M., John W. Meyer, Francisco O. Ramirez, and John Boli. 1987. *Institutional Structure: Constituting State, Society, and the Individual.* Newbury Park, Calif.: Sage Publications.

Thurow, Lester. 1980. *The Zero-Sum Society.* New York: Basic Books.

Tillich, Paul. 1963. *Systematic Theology,* vol. 3: *Life and the Spirit, History and the Kingdom of God.* Chicago: University of Chicago Press.

Tilly, Charles, ed. 1975. *The Formation of National States in Western Europe.* Princeton: Princeton University Press.

Tocqueville, Alexis de. 1945. *Democracy in America.* 2 vols. Translated by Phillips Bradley and Henry Reeve. New York: Vintage Books.

Troeltsch, Ernst. 1931. *The Social Teaching of the Christian Churches.* 2 vols. New York: Macmillan.

———. 1950 [1911]. *The Social Teaching of the Christian Churches.* 2 vols. Translated by O. Wyon. London: George Allen & Unwin.

———. 1986 [1911]. *Protestantism and Progress: The Significance of Protestantism for the Rise of the Modern World.* Philadelphia: Fortress.

Turnbull, Colin. 1972. *The Mountain People.* New York: Simon & Schuster.

Turner, Stephen Park, and Jonathan H. Turner. 1990. *The Impossible Science: An Institutional Analysis of American Sociology.* Newbury Park, Calif.: Sage Publications.

Turner, Victor. 1967. *The Forest of Symbols: Aspects of Ndembu Ritual.* Ithaca, N.Y.: Cornell University Press.

———. 1969. *The Ritual Process: Structure and Anti-Structure.* Ithaca, N.Y.: Cornell University Press.

Updike, John. 1992. "Where Is the Space to Chase Rainbows?" *Forbes,* 14 September, pp. 72-84.

Veblen, Thorstein. 1899. *The Theory of the Leisure Class: An Economic Study in the Evolution of Institutions.* New York: Macmillan.

Volf, Miroslav. 1988. *Zukunft der Arbeit — Arbeit der Zukunft: Der Arbeitsbegriff bei Karl Marx und seine theologische Wertung.* Munich: Kaiser.

———. 1991. *Work in the Spirit: Toward a Theology of Work.* New York: Oxford University Press.

Wachtel, Paul L. 1983. *The Poverty of Affluence; A Psychological Portrait of the American Way of Life.* New York: Free Press.

Wallace, Anthony. 1978. *Rockdale: The Growth of an American Village in the Early Industrial Revolution.* New York: Alfred A. Knopf.

Walras, Leon. 1954 [1874]. *Elements of Pure Economics.* Translated by W. Joffe. London: Allen & Unwin.

Weber, Max. 1946 [1906]. *From Max Weber: Essays in Sociology.* Translated and edited by H. H. Gerth and C. Wright Mills. New York: Oxford University Press.

—. 1958 [1904-5]. *The Protestant Ethic and the Spirit of Capitalism.* Translated by Talcott Parsons. New York: Charles Scribner's Sons.

—. 1968. *Economy and Society: An Outline of Interpretive Sociology.* 3 vols. Edited by Guenther Roth and Claus Wittich. New York: Bedminster Press.

—. 1978 [1921]. *Economy and Society.* 2 vols. Edited by Guenther Roth and Claus Wittich. Berkeley and Los Angeles: University of California Press.

Weinstein, Jeff, and Krisan Kumar. Forthcoming. *Public and Private in Thought and Practice: Reflections on a Grand Dichotomy.* Chicago: University of Chicago Press.

Wells, William W. 1989. *The Agony of Affluence.* Grand Rapids: Zondervan Publishing House.

White, John. 1993. *Money Isn't God: So Why Is the Church Worshiping It?* Downers Grove, Ill.: InterVarsity Press.

Whyte, William H. Jr. 1956. *The Organization Man.* Garden City, N.Y.: Doubleday.

Wilentz, Sean. 1988. "Many Democracies: On Tocqueville and Jacksonian America." Pp. 207-28 in *Reconsidering Tocqueville's "Democracy in America,"* edited by Abraham S. Eisenstadt. New Brunswick, N.J.: Rutgers University Press.

Wilkinson, Rupert. 1988. *The Pursuit of American Character.* New York: Harper & Row.

—. 1992. *American Social Character: Modern Interpretations from the Forties to the Present.* New York: HarperCollins.

Williams, William Appleman. 1964. *The Great Evasion.* Chicago: Quadrangle Books.

Williamson, Oliver. n.d. "Calculativeness, Trust, and Economic Organization." Working Paper OBIR-59, Walter A. Haas School of Business, University of California, Berkeley.

Wilson, James Q. 1993. *The Moral Sense.* New York: Free Press.

Wilson, John. 1978. *Religion in American Society: The Effective Presence.* Englewood Cliffs, N.J.: Prentice-Hall.

Witten, Marsha. 1993. *All Is Forgiven: The Secular Message in American Protestantism.* Princeton: Princeton University Press.

Wolfe, Alan. 1989. *Whose Keeper? Social Science and Moral Obligation.* Berkeley and Los Angeles: University of California Press.

————. 1992. "Democracy Versus Sociology: Boundaries and Their Political Consequences." Pp. 309-25 in *Where Culture Talks: Exclusion and the Making of Society,* edited by Michele Lamont and Marcel Fournier. Chicago: University of Chicago Press.

————. 1993. *The Human Difference: Animals, Computers, and the Necessity of Social Science.* Berkeley and Los Angeles: University of California Press.

Wuthnow, Robert. 1987. *Meaning and Moral Order: Explorations in Cultural Analysis.* Berkeley and Los Angeles: University of California Press.

————. 1988a. *The Restructuring of American Religion: Society and Faith Since World War II.* Princeton: Princeton University Press.

————. 1988b. "Sociology of Religion." Ch. 15 in *Handbook of Sociology,* edited by Neil J. Smelser. Newbury Park, Calif.: Sage Publications.

————. 1991. *Acts of Compassion: Caring for Others and Helping Ourselves.* Princeton: Princeton University Press.

————. 1993. "Pious Materialism: How Americans View Faith and Money." *Christian Century,* 3 March 1993, pp. 238-42.

————. 1994a. "Religion and Economic Life." Pp. 620-46 in *Handbook of Economic Sociology,* edited by Neil J. Smelser and Richard Swedberg. Princeton: Princeton University Press.

————. 1994b. *God and Mammon in America.* New York: Free Press.

Wuthnow, Robert, and Tracy L. Scott. Forthcoming. "Protestants and Economic Behavior." In *New Dimensions in American Religious History: The Protestant Experience,* edited by Darryl Hart and Mark Noll.

Yalom, Irvin D. 1992. *When Nietzsche Wept: A Novel of Obsession.* New York: Basic Books.

Yinger, Milton J. 1971. *The Scientific Study of Religion.* New York: Macmillan.

Young-Bruehl, Elisabeth. 1982. *Hannah Arendt: For Love of the World.* New Haven: Yale University Press.

Zelizer, Viviana A. 1983. *Pricing the Priceless Child: The Changing Social Value of Children.* New York: Basic Books.

————. 1987. *Morals and Markets: The Development of Life Insurance in the United States.* New Brunswick, N.J.: Transaction Books.

————. 1988. "Beyond the Polemics on the Market: Establishing a Theoretical and Empirical Agenda." *Sociological Forum* 3:614-34.

Zerubavel, Eviatar. 1991. *The Fine Line: Making Distinctions in Everyday Life.* New York: Free Press.

Zuckerman, Michael. 1991. "Holy Wars, Civil Wars: Religion and Economics in Nineteenth-Century America." *Prospects* 16:205-40.

Contributors

ALBERT BERGESEN is professor of sociology at the University of Arizona. He is the author of *The Sacred and the Subversive*, the co-author of *Cultural Analysis: The Work of Peter L. Berger, Mary Douglas, Michel Foucault, and Jürgen Habermas*, and the editor of *Studies of the Modern World System*.

JOHN BOLI is professor of sociology at Emory University. He has also been a visiting professor at Stanford University and at Lund University in Sweden. His writings include *New Citizens for a New Society: The Institutional Origins of Mass Schooling in Sweden*.

MARTIN E. MARTY is the Fairfax M. Cone Distinguished Service Professor of the History of Modern Christianity at the University of Chicago and the editor of *The Christian Century*. He is author of the multivolume *Modern American Religion* and co-editor (with R. Scott Appleby) of the multivolume Fundamentalism Project Series.

WILFRED M. McCLAY is associate professor of history at Tulane University. He is the author of *The Masterless: Self and Society in Modern America*, and is currently writing a biography of David Riesman.

NEIL J. SMELSER is emeritus professor of sociology at the University of California at Berkeley and director of the Center for Advanced Study in the Behavioral Sciences in Palo Alto, California. A fellow of the

American Academy of Arts and Sciences and an elected member of the American Philosophical Society, Professor Smelser has recently served as editor of the *Handbook of Sociology* and as co-editor of the *Handbook of Economic Sociology*.

MIROSLAV VOLF is professor of systematic theology at Fuller Theological Seminary and a member of the Evangelical Theological Faculty, Osijek, Croatia. He is the author of *Work in the Spirit: Toward a Theology of Work*.

MARSHA G. WITTEN is assistant professor of sociology at Franklin and Marshall College. She has also taught at Temple University. She is the author of *All Is Forgiven: The Secular Message in American Protestantism*.

ALAN WOLFE is University Professor at Boston University. He is the author of *The Human Difference* and *Whose Keeper? Social Science and Moral Obligation*, as well as editor of *America at Century's End*.

NICHOLAS WOLTERSTORFF is the Noah Porter Professor of Philosophical Theology and a fellow of Saybrook College at Yale University. His books include *On Universals, Reason within the Bounds of Religion*, and *Until Justice and Peace Embrace*.

ROBERT WUTHNOW is the Gerhard R. Andlinger Professor of Social Sciences and co-director (with Albert J. Roboteau and John F. Wilson) of the Center for the Study of American Religion at Princeton University. His books include *Christianity in the Twenty-First Century* and *God and Mammon in America*.

291.1785
W973

90839

LINCOLN CHRISTIAN COLLEGE AND SEMINARY

291.1785 W973

Rethinking materialism

DEMCO

3 4711 00090 6794